UNITED NATIONS
U N C T A D

Hochschule für Technik
und Wirtschaft Berlin

University of Applied Sciences

THE FINANCIAL AND ECONOMIC CRISIS
OF 2008-2009 AND DEVELOPING COUNTRIES

Edited by

Sebastian Dullien
Detlef J. Kotte
Alejandro Márquez
Jan Priewe

UNITED NATIONS
New York and Geneva, December 2010

Note

Symbols of United Nations documents are composed of capital letters combined with figures. Mention of such a symbol indicates a reference to a United Nations document.

The views expressed in this book are those of the authors and do not necessarily reflect the views of the UNCTAD secretariat. The designations employed and the presentation of the material in this publication do not imply the expression of any opinion whatsoever on the part of the Secretariat of the United Nations concerning the legal status of any country, territory, city or area, or of its authorities, or concerning the delimitation of its frontiers or boundaries.

Material in this publication may be freely quoted; acknowledgement, however, is requested (including reference to the document number). It would be appreciated if a copy of the publication containing the quotation were sent to the Publications Assistant, Division on Globalization and Development Strategies, UNCTAD, Palais des Nations, CH-1211 Geneva 10.

UNCTAD/GDS/MDP/2010/1

UNITED NATIONS PUBLICATION

Sales No. E.11.II.D.11

ISBN 978-92-1-112818-5

CONTENTS

THE CRISIS – COUNTRY AND REGIONAL STUDIES

LOOKING FORWARD – POLICY AGENDA

The Report of the Stiglitz Commission: A Summary and Comment

Reforming Macroeconomic Policies in Emerging Economies: From Procyclical to Countercyclical Approaches

ABBREVIATIONS AND ACRONYMS

ASEA	African Securities Exchanges Association
ASEAN	Association of Southeast Asian Nations
BIS	Bank for International Settlements
BNDES	Brazil's Development Bank
CPI	consumer price index
CRR	cash reserve ratio
ECB	external commercial borrowing
EMU	European Monetary Union
EU	European Union
FDI	foreign direct investment
FIE	foreign invested enterprise
FII	foreign institutional investor
FTA	free trade agreement
GDP	gross domestic product
IBGE	Brazilian Institute of Geography and Statistics
IMF	International Monetary Fund
IPEA	Brazilian Institute for Applied Economic Research
OECD	Organisation for Economic Co-operation and Development
OTC	over the counter
PSI	Programme for Sustaining Investment (Brazil)
RBI	Reserve Bank of India
RMB	renminbi
SDR	Special Drawing Right
SELIC	Special Settlement and Custody System (Brazil)
SLR	statutory liquidity ratio
SME	small and medium-sized enterprise
SOE	State-owned enterprise
UNCTAD	United Nations Conference on Trade and Development
VAT	value added tax
WTO	World Trade Organization

ABOUT THE AUTHORS

- *Sebastian Dullien*: Co-Director of the DAAD Partnership on Development Studies project at HTW Berlin, Professor of international economics at HTW Berlin and non-resident Senior Fellow at the American Institute for Contemporary German Studies in Washington, DC.

- *Ricardo Ffrench-Davis*: Professor of international economics at the Department of Economics of the University of Chile. Prior to that, he was Chief Economist of the Central Bank of Chile, Principal Regional Adviser at the Economic Commission for Latin America and the Caribbean (ECLAC) and co-founder of the think tank Centre for Latin American Economic Research (CIEPLAN).

- *Cornelius Huizenga*: Consultant at the Partnership on Sustainable, Low Carbon Transport, Shanghai, China.

- *Detlef J. Kotte*: Head of UNCTAD's Macroeconomic and Development Policies Branch, Geneva, Switzerland.

- *Marcos Antonio Macedo Cintra*: Associate Director of Studies on Economic Relations and International Policies of the Institute for Applied Economic Research (IPEA) in Brasilia, Brazil.

- *Daniela Magalhães Prates*: Professor at the Institute of Economics of the State University of Campinas (Unicamp), Brazil. Researcher at the Study Center of Economic Conjuncture and Policy (Cecon/IE/Unicamp) and at Brazil's National Council for Scientific and Technological Development (CNPq).

- *Alejandro Márquez*: Administrative coordinator of the DAAD Partnership on Development Studies at HTW Berlin.

- *Jörg Mayer*: Senior Economic Affairs Officer, Division on Globalization and Development Strategies at UNCTAD, Geneva, Switzerland.

- *André Nassif*: Professor of economics at the Fluminense Federal University (UFF) and Senior Economist of the Planning department of the Brazilian Development Bank (BNDES).

- *Patrick N. Osakwe*: Senior Economic Affairs Officer, Division for Africa, LDCs and Special Programmes at UNCTAD, Geneva, Switzerland. Until recently, the author was Chief of Financing Development at the United Nations Economic Commission for Africa, Ethiopia, where he provided support to the Committee of Ten Ministers of Finance and Central Bank Governors set up by African governments to monitor the impact of the financial crisis on Africa.

- *Jan Priewe*: Co-Director of the DAAD Partnership on Development Studies project at HTW Berlin, Professor of economics at HTW Berlin.

- *Abhijit Sen Gupta*: Associate Professor at the Centre for International Trade and Development of Jawaharlal Nehru University, New Delhi, India.

- *Laike Yang*: Professor and Dean at the Department of International Trade of East China Normal University, Shanghai, China.

- *Jürgen Zattler*: Deputy Director General at the German Federal Ministry for Economic Co-operation and Development, Berlin, Germany. Prior to that, he worked with the European Commission and a private bank.

INTRODUCTION

Sebastian Dullien, Detlef J. Kotte,
Alejandro Márquez and Jan Priewe

Most analyses of the financial and subsequent economic crisis, including those by leading international institutions like the International Monetary Fund, have focused on OECD countries. This can give the (mistaken) impression that the developing world, even sub-Saharan Africa, has been less severely affected by the crisis and is recovering relatively quickly. Most developed countries' governments are preoccupied with their domestic problems. This collection of papers puts the South on centre stage. It examines how the countries of the South were affected by the global economic and financial crisis and how they responded, what lessons the South could learn and what policy agenda needs to be pushed forward to better support the interests of developing countries, least developed countries as well as emerging-market economies.

The financial crisis started in the United States in 2007 and involved financial institutions in many OECD countries. It was only when the crisis turned into a global economic recession that developing and emerging-market economies were affected, mainly through the trade channel, and in some cases through workers' falling remittances. In many developing countries, the economic consequences of these indirect effects were as severe as the direct effects were on developed countries. The worldwide recession, the first since the Second World War, led to a reduction of world gross domestic product (GDP) by 0.6 per cent in 2009 (figure 1). In the absence of countercyclical responses, the slump could have been much stronger. In

Figure 1

ANNUAL GDP GROWTH, 2005–2010[a]

(Per cent)

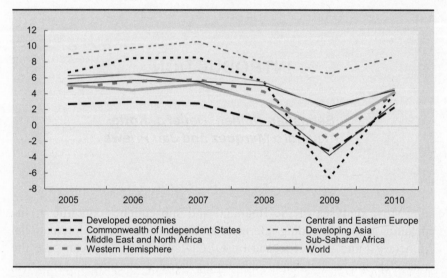

Source: IMF, 2010.
Note: Country categories are those used by the IMF.
  a Data for 2010 are estimates.

2009 global GDP growth was 5.8 percentage points lower than in 2007, and the downturn in emerging and developing countries was almost the same as in developed countries (IMF, 2010). Countries constituting the Commonwealth of Independent States (CIS) and those of Central and Eastern Europe (CEE) were the most severely affected, their GDP growth rates falling by an average of 15.2 percentage points between 2007 and 2009. The corresponding figures for Latin America and sub-Saharan Africa were 7.6 and 4.8 percentage points respectively. In general, countries with large current-account deficits or surpluses, and those with large fiscal deficits prior to the crisis suffered much greater output losses than others. Even in developing Asia growth rates dropped by 4 percentage points between 2007 and 2009.

The significant deceleration of GDP, though varying widely among developing and emerging-market economies, means that the affected countries will take some time to recover. Moreover, the crisis has had various other impacts. A drop in GDP in low-income countries of the same magnitude as in developed countries can have a much more severe social impact on the former. This is particularly evident in the resurgence of poverty, which is likely to hinder the accomplishment of the Millennium Development Goals, especially poverty reduction in Africa and Latin America. The flows of remittances and foreign aid fell, although less than expected. Even though the global economy has rebounded quickly, the prospects for its sustainable recovery are gloomy. The fever of the financial crisis seems to be overcome, but not yet the underlying illness. There is still a high degree of instability and uncertainty in the world economy, which is impeding growth and recovery.

Many financial institutions in developed countries continue to have problems with the quality of assets in their balance sheets, and the capacity and willingness of the financial sector to support the real economy are still limited. A thorough restructuring of banks and non-banks has barely begun, and they appear to be clinging on to their old business models. New legislation for re-regulating the financial sectors is under way, most notably in the United States, where reforms have advanced faster than in Europe. However, ongoing reform efforts are falling short of what is required, and even of what the G-20 summit in Pittsburgh had agreed upon (G-20, 2009). Most importantly, there is no global coherence in the new regulatory efforts; opportunities remain rife for those seeking loopholes and for regulatory arbitrage.

Many OECD countries embarked on countercyclical fiscal policies to an extent not seen for several decades, in addition to providing sizeable rescue packages for banks. Debt-to-GDP ratios in several of them rose by more than 30 percentage points and are currently close to 90 or 100 per cent. Calls for governments to exit from their expansionary stimulus programmes before growth has resumed could result in a premature shift to fiscal austerity and endanger the return to stable growth in 2011 and beyond. It could also lead to a sovereign debt crisis in some critical countries, along with the risk of contagion. Western Europe, in particular, is becoming a hindrance to global economic recovery, with the lowest estimated growth rate among all regions of the world. There is no coherent economic policy in the euro area and a complete lack of global leadership and responsibility. This could have negative repercussions especially for the countries of Eastern Europe, the CIS and Africa. If the Greek fiscal crisis leads to outright sovereign debt default, fears might spill over to other European countries with large current-account and fiscal deficits, and could culminate in a crisis throughout the euro area. Its ultimate cause would be the notorious deficiencies in the bloc's economic architecture, which lacks workable provisions to prevent increasing divergences between member States. The euro area could turn into an example of the type of monetary union not to be emulated by monetary cooperation initiatives in the South.

As the recession threatened to spread globally, many developing and emerging-market economies undertook resolute countercyclical monetary and fiscal actions in parallel with those of developed countries, mainly the United Kingdom and the United States. These policy responses contributed significantly to the recovery of the world economy in 2010, which may continue into 2011. Brazil, China and India, in particular, although hurt by the crisis, responded quicker and with a much higher dose of stimulus than others, which helped to mitigate deflationary risks and avoid a repetition of the Great Depression of the early 1930s. For instance, China took action immediately when it became clear that a sharp drop of output growth was imminent. Other developing countries reacted in similar ways, and stopped monetary and fiscal tightening. Countercyclical fiscal policy was reinvented, and even recommended by the IMF, in contrast to its decade-long policy advice. As a result, growth in these countries picked up rapidly, almost as if the crisis had bypassed them.

Some believe that the so-called emerging economies have turned out to be the winners in the global financial and economic crisis, in the sense that they have returned to their previous paths of high growth, whereas the leading developed economies are stuck on a slow growth path. Although the media often exaggerate this point, there is some truth to it. While the term "emerging economies" is used rather loosely, and there are no clear criteria to identify them, the share of the four BRIC countries (Brazil, the Russian Federation, India and China) in total world production rose by roughly two percentage points, to 19.3 per cent, between 2007 and 2010. However, during the same period the heterogeneous group of 145 other "developing and emerging economies" also expanded its share in world GDP by two percentage points, to 12.6 per cent. The 33 "advanced economies" (following the IMF classification) lost correspondingly four percentage points and now account for 68 per cent of global output, which is nevertheless an overwhelmingly predominant proportion of global production, only slightly changed by the crisis. They also have greater clout in policy-making. Before long the share of the BRIC group is expected to reach that of the United States, which is presently 23 per cent (or 34 per cent of the group of the "advanced" countries' GDP). Stronger and more effective cooperation in economic policy-making among the BRIC and the other developing countries could give them unprecedented economic and political weight that might challenge the long-standing tradition of unipolar policy-making in the world. This should be considered an opportunity for developing and emerging-market economies to voice *their* interests and influence the world economy to move in a more development-friendly direction.

The following are some major lessons that developing countries can learn from the crisis.

- The modern financial sector of the type found in the United States (and in other developed countries) is no longer seen as a general model to be copied by other countries. There is widespread awareness of a growing wedge between financial sector growth and the real economy in many OECD countries that involves high risks. The kind of casino finance practiced by many leading financial institutions on Wall Street should be rejected in favour of a financial sector that operates in support of the real economy, rather than to its detriment.

- Something went terribly wrong in the United States, in the "neoliberal" relationship between the State and business. Unregulated or badly supervised finance, opaque "financial innovations" and minimum State intervention, as well as an unfettered rise in inequality are increasingly seen as detrimental to development. The age of "neoliberalism" now appears to be on the wane.

- Economic and, particularly, financial globalization, can make developing countries more vulnerable and thus impede growth. Countries should be able to shield against negative exogenous shocks from financial markets. A serious reconsideration of the pattern of global integration has become necessary. Crises can spread quickly and painfully resulting in high social costs to countries that had nothing to do with triggering them. This shows that the interdependence of national economies is much closer than had previously been presumed. In the same way as the roles of business and the State need to be rebalanced at the national level, globalization requires enhanced "global governance".

• Developing countries need more policy space for macroeconomic policy-making, for monetary as well as fiscal and exchange rate policy. Their macroeconomic and development strategies need be better tailored to their specific needs, and should go beyond simply ensuring price stability and budgetary discipline as advocated by the Washington Consensus. Many countries have adopted narrow, constantly tight macroeconomic policies, along with liberalization of trade and privatization programmes, which have tended to yield little success in terms of growth and employment creation.

• Countercyclical monetary and fiscal action should be seen as necessary elements in pro-growth macroeconomic policies. Many Asian countries are admired for their generally prudently managed growth. Also, capital controls or capital-account management are back on the agenda, even by the IMF (Ostry et al., 2010), and are no longer seen as "setting the clock back".

• Along with a proactive fiscal policy, promotion of domestic demand should gain more attention compared to the long-standing imperative of export-led growth. Policies of ever growing reserves are unsustainable and need to be reconsidered.

As a consequence of the crisis, the IMF's chief economist, Olivier Blanchard, called for a rethinking of macroeconomic policy (Blanchard et al., 2010) and offered surprisingly new ideas, but these gained only faint support in policy circles and among professional economists. Blanchard and colleagues have questioned the pre-crisis mainstream thinking on macroeconomic policy on several counts. First, they believe that the inflation target should be set higher in developed economies, at about 4 per cent instead of the present 2 per cent, to avoid the zero bound interest rate. Though they do not specifically mention it, this would benefit developing countries, since their inflation target differential vis-à-vis developed countries could become smaller. Second, monetary and regulatory policies should be combined. Thus regulatory policy to control asset prices and financial system stability would evolve as a new policy approach with a macroeconomic impact. Avoiding asset price bubbles would be seen as a new policy goal. Third, they believe "Central banks in small open economies should openly recognize that exchange rate stability is part of their objective function." (Blanchard et al., 2010: 13). In other words, inflation targeting should take into account exchange rates. Fourthly, they call for stronger countercyclical fiscal policy, including better automatic stabilizers, thus rebalancing macroeconomic policy which has long been tilted far too much towards monetary policy. Blanchard et al. emphasize the caveat that their proposals are tailored only for developed economies and that advice to developing countries would follow. Indeed, it is time to reconsider the macroeconomic policy framework for developing countries as well.

From these insights there is still a long way to go before a new policy agenda for developing countries is formulated (for comprehensive policy proposals, see UNCTAD, 2009; Panitchpakdi, 2010 and United Nations, 2009). The G-20 summits in 2009 and 2010 have tended to focus mainly on financial sector reforms. So far, reforms pertaining to developing countries have been only marginally considered in the aftermath of the crisis. In particular, two issues have not been addressed adequately by the G-20: *global imbalances* in trade and capital flows and *reforms of the global exchange rate system*. These were precisely the two areas at the root of the financial crisis, and were addressed by the Stiglitz Commission. It is indeed striking that almost every analysis of the financial crisis refers to the role of global imbalances, but this issue was not on the agenda of the G-20 Pittsburgh summit. Even more striking is absence of the old but unresolved issue of reform of the international exchange rates system within a broader new global order of economic and financial governance. These are issues that need to be addressed from the perspective of developing countries.

Global current-account imbalances have worsened to an unprecedented degree in the past decade. A few countries, mainly the United States, followed by the United Kingdom, Spain and Australia, have built up huge deficits and concomitant external indebtedness, often driven by debt-financed consumption and asset price inflation. The surplus countries, mainly China, Germany, Japan and energy-exporting countries, restrained their domestic demand relative to output and undervalued their currencies in different forms and varying degrees. Like China, but on a smaller scale, many developing countries have built up currency reserves that are invested mainly in United States Treasury bonds. Long before the crisis erupted, a number of economists had warned of the risks that these imbalances implied for financial and macroeconomic stability. Traditionally, the deficit countries were supposed to be responsible for deficit reduction by curbing domestic demand, but more recently very often private or official finance has been provided to finance deficits. UNCTAD, among others, has long called for coordinated international action to unwind global imbalances. A temporary reduction of those imbalances was achieved with the global recession, but new imbalances are expected to occur in coming years. The problem of global imbalances has its mirror image at the regional level in Europe: Germany, together with three smaller EU member States (Austria, Finland, Netherlands), has maximized its current-account surplus through wage and fiscal restraint (thereby minimizing domestic demand growth), whereas others have become overly indebted and have lost international competitiveness. The much needed European governance is lacking, as is global governance to redress global imbalances.

One way to rebalance the global economy is through exchange-rate realignments. Foreign exchange markets do not always behave in line with fundamentals. Free market exchange rates are subject to destabilizing overshooting and undershooting. This is why developing countries fear floating, but on the other hand they cannot defend fixed pegs. They need intermediate regimes with stable but adjustable rates, but these are difficult to accomplish and maintain if done unilaterally. A return to a similar system to Bretton Woods would probably be in conflict with financial globalization and would require fundamental changes in cross-border capital flows. Furthermore, the present dollar standard is likely to systematically overburden the reserve currency country with capital inflows. Some observers are proposing the creation of a new global currency built on Special Drawing Rights and a new global institution in charge of issuing them. Others are proposing a set of multilaterally agreed rules for exchange-rate management that would result in a system of managed exchange rates. These are issues of utmost importance not only for emerging and developing countries, but also for the functioning of the global economy as a whole.

This is the spectrum of issues touched upon in this volume. A number of papers review and compare country experiences; others focus on more general issues relating to the causes of the crisis and the performance of crisis-hit countries and regions. Some address the policy agenda mentioned above, drawing on the work of the Stiglitz Commision and on UNCTAD research. Many of the contributions draw from the two conferences at HTW Berlin in November 2009 and June 2010, while others are contributions by UNCTAD researchers or authors cooperating with HTW in an international network of 12 universities funded by the German Academic Exchange Service (DAAD).[1] The editors wish to express their gratitude to DAAD for funding both conferences.

The following is a brief overview of the various contributions, grouped into three sections: general issues concerning the financial and economic crisis, country or regional case studies, and policy recommendations.

Jan Priewe reviews different interpretations of the global financial crisis of 2008–2009 (and its aftermath), focusing first on the proximate causes in the financial sector of the United States and then on the deeper ultimate causes. The latter were mainly the global imbalances in trade and in cross-border capital flows, the systemic root of which lies in what the author refers to as a "new Triffin dilemma". This dilemma relates to the shortcomings of the present global currency system that uses the United States dollar as the key reserve currency, which has to serve both national and global objectives. Other ultimate causes were the trend towards "finance-driven capitalism" in many OECD countries, most pronounced in the United States, and growing income inequality. The author contends that the confluence of the proximate and ultimate causes paved the way for the crisis.

Daniela Magalhães Prates and *Marcos Antonio Macedo Cintra* suggest that the spread of the current crisis to emerging-market economies shows that the macroeconomic reforms implemented since the financial crises of the 1990s were not sufficient to shelter countries from financial and exchange rate volatility. Even though countries, especially in Latin America and Asia, implemented prudent macroeconomic policies and accumulated large amounts of foreign exchange reserves, they were again hit by large swings in capital flows and subsequent volatility in their exchange rates. The reason for the failure of this policy stance is the hierarchical and asymmetric set-up of the global monetary and financial system, in which the issuer of the key currency, the United States, has a very large degree of freedom in the conduct of fiscal, monetary and exchange rate policies while the resulting volatility has to be borne by other countries. The proposed solution is a tightening or reintroduction of capital controls.

Jörg Mayer describes how the growing importance of financial investors in the markets for primary commodities has led to increased commodity price volatility. He dissects the different types of returns for financial investors and shows how the involvement of this investor group in the markets concerned has led to the prices of a number of commodities moving in tandem with equity prices and with the exchange rates of currencies affected by carry trade. Empirically, he shows that price volatility has increased the most for wheat, maize, soybeans and soybean oil. He asserts that this "financialization" of commodity markets is thus at least partly to blame for the greater price volatility, although he concedes that there are also other factors at play. As a solution, he proposes that the regulation of commodity exchanges as well as the design and viability of physical buffer stocks and intervention mechanisms be reconsidered. In addition, there should be a greater emphasis on policies to increase commodity production and productivity.

Sebastian Dullien takes an empirical look at the transmission mechanisms of the crisis around the world. Countries with large current-account imbalances were especially hard hit by the crisis. Interestingly, not only countries with large deficits but also those with large surpluses were strongly affected. Among the existing exchange-rate regimes, countries with currency boards suffered the greatest impacts. He points out that countries with very open capital accounts run a greater risk of a deep recession, while those with medium inflation rates appear to have performed better during the crisis than those with low inflation rates. He concludes that these facts cast doubts on claims that free capital flows help countries to cushion against shocks and that macroeconomic policies should aim more at current account imbalances.

Laike Yang and *Cornelius Huizenga* analyse how China has coped with the global financial and economic crisis: the crisis affected China's real economy rather than its financial system. It caused a dramatic fall in China's foreign trade and foreign direct investment inflows, higher unemployment rates and strong price fluctuations. The Government responded quickly to tackle the adverse effects of the crisis through a sizeable stimulus package that succeeded in maintaining high growth in both 2009 and 2010.

Abhijit Sen Gupta presents a case study on the impact of the economic and financial crisis on the Indian economy, and outlines the policy reactions of the Indian government to the crisis. He explains that India was already experiencing a domestic downturn when the crisis hit. The fall in exports and capital inflows and a domestic liquidity crunch further exacerbated the downturn. Both monetary authorities and the government reacted swiftly, with expansionary monetary and fiscal policies which contributed to a quick recovery of the Indian economy. However, the effective use of fiscal policy also resulted in a larger budget deficit, and this raises questions about an appropriate exit strategy from the very accommodative monetary policy stance.

André Nassif compares Brazil's and India's responses to the crisis. In an economic environment in which the risk of depression is global, the timeliness and intensity of economic policy responses matter. In September 2008, when the global crisis spread to Brazil and India through the financial channels, it might have been expected that both countries would be negatively affected in a similar manner. However, while the Brazilian economy fell into recession in 2009, India's real GDP grew by over 6 per cent. This remarkable performance meant that India was the second least adversely affected country by the global crisis after China. Nassif shows that the monetary and fiscal policy responses to the global crisis by Indian policymakers were superior to those in Brazil.

Patrick Osakwe describes Africa's exposure to the crisis. He argues that, contrary to common perceptions, the crisis also had adverse impacts on Africa. In many African countries, not only the export volume, but also export prices fell sharply, particularly those of commodities, which account for a large share of Africa's total exports. As a result, foreign exchange earnings as well as government revenues dropped. In addition, exchange rates fluctuated wildly owing to volatile capital flows. While African countries reacted with expansionary monetary and fiscal policies, the poor nevertheless felt the impact acutely, with poverty rising throughout the region. In order to safeguard against the adverse effects of future financial crises that originate elsewhere, Osakwe recommends an explicit policy of diversification of export markets and export products.

Alejandro Márquez presents a summary of the Report of the Commission of Experts of the President of the UN General Assembly on Reforms of the

International Monetary and Financial System, commonly referred to as the Stiglitz Commission Report. He believes that such an exercise is particularly useful since the report, as with many policy documents, is too long and written in jargon that limits its readership. Conveying the main ideas of the report allows a better appreciation of why the financial and economic crisis should be used as an opportunity to reform the international financial and economic system.

Ricardo Ffrench-Davis underlines the difference between what he calls *"financieristic"* macroeoconomic balances and *real* ones. Policymakers who adopt the first type concentrate their efforts on keeping inflation and fiscal deficits low, disregarding the variables relevant for the real balances, namely unemployment, growth and the real exchange rate. These goals have been achieved in many Latin American countries at the expense of growth and more effective employment of both labour and capital, generally under the auspices of the international financial institutions. He alleges that following such types of policies in the spirit of the Washington Consensus led to the current global crisis. The author argues that, in accordance with endogenous growth theory, policymakers should concentrate on achieving growth by aiming at real macroeconomic balances.

Jürgen Zattler examines the role that Special Drawing Rights (SDR), consisting of a kind of artificial basket of four leading currencies, could play in the present global monetary system. Zattler holds that, given the obvious weaknesses of the post-Bretton Woods monetary system, which is basically a "dollar standard", a new role for SDRs needs to be considered. Currency reserves, presently held mainly in dollars, could be diversified by using SDRs. They could also be used for private international transactions rather than only official ones. Emerging countries' bonds might be issued in SDRs, and countercyclical policies could be financed with SDRs. In addition, implementation of climate change policies in developing countries could partly be financed with SDRs.

Detlef Kotte discusses options for improving the structure of international financial governance with a view to reducing the predominant influence of financial markets in determining the conditions for macroeconomic policy-making. He suggests that dependence on the dollar as a reserve currency could be reduced by allowing an independent international institution to create international liquidity to support countries that face externally caused currency crises. He believes the key to greater stability lies primarily in the creation of a multilaterally agreed framework for exchange-rate management that aims at stabilizing real exchange rates in conjunction with a strengthened institutional setting for macroeconomic policy coordination among the systemically important countries. In developing countries and emerging-market economies, the use of capital controls would help stabilize the macroeconomic context for investment in real productive capacity and contribute to their successful integration into the global economy.

Note

1   See http://daadpartnership.htw-berlin.de/.

References

Blanchard O, Dell'Ariccia G and Mauro P (2010). Rethinking macroeconomic policy. IMF Staff Proposition Note, SPN/10/03. Washington, DC, 12 February.

G-20 (2009). Leaders' Statement, the Pittsburgh Summit. 25 September; available at: http://www.g20.org/Documents/pittsburgh_summit_leaders_statement_250909.pdf.

IMF (2009). *World Economic Outlook*. Washington, DC, October.

IMF (2010). *World Economic Outlook*. Washington, DC, July (update).

Ostry JD, Gosh AR, Habermeier K, Chamon,M, Quereshi MS and Reinhardt DBS (2010). Capital Inflows: The role of controls. IMF Staff Position Notes, SPN/10/04. Washington, DC, 19 February.

Panitchpakdi S (2010). Reconstructing economic governance: an agenda for sustainable growth and development. Mumbai, Export-Import Bank of India; available at: http://www.unctad.org/sections/edm_dir/docs/edm_osg_exim2010_en.pdf.

UNCTAD (2009). *Trade and Development Report 2009: Responding to the Global Crisis; Climate Change Mitigation and Development*. New York and Geneva, United Nations; available at: http://www.unctad.org/Templates/webflyer.asp?docid=11867&intItemID =5003&lang=1&mode=toc.

United Nations (2009). Report of the Commission of Experts of the President of the United Nations General Assembly on Reforms of the International Monetary and Financial System. New York.

THE CRISIS

TRANSMISSION, IMPACT AND SPECIAL FEATURES

WHAT WENT WRONG?
ALTERNATIVE INTERPRETATIONS
OF THE GLOBAL FINANCIAL CRISIS*

Jan Priewe

Abstract

This paper first reviews different interpretations of the global financial crisis of 2008-2009 (and its aftermath), focusing on the proximate causes in the financial sector of the United States. However, behind the immediate causes lie ultimate causes without which the crisis cannot be properly understood. These were mainly the global imbalances in trade and in cross-border capital flows, the systemic root of which lies in what the paper refers to as a "new Triffin dilemma". This dilemma relates to the shortcomings of the present global currency system that uses the United States dollar as the key reserve currency, which has to serve both national and global objectives. Other ultimate causes are the trend towards a finance-driven capitalism in many OECD countries, most pronounced in the United States, and the trend towards greater income inequality, which dampens aggregate demand and contributes to financial instability as well as global imbalances. The confluence of the proximate and ultimate causes paved the way for the crisis.

---

*   This article is published in a slightly different version in Dullien, S., Hein, E., Truger, A., van Treeck, T. (eds.): The World Economy in Crisis – the Return of Keynesianism? Metropolis: Marburg/Lahn 2010.

Introduction: What went wrong?

The financial and economic crisis of 2008–2009 is not well understood in the media, in politics or in academic discourse, like the Great Depression, the causes of which continue to be discussed today. The public tends to search for the guilty without necessarily understanding the complex causes of the disaster. Many believe that the culprits were the bankers, their bonuses, their greed, fraud, corruption and speculation. Others hint at human failures: contingent decisions like the refusal to bail out the investment bank Lehman Brothers, which triggered an avalanche of failing financial institutions. According to Alan Greenspan, it was hard to avoid this "hundred year flood" (Greenspan, 2010). Much of this is neither right nor wrong. We have witnessed a systemic crisis in which many factors interacted. How could such greed emerge that did not exist before? How could a crisis in a small segment of the financial markets (i.e. subprime mortgages) turn into a deep global recession, with losses of gross domestic product (GDP) amounting to nearly 10 per cent of global output in 2008–2010,[1] not to mention the loss in values of assets and the astronomical bills to be paid later? Why do the shareholders of profit maximizing corporations tolerate such high bonus payments? It seems that the search for scapegoats targets only the tip of the iceberg. Is the gist of the matter still hidden?

In academic discourse, other interpretations of the causes of the crisis predominate, which focus on the financial sector – primarily in the United States – or on supervisory authorities, or on the trend towards deregulation since the 1970s – especially under the George W. Bush Administration. Others blame what they consider the excessive monetary policy of the Federal Reserve between 2002 and 2004 (Hellwig, 2008; Krahnen and Franke, 2009; Sinn, 2009; Posner, 2009; Taylor, 2009). Yet others, like Borio and Drehmann (2009) and Reinhart and Rogoff (2009), hold that most financial crises in history evolved from previous excessive credit lending and asset price bubbles. The patterns of emergence and unwinding of the major financial crises in emerging and industrialized economies in the past few decades (e.g. Japan in 1992, the Asian crisis in 1997–1998 and Argentina in 2001) are similar to those of the subprime crisis. In phases of boom, the confidence that "this time is different" prevails until the crash disabuses all. Those who cite a lack of macroprudential surveillance by banks have emphasized that the risks of the bubble were not recognised in time (Brunnermeier et al., 2009; Goodhart, 2009). Here, in the lack of macroprudential surveillance lies the predominant answer, as expressed by the G-20 meeting in Pittsburgh in 2009 and by the Financial Stability Forum (2009). Although interesting, it falls short of explaining the full scope of what happened.

Most observers exclude the role of global imbalances in trade and capital flows as a major cause of the crisis. Some cite a "global saving glut" as one of the causes, but fail to explain what this really means. Furthermore, most observers fail to consider that the roots of the financial crisis lie in a pattern of macroeconomic and structural development that has been described as finance-driven capitalism. This pattern has led to seemingly ever-increasing income inequality in most OECD countries. Here, some deeper underlying causes are addressed, which emerged in the past decades with the concomitant financial vulnerability of developed economies. It can demonstrate only that a financial crisis of this type *could* happen, but not that it *did* happen and in the specific manner of the latest crisis.

This paper distinguishes between proximate and more structural or ultimate causes of the financial crisis (see box 1). Global imbalances in trade and capital flows, globalization of financial markets, the trend towards a new finance-led capitalism and the related pattern of income distribution constitute what I consider to be the ultimate causes. If these ultimate causes prove valid, different conclusions can be drawn as to how to prevent similar crises in the future, including rebalancing the global economy, reconsidering globalization, definancialization of the advanced type of capitalism, and new patterns of income distribution. This paper focuses on global imbalances. Those who emphasize only the proximate causes tend to adopt a narrow view that focuses on what happened in the United States. They view the United States (with some careless free-riders from abroad) as being at the origin of the crisis, which was then transmitted via different channels of contagion into a global crisis affecting the real economy. However, from the structural point of view, the turmoil in the United States occurred in a

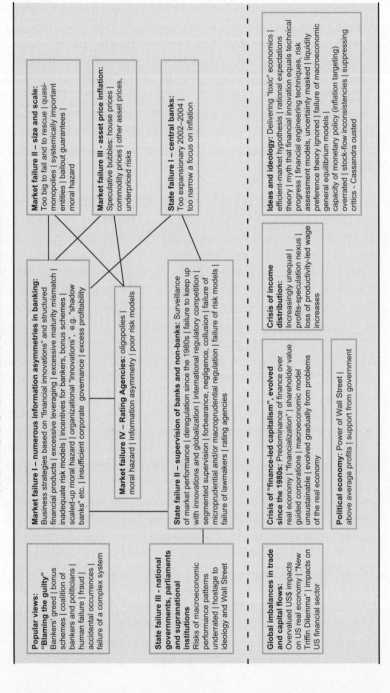

Box 1

CAUSES OF THE SYSTEMIC CRISIS: MARKET AND STATE FAILURES,
AND BASIC UNDERLYING STRUCTURAL DISTORTIONS

Popular views: "Blaming the guilty"
Bankers' greed | bonus schemes | coalition of bankers and politicians | human failure | fraud | accidental occurrences | failure of a complex system

State failure III - national governments, parliaments and supranational institutions
Risks of macroeconomic performance patterns underrated | hostage to ideology and Wall Street

Global imbalances in trade and capital flows:
Overvalued US$ impacts on US real economy | "New Triffin Dilemma" | impacts on US financial sector

Market failure I – numerous information asymmetries in banking:
Business strategies based on "financial innovations" and structured financial products | excessive leveraging | excessive maturity mismatch | inadequate risk models | incentives for bankers, bonus schemes | scaled-up moral hazard | organizational "innovations", e.g. "shadow banks" etc. | insufficient corporate governance | excess profitability

Market failure IV – Rating Agencies: oligopolies | moral hazard | information asymmetry | poor risk models

State failure II – supervision of banks and non-banks: Surveillance of market performance | deregulation since the 1980s | failure to keep up with innovations and globalization | international regulatory competition | segmented supervision | forbearance, negligence, collusion | failure of microprudential and/or macroprudential regulation | failure of risk models | failure of lawmakers | rating agencies

Crisis of "finance-led capitalism", evolved since the 1980s: Predominance of finance over real economy | "financialization" | shareholder value guided corporations | macroeconomic model unsustainable | evolved gradually from problems of the real economy

Political economy: Power of Wall Street | above average profits | support from government

Market failure II – size and scale: Too big to fail and to rescue | quasi-monopolies | systemically important entities | bailout guarantees | moral hazard

Market failure III - asset price inflation: Speculative bubbles: house prices | commodity prices | other asset prices, underpriced risks

State failure I – central banks: Too expansionary 2002–2004 | too narrow a focus on inflation

Crisis of income distribution: Increasingly unequal | profits-speculation nexus | loss of productivity-led wage increases

Ideas and ideology: Delivering "toxic" economics | efficient-market hypothesis | rational expectations theory | myth that financial innovation equals technical progress | financial engineering techniques, risk assessment models, uncertainty masked | liquidity preference theory ignored | failure of macroeconomic general equilibrium models | capacity of monetary policy (inflation targeting) overrated | stock-flow inconsistencies | suppressing critics - Cassandra ousted detrimental global environment. Hence the origin of the crisis can only be understood as the confluence of national and global determinants.

Finally, part of the ultimate causes are the power distribution with respect to the financial sector, relative to the State/government and relative to other sectors, and the negative impact of "toxic ideas" – economic theories and concepts that provide the dominant wisdom shared by the majority of academic professionals, practitioners in the financial industry and policymakers. However, a discussion of these aspects is beyond the scope of this paper.

The paper is organized as follows: section I reviews prevailing analyses of the proximate causes, followed by an analysis of global imbalances (section II) and the insufficient global financial architecture, characterized here as a "new Triffin dilemma" (section III). The role of finance-led capitalism and an increasingly skewed income distribution is roughly sketched in section IV, and section V concludes.

I. Prevailing explanations of the causes of the crisis

A.   Various explanations focusing on financial markets

Apart from apportioning blame to greedy and, in some cases, fraudulent bankers,[2] most analyses focus on proximate causes within the financial sector, especially in the United States. These mainly relate to four forms of market failure and three types of state failure.

1.   Market failures

The classical market failure (see item I in box 1) stems, first of all, from the typical information asymmetry in financial markets, normally discussed as prevailing between banks and debtors. Generally speaking, it can be conceived of as information asymmetry between banks and all their customers, which can lead – intentionally or unintentionally – to obscuring risk. A very important information asymmetry concerns risk assessment of financial products by financial institutions. This knowledge is, similar to a patent, only partly available to the public, and perhaps is not completely known even by rating agencies. Furthermore, risk assessments are normally of a microeconomic nature: they do not capture *mass* undervaluation of risk in good times. This is prone to creating the risk of moral hazard unless banking regulations can prevent it. A related type of market failure can stem from financial innovations which are inherently opaque instruments prone to risk, especially if there is no prior experience of using such instruments. This can be considered a special form of information asymmetry.

If banks or non-banks have become too big to fail, or too big to be rescued (e.g. Lehman Brothers), exit strategies become either intolerable due to extreme collateral damage, or bailouts are so costly that there is no alternative to allowing bankruptcy. This dilemma, beyond all principles, underlies a competitive market economy. Often, it is associated with a high degree of monopoly in the financial sector (see item II in box 1).

Speculative asset price inflation can be considered another type of market failure, which can induce large-scale misallocation of capital and huge collateral damages after the bursting of a bubble (item III). In this respect, the inefficiency of financial markets may be viewed as a market failure, in addition to traditional typologies of market failure in microeconomics. Finally, oligopolistic rating agencies which collude with their clients are likely to be biased, and if they suffer from information asymmetry, they may tend to spread false information with highly negative external effects (item IV).

2.   State failures

If market failures exist, they should be cured or mitigated by government regulations, specifically in the financial sector. Three types of state failures, including false policies, are under discussion. First, many observers believe that monetary policy was too expansionary after the terrorist attacks in New York in September 2001 and the bursting of the dot-com bubble. Too much money in circulation had fuelled asset price increases, and not inflation, which was checked by global competition (Taylor, 2009). Implicitly it is held that the Federal Reserve, or central banks in general, can avoid both inflation *and* asset price bubbles if they strictly follow the Taylor rule.[3] However, if this proposition does not hold, and if neither the Federal Reserve nor the government cares about asset inflation, and if the central bank narrowly focuses on inflation-targeting (i.e. consumer prices), there would be no instrument to counter speculative bubbles, although these can have a severe macroeconomic impact. In the case of the Federal Reserve, its former chairman, Alan Greenspan, and his successor, Bernanke (and many others), believed that monetary policy should target only inflation, and that burst bubbles could be dealt with by a proactive monetary policy of low interest rates, as in 2001–2002, sometimes referred to as the "Jackson Hole doctrine". This doctrine believes in the omnipotence of monetary policy, categorically ruling out such problems as liquidity traps, credit crunches and systemic financial instability.[4] In short, modern central banking claims that "it cannot happen again".

A second, much-discussed state failure is the shortcomings of banking supervision, not only in the United States,[5] due to gradual deregulation over several decades, segmented authorities and lack of international cooperation causing regulatory arbitrage – all promoted and legitimated in the belief that financial markets need to be free in order to thrive. A number of authors (e.g. Brunnermeier et al., 2009) focus on the lack of macroprudential supervision rather than on traditional microprudential supervision. Even if all banks were sound, there could be risk at the macro level due to small changes on a broad scale – a fallacy-of-composition problem. *Macroprudential* supervision would be a novel type of regulation, probably best undertaken by central banks. This type of regulation would require new instruments, which could be in conflict with monetary policy and involve a number of open issues. Besides, given the number of shortcomings in traditional microeconomic banking supervision, the sudden call for a new regulatory approach is surprising. There is considerable agreement that traditional regulation has not kept up with financial innovations.

A third type of failure pertains to government policy and the respective parliaments, which deliberately promoted financial deregulation in the United States following pressure from the Wall Street lobby, and opposed coordinated international financial regulation. Posner (2009: 269) argues convincingly that the Administration under President George W Bush consistently ignored problems in the financial market, in particular the looming housing bubble. After the eruption of the subprime crisis, the handling of the problems in the initial phases was insufficient and imprudent, culminating in the decision to let Lehman Brothers go bankrupt, and then failing to recognise that not only a liquidity crisis but also a solvency crisis had emerged.

3.   Ongoing debate

There appear to be three areas of ongoing debate about the proximate causes. The first area concerns the massive bonus payments. There can be no question that short-term incentives for bankers contributed to risk taking and speculative behaviour, although the incentives were designed to prevent this and to make bankers accountable for misbehaviour. The underlying questions relate to the corporate governance of financial institutions – why shareholders did not voice concern – and the enormous profits made by them, with much higher returns on equity than elsewhere in the economy. The latter can, in principle, be due to their incurring higher risks, to monopoly power (including rent seeking), windfall profits based on extraordinarily high demand for financial services, technical progress (due to innovations) and/or creative accounting practice, apart from fraud. All of them may have contributed to the crisis, and should have been a matter of concern for regulators and governments, but were not. However, fixed salaries and small bonuses would not have prevented the crisis.

The second area of debate concerns monetary policy. Blaming the Federal Reserve for maintaining excessively low open-market interest rates that triggered an increase in asset prices implies that central banks can and should target money aggregates, and that they know how much money fuels inflation and to what extent asset prices. There is no theoretical or empirical basis for such assumptions. There is no clear-cut causal relationship between short-term rates, broad money and asset prices. Demand for mortgages depends on long-term rates which do not follow one-to-one with short-term rates, and which were somewhat reduced by excessive external demand for bonds, as pointed out rightly by Greenspan (2010) and others, as against Taylor (2009) who criticized the Federal Reserve for an excessively easy monetary policy between 2002 and 2005. But the simple truth is that the arsenal of tools of modern and powerful central banks includes no suitable instruments for fighting housing bubbles or other asset price booms. Commercial banks tend to behave procyclically, with increasing leveraging during business cycle booms. If the Greenspan-Bernanke doctrine – that an activist expansionary policy can easily pull the economy out of recession – is no longer tenable, new tools for a pre-emptive policy to curb speculation need to be invented.

The third issue of debate concerns re-regulation of the financial sector. Some emphasize the necessity for macroprudential supervision, but the design is not yet clear. This could involve a rule- (or principle) based countercyclical leverage prescription for banks, provision of equity buffers or a return to the Glass-Steagall Act,[6] but also asset-based reserve requirements (Palley, 2004). Others call for a better coordinated and stricter conventional form of microeconomic supervision, supported by rules for approval of new financial products (e.g. proposed by the German Chancellor Angela Merkel). Some question the present business model and call for much narrower banking and the abandonment of a number of unnecessary financial services. In their view, today's financial industry is overstretched and constitutes a deadweight for the economy. Many hold that common minimum rules have to be found on an international scale, requiring a global supervisory institution (Reinhart and Rogoff, 2009).

Some in the banking industry argue that very fundamental regulatory reforms could throw the baby out with the bathwater and that only minor reforms are necessary. In their view, it was mainly the failure of Lehman Brothers, based on a disastrous political decision, and the often unprofessional and late policy responses of the Administration of the time, which amplified the crisis (vividly described by Posner, 2009: 269).

B.   Alan Greenspan's view

Of special interest is Alan Greenspan's (2010) interpretation of the crisis, which seems to be shared, more or less, by other influential economists (see, for example, Mankiw, 2010). Greenspan contends that it was the long-standing trend towards low, long-term real interest rates on a global scale that triggered house price inflation worldwide, with a few exceptions (e.g. Germany, Japan and Switzerland). This trend emerged from the aftermath of the Cold War, when countries like China, and later the Russian Federation, started to produce at low prices for the global market, and global saving exceeded global investment,[7] mainly driven by some developing countries which achieved double the GDP growth rate of developed countries between 2000 and 2007 ("saving glut"). All this, sometimes referred to as the "the Great Moderation", led to low global inflation and then to low long-term real interest rates.

The acceleration of house price inflation in the United States, which originated in the initially small subprime market segment, came with widespread securitization activities by financial firms that faced strong demand for such structured, highly profitable products. According to Greenspan, the demand came mainly from the government-sponsored enterprises, Fannie Mae and Freddie Mac, which claimed to have been pressured by the Department of Housing and Urban Development to increase the provision of affordable housing (but with no mention of who pressured the Department). In addition, strong demand came from domestic and European financial investors. Grossly inflated credit ratings, deteriorating loan underwriting standards, underpricing of risks, and a general "irrational exuberance" unfolded. Greenspan claims the bubble was easy to identify relative to historical measures, but not the point in time when it would burst. Besides, almost all experts were sanguine, both inside and outside the United States, including a number of Nobel laureates. There was an overwhelming trust in "our highly sophisticated global system of financial risk management to contain market breakdowns" (Greenspan, 2010: 11), which made use of data covering the past few decades (backward looking), so that signs of systemic risks went undetected.[8] However, as noted by Greenspan (2010: 12), "the risk management paradigm nonetheless, harboured a fatal flaw." Greenspan hints at the "indecipherable complexity of … financial products and markets that developed with the advent of sophisticated mathematical techniques to evaluate risk." In a footnote he adds the telling insight: "I often argued that because of the complexity, we had to rely on an international 'invisible hand' to bring equilibrium to such undecipherable markets. The high level of market liquidity (erroneously) appeared to confirm that the system was working" (Greenspan 2010: 12).

This appears to be no different from the famous 2007 remark by Charles Prince, former chairman of Citigroup: "When the music stops, in terms of liquidity, things will be complicated. But as long as the music is playing, you've got to get up and dance. We're still dancing." Did this represent a stubborn belief in equilibrium instead of a sober analysis and responsible governance? Was Greenspan an ideologue – an "animal spirit" of market-fundamentalist policymakers?

Greenspan continues that the crisis was a "hundred year flood" that, under the circumstances – excessive leveraging, two decades of unrelenting prosperity with low inflation and low real interest rates – was impossible to prevent. He asserts that bank regulation is incapable and fundamentally inferior to big banks. And he proposes mainly higher capital-asset ratios and a requirement for all financial intermediaries to hold contingent bonds that can be converted to equity if more equity is needed, as well as increased collateral requirements for globally traded financial products.

Greenspan's statement is indeed revealing if it is representative of the views of leading central bankers and policymakers. Many questions arise: Why do low real interest rates compellingly ignite housing bubbles? Why did supervisors and the Federal Reserve not take action against excessive financial leverage or propose new tools? Why was the mushrooming of the subprime segment in the mortgage market and the excessive securitization tolerated or even promoted? Why was risk management so fundamentally flawed? Why was there no mention of the unregulated market for derivatives – mainly credit default swaps? Why were all of the many measures of financial deregulation over the past few decades not addressed? And why was the excessive debt-led consumption excluded from analysis? The "saving glut" approach is highly opaque (see below). What is evident, however, is the economic mismanagement in the United States after 2001, the unshaken belief in the wisdom of financial markets and their market makers, as well as a complacent belief in the power of the Federal Reserve, and simply the overwhelming belief that "it" cannot happen again.

C.   Beyond the proximate causes

Without going into the details, summarized below are what could be considered the proximate causes of the financial crisis in five key areas:

1. The starting point was a classical asset price and speculation crisis that emerged in the United States housing market in 1995 and accelerated after 2001. This was facilitated by an ill-designed policy and uncontrolled excessive securitization by the financial industry. The bubble burst due to a monetary stance of increasing interest rates necessitated by global inflationary pressure. This in turn led to a banking crisis, including a liquidity and solvency crisis.

2. The housing bubble translated into the build-up of a financial house of cards comprising multiple securitization, collaterized debt obligations (CDOs) and credit default swaps (CDS). This represented an enormous extension of the derivatives markets, in part facilitated by shadow banks (so-called "special investment vehicles") and non-banks such as hedge and pensions funds. Extreme leveraging, excessive maturity risks and considerable overall risk taking occurred, as in many historical boom-bust cycles.

3. The methods of risk assessment by bank managers for their financial products and for the banks themselves, based on mainstream thinking in the economics profession, were systematically flawed. The underestimation of risk was masked by mass demand for "toxic" assets.

4. Until the failure of Lehman Brothers in September 2008, there was a general misjudgement of the accelerators in the spreading of the financial crisis to the national and global economy, especially the role of vulnerable interbank money markets (Brunnermeier 2009).

5. Traditional banking supervision had not kept up with financial innovations and the ever-increasing complexity of the financial industry, either in the United States or in most other OECD countries. This holds true also for supranational institutions, specifically the IMF, which was not aware of the inherent risks of financial globalization.

However, all the above-mentioned factors do not capture the essential reasons which established the preconditions for the financial crisis and subsequent widespread recession. They are at best half the story. Most of these factors focus on microeconomic aspects and on the supply side of financial products. They neglect to explain the huge demand for risky assets, and thus lead to underestimating the enormous scale of demand and supply – and therefore the magnitude of the financial house of cards. Indeed, the United States banks themselves created a big chunk of the demand for structured financial products, using the Federal Reserve's money creation and the money markets. But private domestic net saving was small and shrank to a negative value, despite huge government budget deficits, even during the upswing after 2001. International saving consistently compensated for the shortfall in domestic saving since the mid-1990s until 2006, which was reflected in a rising capital-account surplus – the flipside of the rising current-account deficit. This international saving flooded the United States economy, providing an enormous, ostensibly infinite, source of funds for the various financial markets. On the one hand, the United States – and to a lesser extent the United Kingdom – became the global magnet for capital flows for risky or semi-risky investments (Gros, 2009). The risks were systematically underestimated as long as masses of financial investors participated; they swam, so to speak, with the tide. On the other hand, the United States also attracted risk-averse finance on a large scale, specifically the currency reserves of surplus countries.

The increasing and cumulating financial inflows enabled private households to lower their saving rate and indulge in a consumption frenzy, encouraged by rising house and other asset prices that signalled a new age of wealth. The growth pattern of the United States in the pre-crisis period, since the 1990s, was grounded in consumption dynamics, housing investment and government spending; whereas domestic non-financial fixed investment remained weak, even though it was urgently needed to cope with problems of deindustrialization. This macroeconomic constellation would not have been possible without massive capital inflows from the rest of the world.

The reputation of the dollar, the main global reserve currency, lowered the currency risk to foreign financial investors. This currency bonus contributed to the taking of excessive risks by financial investors from abroad, since the United States was considered immune to a currency crisis, and since the Federal Reserve and the Government were believed to be capable of managing bailouts should they become necessary. Similar to almost all other financial crises in recent decades, excessive current-account deficits had been early warning signs of macroeconomic turmoil (Reinhart and Rogoff, 2009: 204). The narrow focus on the financial sector blinded observers to the shaky global environment. These problems have been much discussed under the heading of "global imbalances". But the causal nexus of these imbalances with the emergence of the financial crisis needs to be explored in greater depth.

II. The role of global imbalances

Global imbalances are normally understood as the confluence of high and increasing current-account surpluses in some countries and the huge current-account deficit of the United States, along with some other smaller deficit countries (see figure 1). At the peak of the imbalances in 2006, the United States absorbed 60 per cent of all surpluses, whereas China, Germany, Japan and six other countries – mainly oil exporters – generated 75 per cent of all surpluses before the crisis (figure 2). China's much discussed surplus accounted for 19 per cent of the aggregate surplus, while Germany[9] and Japan together accounted for 25 per cent. There were also 45 small, mainly strongly performing developing countries which made up the remaining quarter of total surpluses. In the group of deficit countries, there were a few other developed economies besides the United States (mainly Australia, Italy, Spain, Turkey and the United Kingdom) which had a combined share of 22 per cent of deficits, and 75 small, mainly developing countries, which accounted for another 17 per cent of deficits (figure 3).

The United States deficit grew continuously from 1991, reaching a peak in 2006 (figure 4). Since the mid-1980s, the United States had turned into an ever-growing net debtor country, with a net debt of around 20 per cent of GDP prior to the crisis. During the crisis, imbalances shrank when imports plummeted due to a drop in GDP and an increase in household saving, but imbalances are projected to grow again. The bilateral China-United States

Figure 1

CURRENT-ACCOUNT BALANCES, 2001–2014

(Billions of dollars)

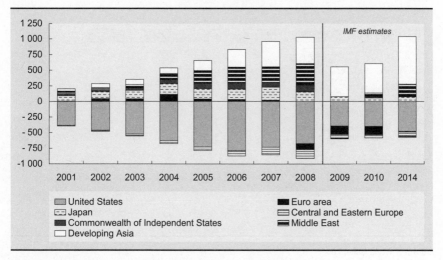

Source: IMF, 2010a.

Figure 2

54 CURRENT-ACCOUNT SURPLUS COUNTRIES, 2006

(Per cent of aggregate surplus)

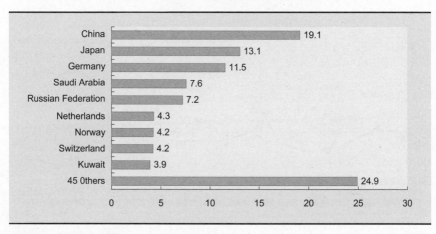

Source: World Bank, 2009.

Figure 3

81 CURRENT-ACCOUNT DEFICIT COUNTRIES, 2006

(Per cent of aggregate deficit)

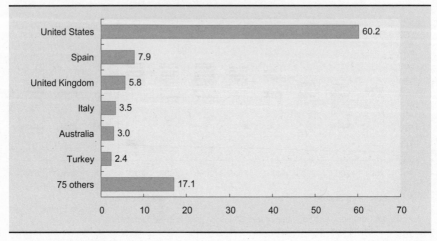

Source: World Bank, 2009.

Figure 4

CURRENT-ACCOUNT BALANCE, 1980–2008

(Per cent of GDP)

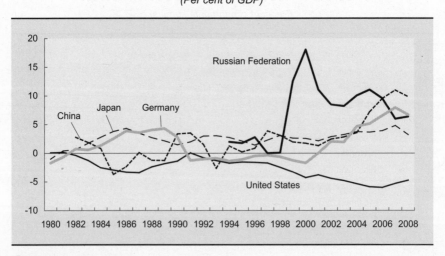

Source: World Bank, 2009.

trade deficit accounts for roughly 30 per cent of the total deficit. Never before had there been global imbalances of this magnitude.

Debates about global imbalances have focused mainly on trade in goods, but have tended to ignore capital flows that reflect financial globalization. This is misleading since capital flows normally are a budget constraint for deficit countries as well as key determinants of exchange rates. The eminent German economist Wolfgang Stützel was among those who contended that, under normal conditions, the capital-account balance determines the current-account balance (Stützel 1978: 125 ff.), in this respect following Böhm-Bawerk. Moreover, the magnitude of gross cross-border capital flows is much bigger than that of trade in goods, specifically because of their short-term nature, and cross-border redeployment of huge capital stocks adds to the flow of capital from current saving. Continuous net capital inflows into a deficit country cumulate and can reach a high, ever-increasing stock level relative to GDP. A large share of capital inflows into the United States financial system was due to increasing official reserves of the central banks of surplus countries which had fixed or managed exchange-rate regimes (e.g. China and Japan).

The general notion that the capital-account balance determines the current-account balance refers to a fully-fledged open-market economy. However, this insight needs to be applied to the special case where the largest economy in the world provides the major reserve currency, where the exchange rates in many emerging-market economies (as well as in Japan) are managed and, as in China, where the capital account is highly regulated or semi-closed so that purely market-determined capital flows play a minor role. Hence the finance that flows into such a surplus country originates from income and money and credit creation in the United States, used mainly for the importation of goods (e.g. from China or oil-producing countries) and returns to the United States as reserves or other capital flows. The reserve-currency country (i.e. the United States) has no budget constraint in the balance of payments if its capital account is open and the leading central bank (i.e. the Federal Reserve) does not intervene in foreign exchange markets. In this specific constellation, it is mainly the finance created in the United States that determines both that country's current-account deficit and a large part of the capital return inflows in the United States capital account. In contrast, for developed countries such as those in the euro area or the

United Kingdom, the origin of financial flows from there to the United States may lie in the portfolio decisions of *their* wealth owners, which influence exchange rates and current-account balances.

Official capital flows from the surplus countries are mainly risk-averse (i.e. directed towards government bonds or similar assets), whereas private investments are often attracted to higher yields that carry higher risk, or simply for the purpose of diversifying portfolios by investing in countries with different risks. The United States financial industry adjusted its offers of financial products to this global demand and attempted to exploit the surging capital inflows, which were driven by a high level of trust in the dollar and seduced by the reputation of the financial system, and, last but not least, by expectations of higher yields than elsewhere. The causes of the emergence of high surpluses vary in each of the different surplus countries.

China, since its accession to the World Trade Organization (WTO) in 2001, followed a more or less neo-mercantilist trade and exchange-rate strategy to boost its net exports through real undervaluation of the renminbi, thus supporting high growth and employment, which were necessary for political stability. In addition, China continued to peg its currency to the dollar (nominal anchor until 2005 and again since mid 2008), accumulated reserves to defend the peg if necessary, successfully sterilized excess money creation and continued to fend off capital inflows other than foreign direct investment. This policy led to more than a 10 per cent current-account surplus at the peak, and to ballooning reserves, mostly invested in the United States.

Since the end of the 1990s, *Germany* was faced with a decoupling of real wages from productivity increases ("wage-restraint"), which led to stagnation of domestic demand. In also following a neo-mercantilist growth path, its trade surplus rose to 7.1 per cent of GDP in 2007. Germany took advantage of the euro: wage restraint and trade surplus could no longer induce appreciation of the exchange rate after the latter was abandoned, but they improved international competitiveness in the same way as a real currency depreciation. Subsequently, capital exports were regarded as more profitable than investing in the real domestic economy, which was suffering from slack aggregate demand. The resulting trade imbalances occurred mainly within the European Union (EU), especially within the euro zone, reflecting deficits in other member countries of the EU. However, capital outflows from Germany did not match the regional structure of trade flows; instead, they were directed, to some extent, to the major financial markets, especially those in the United States. Thus, sluggish domestic demand and higher expected returns abroad triggered capital outflows from Germany to the United States.

Some fluctuations aside, *Japan* tried to maintain a high surplus of its current account with a managed floating exchange-rate regime that sought to curb yen appreciations. To overcome the deflationary pressure, which the country suffered in the mid-1990s and again since 2001, a strong real effective depreciation of the yen was facilitated to offset weak domestic demand. In 2007, Japan's current-account surplus peaked at around 5 per cent of GDP and the trade surplus reached 3.9 per cent of GDP in 2006. Capital outflows from Japan consist of private flows (seeking higher than the low domestic yield), carry trade (i.e. borrowing cheap and short-term in Japan and investing in countries with higher interest rates, see Hattori and Shin 2009), foreign direct investment (mainly targeting emerging Asia) and large official investment of currency reserves.

The role of official reserves in capital flows should not be underestimated. Global currency reserves almost quadrupled from the Asian crisis up to 2008, when they reached more than US$ 7 trillion (figure 5; see also CEA, 2010: appendix B, table B111). The maximum annual increase was in 2007, almost US$ 1.3 trillion. Around two thirds of the global reserves were estimated to be denominated in dollars (Wooldridge, 2006). Considering that the United States capital-account surplus was around 6 per cent of GDP in the peak year 2007, or roughly US$ 800 billion, it is reasonable to assume that more than half of the inflows came from official reserves (Bernanke, 2005). It was not only China and Japan, but many other countries, including developing, that had accumulated reserves.

Capital exports, be they private finance or official reserves, are saving, and do not reflect demand for domestic goods but rather a preference for foreign financial assets. They slow down growth of the world economy unless offset by robust growth, for instance by debt-led consumption or government spending in the deficit countries. Needless to say, this saving does not necessarily translate into higher aggregate demand in the deficit countries.

Figure 5

RESERVES OF MAJOR RESERVE-HOLDING ECONOMIES, 2001–2010

(US$ billion)

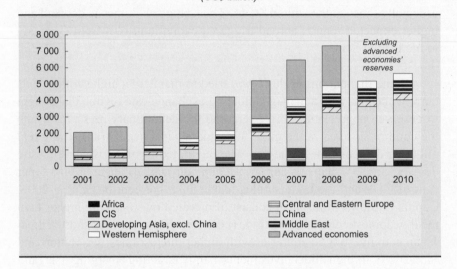

Source: IMF, 2009 and 2010b.
Note: Growth of reserves of emerging and developing economies, 2001–2008: 28.9 per cent per annum. Country categories are those used by the IMF.

While private capital flows to the United States fluctuate according to the expected yield differentials, and thus contribute to exchange-rate volatility, investing official reserves in the United States stabilizes the dollar vis-à-vis other currencies. On average, the real effective exchange rate of the dollar will move up and down only to a limited extent. Indeed, a massive and sustained real depreciation of the dollar has not occurred in the past 25 years, although the United States clearly needed this to lower its current-account deficits (figure 6). From this point of view, the dollar is overvalued in real terms, which has contributed to the much complained about deindustrialization in that country.[10] Structural transformation towards a new export base to offset the exchange-rate disadvantage has failed, as became evident after the bursting of the "new economy" bubble in 2001. The response to this failure has been structural change that favoured the expansion of the financial sector. Wall Street became, so to speak, Main Street; put in simple terms, more and more financial assets, instead of goods, were exported.

Figure 6

REAL EFFECTIVE EXCHANGE RATES IN CHINA, GERMANY, JAPAN AND THE UNITED STATES, 1980–2008

(Index numbers, 2000 = 100)

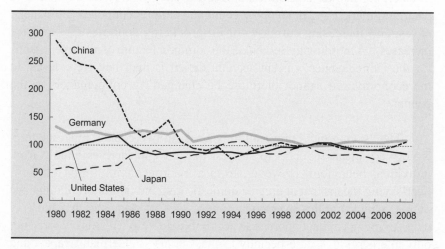

Source: World Bank, 2009.

In the debates about the potential risks of these imbalances, three main opinions predominate (Priewe, 2008). First, that the United States deficit is without risk as it reflects the "saving glut" in Asia and elsewhere, coupled with a high level of trust in the stability of the United States economy (Greenspan, 2004 and 2010; Bernanke, 2005 and 2008). Second, that the combination of deficit and surplus countries was an informal "Bretton Woods II" currency system with a high degree of stability (Dooley, Folkerts-Landau and Garber, 2003). Third, that the imbalances were risky and would lead sooner or later to a strong devaluation of the dollar, which would harm primarily the growth of the surplus economies but also the entire world economy, hence collective action was needed (e.g. Obstfeld, 2005). Some blame China and other surplus countries for their neo-mercantilist exchange-rate policies, while others blame the United States for living beyond its means by tolerating excessive household consumption and high budget deficits. All these positions captured a grain of truth. However, none of them foresaw that the imbalances would trigger financial boom and bust, and the expected currency crisis did not occur.

The notion of a saving glut, as developed by Bernanke (2005), refers to several trends since the mid-1990s, such as an ageing population, fewer investment opportunities in rich countries, excessive household saving in emerging-market economies, strong currency reserve accumulation in emerging-market and developing economies to prevent potential financial crises, and increasing surpluses of oil-producing countries due to price increases.[11] According to Bernanke, the common feature of all these reasons for the United States' current-account deficit is that they are external to the economy and cannot therefore be changed by policymakers in the country.

The "saving glut" proposition is weak on two counts. First, the term is not very clear. It seems to suggest that the glut derives mainly from individual behaviour. However, from a macroeconomic point of view, over-saving means that aggregate domestic demand falls short of domestic output, which implies overproduction or lack of domestic demand (i.e. over-saving or capital export as an accounting identity[12]). This occurred not only in emerging Asia, especially China, but also in Germany, Japan, and oil-producing economies, and even in many poor developing countries. Thus the term saving glut explains nothing, but simply reflects overproduction relative to domestic demand. Second, Bernanke and others overlook the simple fact that the "savings" are transferred mainly to one single country that seems more attractive than all others, namely the reserve-currency country and its financial markets. There must be peculiar pull factors in the United States which exist nowhere else. Hence the reasons for that country's deficit are not only external to it.

It is true that the present global currency system can be compared to the Bretton Woods system, though in a less stable form, with the United States dollar as the main global currency (i.e. the dollar standard as compared to the former gold–dollar standard). An informal system of this kind rests on trust in the dollar and in the United States' financial system, but it is less sustainable than the original Bretton Woods system if inherent contradictions start to unfold. Although "Bretton Woods II" has contributed to the highest worldwide growth (1998–2007) since the breakdown of the original Bretton Woods system, it has been tied to the excessive consumption dynamics of the United States (in the absence of investment-led growth) and to the highly absorptive capacity of that country's financial system. The growth mechanism of the present system is based on an unsustainable and skewed division of labour, where one group of countries produces more goods than it can absorb, while the other generates global aggregate demand and absorbs . more products than it produces. Both sides depend on each other, and no single country or group of countries can be blamed for the imbalances. Thus, the more the imbalances grew, the more likely it was that the system would explode. The Achilles heel was not the value of the dollar, since there was no alternative candidate for a reserve currency, but rather the fragility of the United States financial sector, which was indulging in asset inflation with new financial products. As the growth momentum induced by "Bretton Woods II" overheated and precipitated global inflation, which required a tightening of monetary policy, the bust was only a matter of time, as rising interest rates triggered a fall in prices of housing and other assets.

The global imbalances have contributed to the financial crisis and the subsequent global "grand recession". Whether the core reasons for the imbalances lie in the specific policies of the main surplus and deficit countries or are of a systemic nature, related to the present global currency system, is analysed below.

III. The "new Triffin dilemma"

The crucial weakness of "Bretton Woods II" can be described as a "new Triffin dilemma". Robert Triffin (1960) detected a flaw in the architecture of the original Bretton Woods system that constituted a dilemma and would lead to the demise of this system. And so it happened in the early 1970s. Similar defects, albeit somewhat different, have undermined the "Bretton Woods II" system. As is well known, the old system was a gold-dollar standard with a commitment to maintain a constant price of US$ 35 per ounce of gold in order to reinforce the reputation and credibility of the dollar as the reserve currency. The dollar served both as a national and a global currency, as a unit of account, a means of payment for traded goods and many credit contracts, and as a store of value, in particular for currency reserves of central banks. The Federal Reserve had to provide dollars both for the United

States economy and for the rest of the world; but with a rising demand for dollars in a growing world economy and a more or less constant supply of dollars bound to scarce gold supplies, the promise to change dollars to gold at a constant price would lose credibility. Triffin had proposed a system, governed by the IMF, which would generate Special Drawing Rights (SDRs) as a new artificial basket currency that would substitute more and more for the dollar, thus transforming the IMF into a global central bank, similar to Keynes's original proposal at Bretton Woods.

The Triffin dilemma was aggravated if dollars were allocated to the rest of the world via net imports of the United States, financed with the reserves of central banks outside that country. Whereas a credible dollar standard would require a surplus in the current account, a deficit status would undermine the value of the dollar and sooner or later would lead to devaluation. Furthermore, the Bretton Woods system gave the reserve-currency country the advantage of getting indebted in its own currency, implying a lack of "budget constraint" in its balance of payments which eased the financing of budget deficits – even when inflationary – through capital inflows from abroad. These foreign inflows resulted either from foreign exchange interventions to stabilize the currency pegs to the dollar, or from investing reserves in United States Treasury bills. According to this view, the inflation in the late 1960s that eventually destroyed trust in the dollar and its peg to gold was an indirect result of the Triffin dilemma.

In addition to the Triffin dilemma, a number of similar weaknesses can be mentioned. In the Bretton Woods system, the dollar as the n-th currency could not be depreciated; only n-1 currencies could be appreciated.[13] This created incentives for protracted misalignments of exchange rates, especially in the absence of rules for surplus countries to apply expansionary policies. Moreover, the trend to full capital-account liberalization after the Second World War and the emergence of global financial markets undermined the possibilities of defending exchange-rate pegs. The gist of the matter is that a currency, even if it has by all measures a clear supremacy over others, cannot easily serve both national and global objectives.

What has been called "Bretton Woods II" is a system based on a pure dollar standard (i.e. not a gold-dollar standard), to which a number of mainly emerging-market and developing economies have loosely or even firmly pegged their currencies. This has stabilized the currency system somewhat after the demise of Bretton Woods, although there have nevertheless been wide swings in exchange rates. The preconditions are that the dollar is not threatened by severe inflation, that the Federal Reserve can pursue a fully autonomous monetary policy without regard for the external value of the dollar, and that there is a deep and large financial market sufficiently attractive to allure net capital flows from abroad to finance that country's current-account deficit. The system may be stable in the sense that there is no alternative as long as no other reserve-currency candidate emerges and as long as full and unfettered floating is unacceptable for the majority of countries, in particular developing countries. But it is not stable with regard to growth and financial system stability since it is prone to imbalances.

The system provides a number of adverse incentives. For the United States, it tends to flood the economy with capital inflows and leads to an overvaluation of the real exchange rate relative to a moderate current-account deficit or balance. In principle, this flood of inflows could be reduced by capital exports from the United States, which has happened occasionally (mainly to emerging-market economies). However, this is highly unlikely to happen all the time: the n-th country is a "natural" current-account-deficit country, as it is the main absorber of reserves, offers the largest and deepest capital markets in the world, has a reputation and trust advantage, and involves less currency risks for financial investors. In short, there is a strong systemic pull factor in the reserve-currency country that tends to attract finance (or "over-savings") from the n-1 countries.

If overvaluation of the real effective exchange rate of the n-th country occurs, it hollows out its real economy and its international competitiveness. The risk of a sudden devaluation of the n-th currency is limited, the external budget constraint is soft, and interest rates tend to be depressed, at least in periods of soaring inflows, thus weakening the power of a restrictive monetary policy or requiring a higher Federal Funds rate to fight inflation. In case of a strong current-account deficit, private households and/or the government budget tend to be in high deficit, whereas non-financial corporations resort to self-financing.

For the n-1 countries, in principle, the system provides incentives for them to undervalue their currencies and to embark on neo-mercantilist export-led growth, with pegged exchange rates or strongly managed floating or in other ways such as undervalued exchange rates. Since the pegs are mostly soft and vulnerable, due to the volatility of global capital flows, overly high reserves are built up. Overall, the system tends to result in huge global imbalances in trade and capital flows, especially since there are no rectifying market mechanisms. Not all of the n-1 countries need to be surplus countries, compelled by systemic drivers. Whether a country becomes a surplus country and to what extent, depends very much on the mix of institutions and policies in the particular country. As mentioned above, the reasons for the creation of surpluses in China, Japan, Germany, oil-producing countries and others are quite diverse and appear to be country-specific. But if surpluses occur, they are primarily invested in the n-th country, thus avoiding appreciation of capital-exporting countries' exchange rates.

Moral hazard emerges in the reserve-currency country's financial system as it exploits the inflows of capital through systematic underpricing of risks. The sheer magnitude of the inflowing liquidity fuels asset price bubbles and excessive risk taking by financial institutions. Higher risks are incurred than in the n-1 economies, and the risks are concealed by mass inflows, herd behaviour and exaggerated trust in the leading currency. Moreover, all of this is driven by rational behaviour and policy from a narrow microeconomic or national perspective. Booms are likely to be strong but accompanied by asset price inflation, and severe currency crises can be excluded as there are no other currencies to flee to (Carbaugh and Hedrick 2009). Having the only reserve currency is like a monopoly, whereby the monopolist enjoys certain privileges, though this is not without risks. The n-th currency country has to devote considerable attention to supervision and surveillance of the much expanded financial sector. In conventional understanding, deficit countries are in an inferior position to surplus countries, but the reserve-currency country is a privileged exception. All this does not necessarily lead to a financial crash, but it certainly increases the risks.

In principle, the rebalancing of global trade and capital flows within the "Bretton-Woods II" system can be done either unilaterally by the surplus countries or the deficit country, or through multilateral action. The surplus countries could revalue against the dollar and switch from export-led growth to domestic-demand-led growth. The deficit country could tighten fiscal and monetary policy to contain the current-account deficit, but at the price of a global recession. This is only a likely response in the case of inflation in the n-th country; in the case of asset price inflation the likely result will be a financial crisis. A multilaterally coordinated pre-emptive policy for global rebalancing is the better solution, but this is unlikely in the absence of a system of global macroeconomic governance (Helleiner, 2009; Keynes, 1979: 256–295).

The new Triffin dilemma in the "Bretton Woods II" system requires a particular hard currency as the global reserve currency, but exposes the respective country to comparatively soft budget constraints – much softer than in any n-1 country – in its balance of payments, in its government budget, in its private household sector, in its non-financial industries and, last but not least, in its financial sector. This country is prone to asset price inflation and to a type of finance-led capitalism, distorted by "financialization", which spills over to more and more of the n-1 countries.

IV. Finance-led capitalism and unequal income distribution

Many economists have observed and debated a trend in developed economies, most markedly in the United States, towards financialization and finance-led capitalism (Hein et al., 2008; van Treeck, 2009). Roughly, the central idea is that the traditional managerial and "Fordist" form of capitalism furthered growth of and investment by non-financial firms and productivity-led wage dynamics, but at the expense of shareholders who were unable to discipline managers, often allies of workers. The more bank-based financial system promoted debt financing of enterprises. Now, a more capital-market-based system has emerged which gives greater power of governance to the financial markets and shareholders. This required deregulated financial markets – with stock prices as an efficient guide for corporate development – and the rise of investment banks and other non-banks. It led to increased internal financing of firms, the rise of financial holding structures of corporations, more mergers and acquisitions and less investment in fixed assets, higher cash payouts to shareholders and increased returns to shareholders, lower wage increases (partly due to deregulation of labour markets) and a falling share of wages, stock market dependence on macro performance and higher susceptibility to asset price bubbles – in short, greater financial fragility.

In a Kaldor-Kaleckian framework, in a closed economy, profits (P) can be conceived of as the result of demand for investment (I), and demand from consumption by capitalists (I_p) and workers (i.e. low saving of the latter, S_W).[14] In an open economy that includes economic activity of the government, high aggregate profits can only be achieved, on the condition that there is low corporate investment (I_c) and a negative trade balance (X<M) via high consumption by those who receive profits and by workers (i.e. low saving of workers), high residential investment (I_R) and high budget deficits (G>T): $P = I_c + I_R + G\text{-}T + X\text{-}M + C_p\text{-}S_W$. These were precisely the conditions that prevailed in the United States in previous boom phases. In other countries the features of financialization led to different macroeconomic regimes. For example, in Germany they led to wage restraint and an excessive trade surplus but, overall, to lower growth, and in Japan mainly to high budget deficits.

Over the past two to three decades various trends in financial development in the United States and also in other OECD countries seem to have emerged:

- Money and credit are increasingly used for financial transactions rather than for real transactions (i.e. exchange of goods, services and labour).

- Profit maximization is conceived more and more, at least by joint stock companies, as maximization of shareholder value rather than current profit. Accounting rules have been changing (based on such features as mark-to-market and fair value rather than on the lowest value principle); corporate governance is undertaken more by capital markets than by house banks; there are new forms of pay for management based on stock market performance, and lower barriers to mergers and acquisitions.

- The financial sector has experienced above-average growth in many countries, largely driven by financial innovations, deregulation and globalization of financial markets. Indeed, the financial sector has been considered the boom sector, seemingly without a clear distinction from the real (non-financial) economy, and financial service innovations have been seen as a special form of technical progress.

- Returns on equity – as well as management pay – have been rising relative to non-financial sectors, and have become more and more the benchmark for the real economy. The share of aggregate wages in national income has been falling in most OECD countries, and profits have tilted more towards financial industries than to non-financial sectors.[15]

- Security and other asset markets like real estate have become more susceptible to bubbles and speculation. The number of financial crises has increased, seemingly more in emerging-market economies, although these crises were linked to risk and high-yield-seeking external finance originating in OECD economies.

These trends have been the most pronounced in the United Kingdom and the United States, but are also prevalent in almost all other economies where financial markets tend to emulate the Wall Street model, be they in Frankfurt, Paris, Singapore, Beijing or Johannesburg. Stock prices, rather than accumulation of fixed capital and technical progress, have been seen as heart pacemakers for the entire economy. Differences between the financial industry and the real economy seem to have evaporated. Any misgiving that finance may be deadweight for the "productive", real economy has been increasingly rejected; instead, finance has been praised as growth enhancing (Summers, 2000). Thus, the gradual transformation of the traditional capitalism of the golden age after the Second World War – centred on growth of the real economy – led to the problematic development of the financial sector, which culminated in the subprime crisis.

All this is far beyond the narrow focus on the proximate causes of the financial crisis in section 1 of this paper. These structural, long-standing causes have contributed to the global imbalances, since they are at the root of the absorptive capacity of the United States' financial sector with regard to external capital inflows.

The trend towards financialization has occurred alongside increasing income inequality, arguably the most pronounced in the United States among developed countries. The weak wage increases in low- and middle-income households in the past have led to a falling propensity to save, dissaving and increasing indebtedness, in particular for house purchases. The credit-asset price spiral that was kept in motion basically underpinned macroeconomic growth in the United States since the mid-1990s when house prices started to rise. The background for this development was the widespread delinking of real wage and productivity increases in many OECD countries,[16] with Germany and Japan at the lower end. In Germany, this contributed since the late 1990s to a marked weakness in domestic demand and imports, and, on the flip side, to excessive net exports of goods and high net capital exports. Germany became addicted to wage restraint, in contrast to the majority of the 15 other euro- zone members which followed a different pattern of wage setting. In other countries, the increasingly skewed income distribution is embedded in different macroeconomic patterns, often accompanied by current-account deficits. The common feature in most OECD countries is that growth of the real economy and employment has been weaker than in previous upswing phases of the business cycle. As a result, unsustainable macroeconomic regimes have evolved which directly (in the United States) or indirectly (e.g. China, Germany, Japan,) contributed to the emergence of the financial and economic crisis.

V. Conclusions

Opinions about the causes of the financial crisis differ widely. Most of them focus on the financial sector and blame either the bankers or the supervisory authorities, or an excessively lax monetary policy, and, albeit more seldom, policymakers (although they deserve much of the blame in the United States, particularly in 2001–2005). The main message of this paper is that the crisis cannot be fully understood unless the more fundamental causes are taken into consideration.

The first of these causes is the emerging global imbalances in trade and concomitant capital flows over the past two decades that characterized the distorted pattern of globalization under a financial architecture sometimes termed "Bretton Woods II". The new Triffin dilemma led to the flooding of the United States' financial sector with both risk-seeking and risk-averse external capital flows, and created an enormous demand for financial products of different kinds that promoted an unsustainable, risky macroeconomic regime in that country, based on asset bubbles.

Secondly, over more than two decades the traditional post-war capitalism in the United States has been transformed by financialization into a fragile finance-led form of capitalism with a vastly overstretched financial sector. Alongside this transformation, income distribution has tended towards greater inequality, and the lack of fixed investment dynamics in non-financial sectors has been offset by debt-financed consumption and government spending.

This analysis leads to three major policy conclusions. First, coordinated financial sector reforms in the leading OECD countries are necessary, which would restore regulation of banks and non-banks and tighten microeconomic prudential supervision. In addition, those reforms need to include some kind of prudential macroeconomic supervision with a countercyclical control of leverage, the setting of higher capital-asset ratios, the use of new tools to prevent asset bubbles without endangering the real economy, and new methods of risk management, to name but a few measures that should be part of a giant project in the years to come.

Furthermore, the global currency system needs fundamental reforms that reduce global imbalances and enable orderly adjustments of exchange rates to bolster the real economy. A true "Bretton Woods II" should be on the agenda, in which the dollar should be replaced as the main reserve currency, at least in part by a basket of currencies or Special Drawing Rights.

Finally, the road to ever more financialization should be left behind; instead priority should be given to revitalization of the real economy, supported by a downsized financial sector that is more geared to serving the needs of non-financial enterprises. This includes a departure from excessive export-led or debt-led macroeconomic regimes, and a greater dependence than in the past on sustainable domestic demand dynamics, based on more equal distribution of income.

These are three enormous tasks for institutional reform which cannot be implemented overnight, require much more global coordination and governance, and, last but not least, need better economics than that of the mainstream economics of the past. All this is clearly uncharted territory.

Notes

1   If global growth had continued at the 2007 rate of 5.2 per cent, world GDP would have been 16.4 per cent higher in 2010. However, it grew by only 3 per cent in 2008 and by 0.8 per cent in 2009, and is expected to recover somewhat with a projected 3.9 per cent growth in 2010, according to the IMF (2010a). This means a loss of about 10 percentage points of GDP relative to the previous growth trend. Moreover, without countercyclical policies the losses would have been much higher.

2   At the time of writing, there are ongoing investigations by the United States Securities and Exchange Commission (SEC) against Goldman Sachs and other major banks. Also, the United States Senate Judiciary Committee's Subcommittee on Crime, is looking into the practices of these institutions. Yet most conventional economists have tended to ignore the issue of financial crime and fraud (Galbraith, 2010).

3   The Taylor rule stipulates that the interest rate should be determined solely by the equilibrium short-term interest rate plus the weighted average of the inflation gap and the output gap. The Federal Funds Rate, which should have averaged 3.8 per cent during the period 2002–2005, according to the Taylor rule, averaged in actual fact 1.8 per cent (Taylor 2009).

4   To cite Alan Greenspan's take on bursting bubbles: "Assuaging their aftermath seems the best we can hope for" (2010: 46).

5   Although the United States was at the epicentre of the crisis, and banking regulation in most other OECD countries was not as lax as in the United States, the high level of financial integration in the world today resulted in immediate contagion. With financial globalization, national regulation becomes extremely porous due to open borders and a lack of transnational regulatory institutions.

6   This Act, which took effect in 1933, introduced the separation of commercial and investment banking, and it founded the Federal Deposit Insurance Corporation (FDIC) for insuring bank deposits.

7   Greenspan (2010) refers to intended saving and investment.

8   IMF staff wrote in April 2007: "... global economic risks have declined since ... September 2006 ... [T]he overall U.S. economy is holding up well ... [and] the signs elsewhere are very encouraging" (IMF, 2007, xii). See also Reinhart and Rogoff, 2009: 214.

9   Germany's huge surplus is mainly absorbed by deficits in the euro zone, which has an almost balanced current account.

10   The United States dollar appreciated continuously by about 20 per cent (in real effective terms) from 1990 to 2002, and devalued from then until 2008 at the same rate. For different measures of the real effective exchange rate, see CEA, 2010, annex table B 110.

11   Bernanke (2005) suggested that the United States' current account could run out of control, but he believed, optimistically, in medium-term moderation of the deficit.

12   The ex post accounting identity can be expressed as: $X-M = (S-I) - (G-T)$, where X represents exports, M imports, S private saving, I private investment, G government expenditure in final goods and T tax receipts. With a negligible budget deficit, $X-M = S-I$. A trade surplus implies that part of aggregate output is neither invested nor consumed (S as non-consumption) at home, due to a lack of demand; instead, it is exported. Therefore, to term this a "saving glut" seems misleading.

13   It is assumed that there are n currencies, and the n-th currency is the major reserve currency (here the United States dollar), in which the value of the other n-1 currencies is expressed.

14   This follows Kalecki's famous statement: "Capitalists earn what they spend and workers spend what they earn." It can be expressed as: $P = I + C_p - S_w$.

15   The value added of the United States financial sector rose from 4 per cent of GDP to 8 per cent from the mid-1970s to 2007, compared with 2.5 per cent in 1947 (Reinhart and Rogoff, 2009: 210; Greenspan, 2010: exhibit 8). In 2007, 30 per cent of corporate profits accrued to the financial sector, compared with 23 per cent in 1970 (author's calculations, based on CEA, 2009: table B91). In the United States since the 1990s, net income of commercial banks as a percentage of equity has clearly reached higher levels than before, peaking at 15 per cent in 2005 (see Greenspan, 2010: Exhibit 14).

16   To illustrate this, the average real hourly wage in private enterprises outside agriculture rose in the United States by only 5.9 per cent from 1964 to 2007 in total, whereas labour productivity grew by 1.9 per cent per annum (CEA, 2009: tables B47 and B49).

References

Bernanke BS (2005). The global saving glut and the U.S. current account deficit. Sandridge Lecture (10 March), Richmond, VA. Available at: http://www.federalreserve.gov/boarddocs/speeches/2005/200503102/.

Bernanke BS (2008). Global imbalance: Recent developments and prospects, Bundesbank Lecture, Berlin, 11 September. Available at: www.federalreserve.gov/newsevents/speech/bernanke2007091a.htm.

Borio C and Drehmann M (2009). Assessing the risk of banking crises – revisited. *BIS Quarterly Review*, March, 29–46.

Brunnermeier MK (2009). Deciphering the liquidity and credit crunch, 2007-2008. *Journal of Economic Perspectives*, 23(1), 77–100.

Brunnermeier MK et al. (2009). The fundamental principles of financial regulation. *Geneva Report on the World Economy,* 11/2009. Geneva, International Center for Monetary and Banking Studies.

Carbaugh RJ and Hedrick DW (2009). Will the dollar be dethroned as the main reserve currency? *Global Economy Journal*, 9(3): 1–14.

CEA (Council of Economic Advisers) (2009). *Report to the President 2009*. Washington, DC.

CEA (2010): *Report to the President 2010*. Washington, DC.

Dooley MP, Folkerts-Landau D and Garber PM (2003). An essay on the revived Bretton Woods system. NBER Working Paper, No. 9971, Cambridge, MA.

Eichengreen B (2007). Global Imbalances and the Lessons of Bretton Woods, Cambridge, MA, MIT Press.

Financial Stability Forum (2009). Report of the Financial Stability Forum on addressing procyclicality in the financial system. Available at: http://www.financialstabilityboard.org/publications/r_0904a.pdf (accessed 15 May 2010).

Galbraith J (2010). Statement to the Subcommittee on Crime, Senate Judiciary Committee, 4 May 2010. Available at: http://utip.gov.utexas.edu/Flyers/GalbraithMay4SubCommCrimeRV.pdf.

Goodhart CAE (2009). *The Regulatory Response to the Financial Crisis*. Cheltenham, Edward Elgar.

Greenspan A (2004). Evolving U.S. payments imbalance and its impact on Europe and the rest of the world. *Cato Journal*, 24(1–2): 1–11.

Greenspan A (2010). The crisis. Available at: http://www.brookings.edu/~/media/Files/Programs/ES/BPEA/2010_spring_bpea_papers/spring2010_greenspan.pdf, 9 March (accessed 3 May, 2010).

Gros D (2009). Global imbalances and the accumulation of risk. CEPS Policy Briefs, No.189. Brussels, Centre for European Policy Studies.

Hattori H and Shin HS (2009). Yen carry trade and the subprime crisis. IMF Staff Papers, No. 56: 384–409.

Hein E et al., eds. (2008). Finance-led Capitalism? Macroeconomic Effects of Changes in the Financial Sector. Marburg/Lahn, Metropolis.

Helleiner E (2009). The contemporary reform of global financial governance: Implications and lessons from the past. UNCTAD, G-24 Discussion Paper Series, No. 55. Geneva, United Nations Conference on Trade and Development.

Hellwig M (2008). Systemic risk in the financial sector. An analysis of the subprime-mortgage financial crisis. Preprints of the Max Planck Institute for Research on Collective Goods, No. 43.

IMF (2007). *World Economic Outlook*. Washington, DC, April.

IMF (2009). *World Economic Outlook*. Washington, DC, April.

IMF (2010a). World Economic Outlook (update 26 January). Available at: http://www.imf.org/external/pubs/ft/weo/2010/update/01/index.htm.

IMF (2010b). Currency composition of official foreign exchange reserves (COFER database). Available at: http://www.imf.org/external/np/sta/cofer/eng/cofer.pdf (accessed 10 May, 2010).

Keynes JM (1979). *Collected Writings of John Maynard Keynes*, vol. XXIV (edited by Moggridge D) Cambridge, Cambridge University Press.

Krahnen JP and Franke G. (2009). Instabile Finanzmärkte. CFS Working Paper, No. 2009/13, Goethe-Universität Frankfurt.

Mankiw NG (2010). Insuring against the next crisis. *International Herald Tribune*, 27–28 March.

Obstfeld M (2005). America's deficit, the world's problem. Working Paper, No. C05-144. Berkeley, CA, Center for International and Development Economics Research, University of California, Berkeley.

Obstfeld M and Rogoff KS (2005). Global current account imbalances and exchange rate adjustments. *Brooking Papers on Economic Activity*, 1, 67–146. Baltimore, Brookings Institution Press.

Palley TI (2004). Asset-based reserve requirements: Reasserting domestic monetary control in an era of financial innovation and instability. *Review of Political Economy*, 1: 43–58.

Posner RA (2009). A Failure of Capitalism: The Crisis of '08 and the Descent into Depression. Cambridge, MA, Harvard University Press.

Priewe J (2008). Leistungsbilanzdefizit der USA. *Aus Politik und Zeitgeschichte*, 7: 21–26.

Reinhart CM and Rogoff KS (2009). *This Time is Different: Eight Centuries of Financial Folly*. Princeton, Princeton University Press.

Sinn HW (2009). Kasino Kapitalismus. Wie es zur Finanzkrise kam und was jetzt zu tun ist, 2nd edition, Berlin, ECON.

Stützel W (1978). Saldenmechanik. Ein Beitrag zur Geldtheorie. Tübingen, Mohr.

Summers LH (2000). International financial crises: Causes, prevention, cures. *American Economic Review*, Papers and Proceedings, 90(2): 1–16.

Taylor JB (2009). *Getting Off Track*. Stanford, CA, Hoover Institution Press.

Triffin R (1960). *Gold and the Dollar Crisis*. New Haven, Yale University Press.

van Treeck T (2009). The macroeconomics of "financialisation" and the deeper origins of the world economic crisis. IMK Working Paper, No. 9. Dusseldorf, Hans Boeckler Foundation, Macroeconomic Policy Institute.

World Bank (2009). *World Development Indicators*. Washington, DC.

Wooldridge PD (2006). Veränderte Zusammensetzung von Währungsreserven. *BIZ Quartalsbericht,* September: 29–45.

THE EMERGING-MARKET ECONOMIES IN THE FACE OF THE GLOBAL FINANCIAL CRISIS

Daniela Magalhães Prates and Marcos Antonio Macedo Cintra

Abstract

This paper discusses the implications of the global financial crisis for emerging-market economies. The crisis, through deleveraging and/or flight to quality, spread to those economies whose companies and banks had no connection with the securities linked to the subprime mortgages that triggered the crisis. We argue that the hierarchical and asymmetrical nature of the present international financial and monetary architecture caused these movements to have much greater destabilizing effects on the foreign exchange markets of the emerging-market economies. The latest crisis has shown that the strategies implemented by emerging-market economies following the financial crises of the 1990s (e.g. adoption of prudent macroeconomic policies and the accumulation of foreign currency reserves) have been insufficient to immunize them against the systemic risks inherent in financial globalization. Therefore, these economies need to review those strategies and adopt appropriate instruments for better management of capital flows.

Introduction

The financial crisis, which started in mid-2007 with soaring insolvencies and the devaluation of real estate and assets related to high-risk (subprime) mortgages in the United States, reached systemic proportions following the bankruptcy of many banking and non-banking institutions. Investors' distrust in financial systems became widespread, leading to panic-driven movements in stock exchanges and in derivative and credit markets worldwide. Given the magnitude of the losses and of the public resources raised in order to re-establish trust, weaknesses in the deregulated and liberalized financial system and in the model of credit generation and distribution involving a large number of institutions and markets – the so-called "global shadow banking system" – have become evident (Farhi and Cintra, 2008).

The crisis spread to developing countries, many of which were forced to provide rescue package to bolster their respective financial systems and/ or to implement expansionary monetary policy. Further aggravating the scenario of uncertainty, commodity prices collapsed during the second half of 2008 due to the financial turmoil and to a sharp deterioration of global economic prospects, reinforcing pressures for currency depreciation in these countries.

Therefore the current crisis has shown that the adoption of prudent macroeconomic policies and the accumulation of foreign currency reserves by emerging-market economies have been insufficient to immunize them against the systemic risks inherent in financial globalization. Yet so far, proposals for improving regulatory mechanisms have focused on the configuration of financial systems in developed countries without taking into account the hierarchical and asymmetrical nature of the present international financial and monetary architecture and its implications for the emerging-market economies.

The purpose of this paper is to discuss these implications. It is organized as follows. The first section presents a brief agenda for improvement of the regulatory system in developed countries. The second section analyses the impacts of the crisis on the emerging-market economies. It argues that proposals for reform have so far ignored these implications, which are specific to and associated with these countries' subordinate position in the international monetary and financial system. Finally the third section offers concluding remarks and argues that emerging-market economies should review their strategies implemented after the financial crises of the 1990s (which have proved insufficient to protect them from the intrinsic volatility of international capital flows) and adopt instruments of capital flow management.

I. Proposed agenda for improving the governance of the international financial system

The implications of the crisis for the governance of the international financial system still remain uncertain. So far, no solution has been found to overcome the inherent technical deficiency of this governance, namely the lack of an international regulatory system. Regulators and institutions concerned with the financial market are still organized on a national basis. While regulation is national, finance is increasingly multinational. However, even with the current status quo, it is possible to formulate a few proposals to improve the existing mechanisms available for regulating the global financial system.

First, it would be necessary to consolidate or to coordinate the work of the different regulatory agencies, both in Europe and in the United States. The subprime crisis has revealed the obsolescence of the decentralized structure of supervision as a result of the close interrelationships that have developed among the different financial institutions (banks, pension funds and investment funds) and markets (credit, capital and derivative markets).

Second, initiatives should include imposing limits on the process of securitization. For instance: (i) regulators could impose restrictions on the kind of instruments that can be issued and acquired by regulated entities; (ii) central banks should only be able to accept as collateral for loan commitments or rediscount operations sufficiently transparent classes of asset-backed securities; (iii) a regulation could be enforced that requires the originator to retain the equity tranche; and (iv) re-intermediation could be promoted through the incorporation of off-balance-sheet institutions on banks' balance sheets.

Third, the role of rating agencies and banks' models of internal ratings (proposed in the Basel II Accord) should be reconsidered. As Buiter (2008a) suggests, the regulatory role of these institutions should be eliminated. Rating agencies ought to become one-product firms, only offering the service of credit-risk rating. The existence of specialized companies should also reduce entry barriers and enhance competition. Payment by the issuer should be disallowed and payment by the investor is not an ideal solution (because it would create a free-rider or collective action problem) and should be discouraged. Instead, rating agencies would be paid by an organism representing institutional investors, financed through a fee paid by these agents and by the issuers of securities.

Fourth, internal models of risk pricing have proved to be of little use in times of turbulence, since they are built on parameters drawn from past information. They assume that the prices of assets are not correlated and that oscillations are of relatively little consequence. However, when a crisis breaks out, the prices of assets become correlated and oscillations become sharp, resulting in huge losses. What fuels the boom are market estimates that risks are low. Market-price-based models suggest to banks in the upturn that risks have fallen and capital is sufficient for more risk-taking (Goodhart and Persaud, 2008), when in fact the opposite should be done. In other words, boom time is the best time for financial institutions to make provisions.

II. The implications of the crisis for emerging-market economies

---

So far, proposals for improving regulatory mechanisms have focused on the configuration of financial systems in developed countries and on the international financial system (Aglietta and Rigot, 2008; Buiter, 2008b).[1] In so doing, they have failed to take into account two fundamental issues, noted by Keynes (1943), which are closely related: the hierarchical and asymmetrical nature of the international monetary system, and the characteristics of that system (besides its nature, the form of international currency, the exchange rate regime and the degree of capital mobility), which have shaped the nature of international finances of each historical epoch.

In spite of the different characteristics of the international monetary system which has been evolving since the nineteenth century, the practical solution to overcome/tackle the absence of a truly international currency has remained the same. Through a financial market process, a key currency, historically that of the hegemonic country (at present, the United States dollar),[2] is established and performs the role of an international currency (i.e. it serves as a means of payment, unit of account and of denomination of contracts and value reserve). There is, however, an inherent ambiguity in this agreement, since the key currency, set-up at the top of the pyramid, is also a financial asset that is in competition with other currencies.

As pointed out by Herr (2006), "Keynes's concept of a liquidity premium can be transferred to the international level. Each currency in the world (...) with [its] own exchange rate earns a specific non-pecuniary rate of return (a country specific liquidity premium)." The key currency has the higher currency premium that reflects economic considerations (like trust and reputation). It also reflects the nature of the State, its political stability, international role and economic and military power.

Besides the superior position of the key currency, there is an asymmetry in the international monetary system between two kinds of currencies. First, there are the convertible currencies of developed countries, which occupy an intermediary position in the hierarchy, since they perform, in a secondary way, the role of international currencies and they too have a high liquidity premium though smaller than the liquidity premium of the key currency. Second, there are the currencies of those developing countries which are increasingly participating in the global financial system and have thus become emerging-market economies. These low-quality currencies, situated at the bottom of the hierarchy, are generally incapable of performing roles of international currencies, which makes them non-convertible currencies, with the lowest liquidity premium.

In the international monetary system which emerged after the breakdown of the Bretton Woods system and which was consolidated by the regained hegemony of the United States, the hierarchy of currencies has become even more asymmetrical. This is because of the key currency's fiduciary character, which secures the United States a practically unlimited degree of liberty in the management of its exchange, monetary and tax policies. The other characteristics of this system – flexible exchange rates and free capital mobility – have reinforced this autonomy, and at the same time have created an inherent instability in the system, which has had adverse effects on the countries that issue non-convertible currencies.

This is because these countries are subject to two closely associated asymmetries: monetary asymmetry, which is related to the hierarchical nature of the international monetary system, and the asymmetry of the international financial system, comprising two dimensions. The first is related to the determinants of capital flows directed to the emerging-market economies. These flows ultimately depend on a dynamic that is exogenous to these countries, making them constantly vulnerable to the reversal of such flows, caused either by changes of phase in the economic cycle and/or changes in the monetary policy of the developed countries, or by a greater preference for liquidity on the part of global investors. The second dimension relates to these countries marginal participation in global capital flows (Obstfeld and Taylor, 2004).

Monetary and financial asymmetries, which reinforce each other, have two important consequences for the dynamics of the foreign exchange market of emerging-market economies. First, these markets are particularly vulnerable to the inherent volatility of capital flows. At times (as in the fourth quarter of 2008) of a reversal of the economic cycle and of an increase in the preference for liquidity, financial assets of emerging-market economies that do not play the role of store of value in the international system are the first to be sell by global investors.

Second, the fact that these markets account for only a marginal proportion of capital flows also contributes to their greater volatility. This is so because the degree of instability of investments is generally higher for foreign than for domestic assets (Plihon, 1996) and, in the case of assets of emerging-market economies, this instability is still more pronounced as a result of the equally marginal effects of the sale of these assets on the profitability of global portfolios. However, in spite of their residual nature, the potentially destabilizing effects of capital flows on the emerging-market economies' foreign exchange and financial markets are considerable, given that, in relation to the size of these markets, the volume allocated by global investors is not marginal (Akyüz and Cornford, 1999). Because these markets are not very liquid and deep, sales by these investors can result in currency depreciations and significant reductions in the prices of assets, with potentially harmful effects on other segments of the financial market, as well as on the macroeconomic dynamics and on the level of activity. Such effects are also related to the so-called currency mismatch in the balance sheets of banks, companies and governments that hold debt in foreign currency, which is one of the consequences of monetary asymmetry.

These adverse consequences have been rendered even more conspicuous by the current crisis, which, contrary to the financial crises of the 1990s, originated at the centre of the system – the United States. This crisis has become a systemic one which, by means of deleveraging and/or flight to quality, has spread to developing countries whose companies and banks had no connection with the securities linked to subprime mortgages. However, exactly because of the asymmetries, these movements had much greater destabilizing effects on the foreign exchange markets of the emerging-market economies (figure 1). As discussed below, not even those emerging-market economies with relatively solid macroeconomic foundations have remained untouched by the contagion effect of the crisis (*The Economist*, 2008; Slater, 2008).

Figure 1

**VARIATION IN EXCHANGE RATES BY GROUPS OF COUNTRIES,
SELECTED PERIODS**

(Per cent)

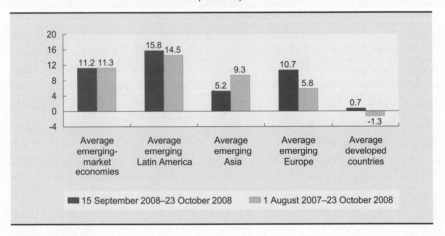

Source: Bloomberg.

After these considerations on the hierarchical and asymmetrical nature of the contemporary international financial and monetary system, it is important to recall Keynes' proposal at the Bretton Woods Conference. Keynes' basic idea was to extend to the international sphere the banking principles applied in the national sphere. According to his proposal, an International Clearing Union, a central bank of central banks, would issue an international banking currency of a public nature, the "bancor", which would liquidate positions among the central banks: countries' deficits and surpluses would result in reductions and increases of the national banks' bancor in the International Clearing Union. Private business would be conducted in national currencies, which would be tied to the bancor by means of a system of fixed, but adjustable, exchange rates (Keynes, 1943). Since the bancor would not be subject to hoarding on the part of private agents, there would be no demand for the key currency as a financial asset and as an instrument of preference for liquidity.

In this system, problems of liquidity or solvency in countries with less financial power – that is to say, those that occupy lower positions in the monetary hierarchy (in the present context, emerging-market economies), whose currencies remain non-convertible and are unable to perform monetary functions in the international sphere – would no longer have to be solved through efforts to gain the confidence of capital markets. The central bank of central banks would have the role of consciously managing the needs for liquidity in international trade and the imbalance in the balance sheets of creditors and debtors. This would enable deflationary adjustments to be avoided and national economies would be able to sustain their trajectories towards full employment.

One of the central elements of this proposal was thus to reduce the asymmetries between creditor and debtor countries, avoiding the deflationary adjustments that hindered economies from achieving full employment. In today's world, reform of the international monetary and financial system as proposed by Keynes which aims at alleviating the system's asymmetries would certainly contribute to increasing the autonomy of macroeconomic policy and reducing the vulnerability of peripheral countries to the sudden stops in capital flows and to episodes of exchange rate instability that can lead to serious financial crisis.

However, this sort of reform is still a "monetary utopia", even after the outbreak of the current crisis, which is undoubtedly the most severe since that of 1929. The tendency of flight-to-the-dollar clearly shows that the American currency still acts as the system's key currency. This being said, what would be the alternative to allowing emerging-market economies to widen their scope for macroeconomic management aimed at attaining high levels of employment and achieving social advancement while minimizing their susceptibility to the ups and downs of the international financial market?

The current crisis has shown that the adoption of prudent macroeconomic policies and the accumulation of significant amounts of foreign currency reserves (the "precautionary demand" for reserves) by emerging-market economies was insufficient to immunize them against the systemic risks inherent in financial globalization. It is worth recalling that after the regional financial crises of the 1990s in Latin America and in Asia, the administered exchange rate regimes (fixed or currency bands) – which proved to be extremely susceptible to exchange rate appreciation and to speculative attacks – were replaced by floating exchange rate regimes, with different degrees of intervention.[3] That is to say, they were replaced by an intermediate system, the "dirty float" regime, in which the intervention by central banks became the rule and not the exception (BIS, 2005).

The constant and significant interventions of the central banks in foreign exchange markets through the purchase of foreign currency were based on the so-called "mercantilist motive" (i.e. manipulation of the exchange rate in order to ensure a virtuous commercial participation in the international trade) and/or to increase national capacity for sustaining external liquidity at times of a reversal of capital flows. Whereas, between 1998 and 2002, such a trend was more evident in East Asian countries (Aizenman, Lee and Rhee, 2004; Dooley, Folkers-Landau and Garber, 2004), after 2003 many Latin American economies, benefiting from the increase in commodity prices, began to imitate the Asian strategy of reserve accumulation (IMF, 2006). This increase also enabled the region to maintain a current-account surplus between 2003 and 2007. The Eastern European countries, however, have not followed their Asian and Latin American counterparts. On the contrary, with the stability of their exchange rate regimes in relation to the euro, as a result of the European Union's strategy of integration, these countries accumulated significant current-account deficits, causing them to become dependent on external capital flows to adjust their balance sheets (see table 1).

Even though some analysts argue that "precautionary demand", and not the "mercantilist motive", is the greater determinant of the policy of reserve accumulation followed in the Asian countries and, to a lesser extent, in the Latin American ones (Aizenman, Lee and Rhee, 2004), the two are closely related and reinforce each other. This is so because exchange rate manipulation is crucial for obtaining current-account surpluses and reserves accumulated on the basis of such surpluses (and from foreign direct investment flows) are more robust than those obtained through the entry of portfolio investments and short-term bank loans, which are very volatile and susceptible to sudden stops or reversals, causing a reduction or even a complete exhaustion of the foreign currency reserves.

The importance of the composition of capital inflows was made clear by the different impacts of the current crisis on the exchange rates of emerging-market economies. These impacts were more significant not only in countries such as South Africa and Turkey, which had high current-account

Table 1

PRIVATE CAPITAL FLOWS AND CURRENT-ACCOUNT POSITIONS IN EMERGING-MARKET ECONOMIES, 2000–2008

(US$ billion)

	2000	2002	2003	2004	2005	2006	2007	2008ᵃ
Net flow of private capital	**79.9**	**60.6**	**178.6**	**230.3**	**289.3**	**254.2**	**689.3**	**179.2**
Foreign direct investment	149.1	150.0	147.8	186.7	252.1	255.8	412.1	439.9
Portfolio	-6.2	-45.8	3.1	23.1	36.5	-43.4	88.6	-84.7
Other flowsᵇ	-62.9	-43.5	27.7	20.5	0.7	41.8	188.6	-176.0
Net official capital flows	-58.0	17.6	-54.4	-63.0	-105.8	-193.6	-98.4	-116.9
Current-account balances	**92.9**	**80.5**	**149.0**	**222.3**	**449.7**	**665.6**	**657.9**	**709.2**
Development Asia	41.7	66.9	85.0	92.9	167.5	289.2	414.7	424.1
Western Hemisphere	-48.6	-16.2	9.2	21.4	36.7	49.8	14.8	-26.7
Middle East	78.2	31.4	63.9	106.2	219.2	286.4	279.2	347.8
Africa	2.0	-12.6	-12.7	-8.5	-2.7	31.0	10.1	8.6
Memo item:								
Fuel exporters	48.3	30.3	35.7	63.6	87.5	96.3	71.7	107.5
Central and Eastern Europeᶜ	-28.6	-19.3	-32.2	-53.2	-58.5	-87.1	-132.6	-152.1
International reserves	**801.1**	**1032.7**	**1363.7**	**1815.3**	**2310.6**	**3080.8**	**4377.3**	**4961.4**

Source: IMF, *World Economic Outlook*, April 2008.
a Estimates.
b Including bank loans and issues of bonds, commercial papers, notes, etc.
c Excluding the Russian Federation, which has not had a current-account deficit since 1999.

deficits, but also in those that increased their degree of financial openness up during the phase of abundant international liquidity (2003–2007) and absorbed significant amounts of speculative capital inflows (and/or allowed hedging and speculative transactions on the foreign exchange derivative markets). Brazil and the Republic of Korea, two countries that suffered strong devaluations since the outbreak of the crisis and its aggravation, belong to this latter group (figure 2). They were significantly affected by the crisis in spite of their current-account surpluses in 2007 (which turned into deficit in 2008) and their possession of significant international reserves: US$ 205.5 billion and US$ 239.7 billion, respectively, in September 2008 (*The Economist,* 2008).

The Brazilian economy, better protected than at other moments of global turbulence, was touched by some contagion effects, largely associated with its high degree of financial opening, which has allowed foreign investors unrestricted access to the spot and derivative segments of its domestic financial markets. First, the maturities of international credit lines for Brazilian banks and companies were cut short and interest rates were raised, making access to new loans for working capital and investment more difficult. Brazilian banks and companies started encountering difficulties in accessing credit lines, even to support foreign trade operations, which are considered low risk. According to Brazil's central bank, short-term credit lines – including those for imports and exports – amounted to US$ 46.1 billion in August 2008. If considered together with the operations of the multinational companies in the country, which amounted to US$ 59 billion, this represents a considerable amount of foreign resources that were fuelling the Brazilian economy. Second, the devaluation of stocks negotiated on the Sao Paulo Stock Exchange (Bovespa) reduced the price of companies' assets (to 1 trillion Brazilian real as on October 2008). Third, the weakening of industrialized economies reduced the demand for Brazilian exports, many of which have also suffered from a fall in prices, particularly agricultural, mineral and industrial commodity exports.

Fourth, the Brazilian currency registered a sharp devaluation due to the flight of foreign investors and to major losses incurred by 220 companies (mostly, exporters) which had performed high-risk operations in both the domestic foreign exchange derivative market (which are undertake in Brazilian real) and the international foreign exchange derivative market

Figure 2

VARIATIONS IN THE EXCHANGE RATES OF EMERGING-MARKET ECONOMIES, SELECTED PERIODS

(Per cent)

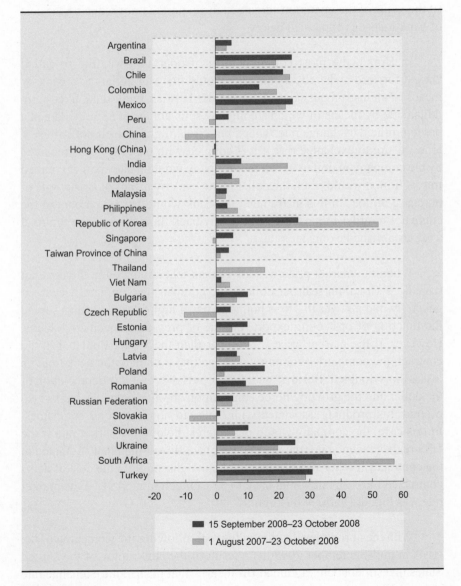

Source: Bloomberg.

(where non-deliverable forwards (NDFs) are negotiated). These operations were performed in the context of an uninterrupted appreciation of the Brazilian real since 2003, with the aim of offering protection to the estimated amount of exports against the devaluation, or of obtaining speculative gains (if the value of the operation surpassed the exports), or of reducing the cost of bank loans, as explained below.

In Brazil, the most common form of operation was the so-called "target forward" whereby a company would first sell dollars to a bank by means of an instrument called a "forward". This is a traditional, fixed-term dollar sale by means of which a company sells dollars at a future date at a predetermined exchange rate. This transaction might in itself not represent an exposure to exchange risk if it is coupled with earnings to be received by the company in dollars. Then the company would make another coupled transaction: it would resell the dollar to the bank by means of a risky sale of purchase option. In this instrument, the bank would pay an amount to the company in order to have the right to buy back the dollars in the future at a pre-established exchange rate.

When the market price was lower than that stipulated in the contract (usually 2 Brazilian real per dollar), the company would gain because it generally had a buyer that was bound to pay a higher value. It thus served the function of protecting export revenue or providing speculative gains. However, if the market price was higher than the value stipulated in the contract, the company's commitment to selling dollars to the bank (and its losses) was doubled. Besides, with the surplus of credit, the depreciation of the dollar and the growing fierce competition among banks, the banks also offered this product, associated with loans, to non-exporting companies. In this case, the company would pay interest below the market rate if the US$/real exchange rate (the market price) was lower than that stipulated in the contract (in other word, it would obtain a discount on the cost of debts contracted in real), but would have to pay a much higher rate if the market rate was higher (Farhi and Borghi, 2009).

With the abrupt devaluation of the real following the worsening of the crisis in mid-September 2008 (as a result of the bankruptcy of the United States investment bank, Lehman Brothers) – that pushed the exchange rate above R$ 2 per dollar – company losses piled up, whereas banks were under the threat of breach of contract (counterpart risk). There were also rumors that medium-sized companies, including constructors and smaller sized banks, had also undertake these very high-risk operations. A crisis of trust in the domestic financial system was thus generated, resulting in a sudden contraction of domestic credit, both for companies and for small banks, causing them difficulties in adjusting their balance sheets. In spite of the sudden drop in the amount of compulsory deposits, which had allowed the purchase of loan portfolios, liquidity remained concentrated in the large banks and increased the amount of overnight operations with the central bank. Faced with this situation, the Brazilian Government allowed public banks to temporarily purchase loans portfolios and to take over financial institutions that were experiencing liquidity problems with a view to avoiding bankruptcy and a consequent spread of panic in the country.

In this context, companies started buying foreign currency, either to honor future contracts with suppliers of imported parts and raw materials or in an attempt to cover their losses in foreign exchange derivative markets. This resulted in a sharp devaluation of the real – a trend amplified by foreign investors' aversion to risk. In response, the central bank started selling foreign currency in swap auctions on the Brazilian Mercantile and Futures Exchange (BM&F) and on the spot market, in an attempt to contain the sharp devaluation of the real. It also began granting loans in foreign currency, drawing on exchange reserves, in order to ensure the supply of credit to exporters.

In the case of the Republic of Korea (upgraded by the IMF from the classification of a newly industrializing Asian economy to a developed economy), the Government initiated a US$ 130-billion rescue plan with a view to stabilizing the financial markets (especially the foreign exchange market, because of the huge foreign currency liabilities of its banks). It also adopted other policies aimed at alleviating the harmful effects of the crisis on the domestic financial system, including the supply of liquidity in United States dollars on the foreign exchange market and a lowering of the basic interest rate (from 5 per cent to 4.25 per cent, agreed at an extraordinary meeting on 27 October 2008). After the South African rand, the Korean won was the emerging-market economy currency which suffered the sharpest devaluation between the outbreak of the crisis and 23 October (see figure 2).

As in Brazil, the sharp devaluation of the Korean currency was associated with companies' operations with exchange derivatives. Another similarity was the gradual appreciation of the Korean won in earlier years, which, just as in Brazil, was the main mechanism used to alleviate inflationary pressures associated with the rise in commodity prices and which ensured the efficiency of the inflation target regime. Nevertheless, the cost of this strategy in both countries was that exports became less competitive, inducing exporting companies to search for hedges and/or speculative gains in an attempt to remedy their situation. Besides, in the Republic of Korea, which is a large importer of commodities, deterioration in its terms of trade contributed to a current-account deficit.

In the Republic of Korea, the largest depreciation of the country's currency in relation to the dollar between August 2007 and October 2008 was the result of the relationship between derivatives operations and the large short-term debt contracted by the country's banks. This linkage is a consequence of the country's institutional framework for its foreign exchange derivative market, wherein gains or losses are liquidated in United States dollars (i.e. they are deliverable), as in most countries. Brazil, where such gains and losses are paid in the domestic currency, is an exception.

In the Republic of Korea, the banks sold to companies (mainly exporters) so-called "knock-in-knock-out" (KIKO) foreign exchange options, a derivative for hedging against the appreciation of the local currency in relation to the dollar. As Farhi and Borghi (2009) explain, this option allowed firms to sell dollars at a fixed won-dollar exchange rate in case the won fluctuated within a range pre-stipulated in the contract. However, if the value of the won fell below that range, they would have to sell dollars below the market price, thus incurring enormous losses.

To make operations on the over-the-counter derivative markets possible and profitable, the banks borrowed in United States dollars to sustain their positions on these markets. With the outbreak of the crisis and the credit crunch in international financial markets, banks faced growing difficulties in refinancing these loans and consequently started buying dollars to liquidate their external liabilities, thus exerting pressure for devaluation of the won. This devaluation led to losses by the companies that relied on the currency's appreciation, forcing them to hand over the corresponding dollars to the banks, part of which had to be obtained on the foreign exchange market. This added further pressure on the won to depreciate (Kim and Yang, 2008). With the depreciation of the won in 2008, more than 520 small and medium-sized exporting companies which had purchased KIKO options were on the verge of insolvency (Jong-Heon, 2008).

In open economies, with ample capital flows and derivative markets, which enable the establishment of speculative positions of liquid and deep derivatives on those markets (i.e. contaminating the evolution of prices in spot markets), the exchange rate reflects the demand and supply of currencies as financial assets, and not the relative prices of internally and externally produced goods. Therefore the exchange rate does not move as a function of the current-account position; that is to say, it does not react to a current-account surplus or deficit. Always procyclical and tending to exaggeration, expectations of price variation provoke adjustments between the domestic and the international currency that are disconnected to foreign trade results. In the case of non-convertible currencies, these adjustments are particularly rough, given their asymmetrical position in the contemporary monetary and financial system.

Those countries that manage convertible currencies are relatively better protected against fluctuations in their exchange rates. For them, there is generally a "point of purchase", or there are markets of liquid and deep hedges where purchasers and sellers of the different currencies seek protection against possible fluctuations in exchange rates at a convenient cost. Even then, at times of abrupt flight to liquidity, the possessors of wealth run to the reserve currency with the higher liquidity premium. On the other hand, in the globalized world, those that issue non-convertible currencies are forced to hold on to reserves of strong currencies to compensate for the lowest liquidity premium; in other words, an international reserve functions as a cushion against the flight of foreign capital. However, such a cushion might prove insufficient to prevent a massive sale of domestic currency. Exposed to this flight, the countries with non-convertible currencies are unlikely to be able to prevent an abrupt devaluation of their domestic currency by raising the interest rate. In sum, the high value of liquidity, implicit in the possession of an international reserve currency, is, at times of low confidence and panic, the most coveted object in global markets.

III. Conclusion

The inability of a currency reserve to cushion or immunize many emerging-market economies against the adverse effects of the current financial crisis and against the potentially harmful effects of the previous appreciation of their currencies, as evident from the experiences of Brazil and the Republic of Korean, shows the urgent need for resuming discussions on the importance of maintaining a competitive exchange rate and on the role of capital controls. Rodrik (2006: 12) has drawn attention to the "unbalanced" integration of these countries into financial globalization. According to Rodrik, developing countries "responded to financial globalization in a highly unbalanced and far-from-optimal manner. They have over-invested in the costly strategy of reserve accumulation and under-invested in capital account management policies to reduce short-term foreign liabilities."

Our hypothesis is that changes in international financial regulations (expected in the next few years) are unlikely to include structural reform of the international monetary and financial system and a reversal of the trend towards increased globalization, partly because the United States would be reluctant to relinquish its exclusive management of the international reserve currency. It is thus of the utmost importance to consider not only these capital controls, but also others instruments of capital flow management, which also include the prudential regulation of banks' operations in foreign currencies (Epstein, Grabel and Jomo, 2004). These instruments, by affecting an economy's degree of financial opening, widen the space for the exercise of exchange rate policies (thus reducing conflicts with monetary policy) and for efficient intervention at moments of excess or shortage of currency supply.

This means that the relationship between the accumulation of foreign reserves and capital controls is not necessarily one of substitution, as suggested by Rodrik (2006). Instead, since the adoption of "dirty float" regimes by many emerging-market economies, a new role has emerged for the management of capital flows. Besides increasing the degree of autonomy for economic policy-making and reducing these countries' vulnerability to financial crises, these capital controls, along with instruments of prudential regulation, have proven to be a *sine qua non* for the adoption of more flexible exchange rate policies: they can cushion the destabilizing effects of short-term capital flows. Regulation of capital flows is a supporting instrument in interventions on foreign exchange markets for the management of floating exchange rate regimes in emerging-market economies, since they reduce the minimum level of reserves needed to restrain speculative movements and alleviate pressures on the interest rate at times of flight of foreign capital.

Notes

1   Proposals developed by UNCTAD have been the exception.
2   De Brunhoff (1996) argues that the establishment of the key currency is also the result of an implicit agreement among developed countries that reflects the underlying power relations.
3   An exception was the fixed exchange rate regime adopted by Malaysia between September 1998 and July 2005 and the Chinese exchange rate regime.

References

Aglietta M and Rigot S (2008). La réglementation des hedge funds face à la crise financière: une contribution au débat. Paris, Ouest la Défense/EconomiX and Centre d'Etudes Prospectives et d'Informations Internationales (CEPII).
Akyüz Y and Cornford A (1999). Capital flows to developing countries and the reform of the international financial system. UNCTAD Discussion Paper no. 143. Geneva, United Nations, Conference on Trade and Development, November.
Aizenman J, Lee Y and Rhee Y (2004). International reserves management and capital mobility in a volatile world: Policy considerations – a case study of Korea. NBER Working Paper, no.10534. Cambridge, MA, National Bureau of Economic Research.
BIS (2005). Foreign exchange market intervention in emerging markets: Motives, techniques and implications. BIS Papers, no. 24, Basel, Bank for International Settlements, May.

Buiter W (2008a) The Fed as market maker of last resort: Better late than never. *Financial Times*, London, 12 March. Available at: http://blogs.ft.com/maverecon/2008/03/the-fed-as-market-maker-of-last-resort-better-late-than-never/.

Buiter W (2008b). A damp squib from the G-7 in Washington DC. *Financial Times*, London, 11 October.

de Brunhoff S (1996). L'instabilité monetaire internationale. In: Chesnais F, ed. *La Mondialisation Financière: Genèse, Coût et Enjeux*. Paris, Syros.

Dooley MP, Folkers-Landau D and Garber P (2004). The revived Bretton Woods system: the effects of periphery intervention and reserve management on interest rates and exchange rates in center countries. NBER Working Paper no. 10332. Cambridge, MA, National Bureau of Economic Research.

The Economist (2008). Into the storm. 23 October: 23–30.

Epstein G, Grabel I and Jomo KS (2004). Capital management techniques in developing countries: an assessment of experiences from the 1990s and lessons for the future. G-24 Discussion Paper no. 27. Geneva, United Nations Conference on Trade and Development.

Farhi M and Borghi R (2009). Derivatives operations of corporations from emerging economies in the recent cycle. 4th International Colloquium, Université of Bourgogne, Dijon, 10–12 December.

Farhi M and Cintra MAM (2008). A crise financeira e o global shadow banking system, *Novos Estudos* no.82. São Paulo, Centro Brasileir de Análise e Planejamento (Cebrap), November.

Goodhart C and Persaud A (2008). How to avoid the next crash. *Financial Times*, London, 30 January.

Herr H (2006). The theories of financial globalization. Berlin, Berlin School of Economics, July.

IMF (2006). *World Economic Outlook*. Washington, DC, October.

IMF (2008). *Global Financial Stability Report*. Washington, DC, October.

Jong-Heon L (2008). South Korean firms suffering cash crunch. *UPI Asia*, 18 November.

Keynes JM (1943). A União Internacional de Compensação. In: Szmrecsányi T, ed. (1984). *Keynes*. São Paulo, Editora Ática:197–207.

Kim S and Yang DY (2008). Managing capital flows: the case of the Republic of Korea. ADB Discussion Paper no. 88. Tokyo, Asian Development Bank Institute.

Obstfeld M and Taylor AM (2004). *Global capital markets: Integration, Crisis and Growth*. Cambridge, Cambridge University Press.

Plihon D (1996). Desequilibres mondiaux et instabilité financière: les responsabilité des politiques libérales. In: Chesnais F, ed. *La Mondialisation Financière: Genèse, Coût et Enjeux*. Paris, Syros.

Rodrik D (2006). The social cost of foreign exchange reserves. NBER Working Paper no. 11952. Cambridge, MA, National Bureau of Economic Research. Available at: http://www.nber.org/papers/w11952.

Slater J (2008). Tumult touches emerging nations. *Wall Street Journal*, 23 October: 4.

THE FINANCIALIZATION OF COMMODITY MARKETS AND COMMODITY PRICE VOLATILITY

Jörg Mayer*

Abstract

Financial investors have increasingly been treating commodities as an alternative asset class in order to optimize the risk-return profile of their portfolios. In doing so, these investors, particularly so-called index traders who tend to take only long positions that exert upward pressure on prices, have paid little attention to fundamental supply and demand relationships in the markets for specific commodities. As a result, commodity prices, equity prices and the exchange rates of currencies affected by carry-trade speculation have moved in parallel during much of the period since 2005. Moreover, the greater presence of index traders on commodity exchanges has led to higher commodity price volatility. There is a need to reconsider regulation of commodity exchanges, the design and viability of physical buffer stock and intervention mechanisms, as well as incentives to increase production and productivity, particularly of food commodities.

*   Part of this paper draws on the author's contributions to UNCTAD's *Trade and Development Report 2009*. The author is grateful to Makameh Bahrami for help with the data, and to Johannes Gareis and Juan Pizzaro for research assistance.

Introduction

The build-up to and eruption of the current global financial crisis was paralleled by an unusually sharp increase and subsequent strong reversal in the prices of internationally traded primary commodities. Recent developments in commodity prices have been exceptional in many ways. The price boom between 2002 and mid-2008 was the most pronounced in several decades – in magnitude, duration and breadth. It placed a heavy burden on many developing countries that rely on food and energy imports, and contributed to a food crisis in a number of countries in 2007–2008. The subsequent price decline stands out both for its sharpness and for the number of commodity groups affected. It was one of the main channels through which the dramatic slowdown of economic and financial activity in the major industrialized countries was transmitted to the developing world.

The strong and sustained increase in primary commodity prices between 2002 and mid-2008 was accompanied by the growing presence of financial investors in commodity futures exchanges. This financialization of commodity markets has caused concern that the steep increase in 2007–2008 and the subsequent strong reversal, was largely driven by financial investors' use of commodities as an asset class.

Much of these recent commodity price developments have been attributed to changes in fundamental supply and demand relationships. However, the extreme scale of the recent changes in primary commodity prices, and the fact that prices increased and subsequently fell across all major categories of commodities, suggests that, beyond the specific functioning of commodity markets, there are broader macroeconomic and financial factors that operate across a large number of markets. These factors need to be considered to fully understand recent commodity price developments. The depreciation of the dollar was clearly one general, albeit minor, cause of the surge in commodity prices. But a major new element in commodity trading over the past few years has been the greater presence on commodity futures exchanges of financial investors that treat commodities as an asset class. The fact that these market participants do not trade on the basis of fundamental supply and demand relationships, and that they hold, on average, very large positions in commodity markets, implies that they can exert considerable influence on commodity price developments.

This paper addresses the potential impact of the increasing presence of financial investors in commodity exchanges[1] on commodity price developments. It is structured as follows. Section I provides aggregate evidence of financial investment in commodity markets, and discusses the general motivation behind such investment. Section II examines the implications of financial investment for commodity price developments by looking at the correlation between commodity prices, on the one hand, and equity prices and exchange rates on the other. Section III analyses commodity price volatility. Section IV concludes by presenting options for regulatory measures and reserve and intervention mechanisms designed to guarantee the appropriate functioning of commodity exchanges.

I. The increasing presence of financial investors in commodity markets

A.   Primary commodities as an asset class

Most financial investors in commodities take positions on commodity futures and options markets.[2] Financial investors have been active in such markets since the early 1990s. However, in the aftermath of the dot-com crash on equity markets in 2000, their involvement increased, rising dramatically in early 2005, as reflected in aggregate measures of financial investment in commodity markets: the number of futures and options contracts outstanding on commodity exchanges worldwide rose more than threefold between 2002 and mid-2008 (figure 1), and, during the same period, the notional value of commodity-related contracts traded over the counter (OTC) (i.e. contracts traded bilaterally, and not listed on any exchange) increased more than 14-fold, to $13 trillion (figure 2).[3] Financial investments in commodities

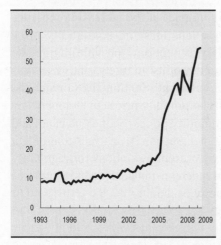

Figure 1

FUTURES AND OPTIONS CONTRACTS OUTSTANDING ON COMMODITY EXCHANGES, DEC. 1993 – DEC. 2009

(Number of contracts, million)

Source: BIS, *Quarterly Review*, March 2010, table 23B.

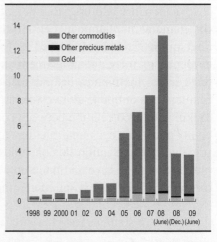

Figure 2

NOTIONAL AMOUNT OF OUTSTANDING OVER-THE-COUNTER COMMODITY DERIVATIVES, DEC. 1998 – JUNE 2009

($ trillion)

Source: BIS, *Quarterly Review*, March 2010, table 22A.

fell sharply starting in mid-2008 before picking up again in the first half of 2009.

Financial investors in commodity futures markets regard commodities as an asset class, comparable to other asset classes such as equities, bonds and real estate. They take positions in commodities as a group based on the risk-return properties of portfolios that contain commodity futures relative to those that are limited to traditional asset classes. This strategy supposes that commodities have a unique risk premium which is not replicable by combining other asset classes, and that they form a fairly homogeneous class which can be grouped together through a few representative positions (Scherer and He, 2008). Indeed, long-term empirical evidence indicates that commodity futures contracts exhibit the same average return as investments in equities, but over the business cycle their return is negatively correlated with that from investments in equities and bonds. Moreover, the returns on commodities are less volatile than those on equities or bonds, because the pair-wise correlations between returns on futures contracts for various commodities (e.g. oil and copper, or oil and maize) traditionally have been relatively low (Gorton and Rouwenhorst, 2006).[4]

Contrary to equities and bonds, commodity futures contracts also have good hedging properties against inflation (i.e. their return is positively correlated with inflation). This is because these kinds of contracts represent a bet on commodity prices, such as those of energy and food products which have a strong weight in the goods baskets that are used for measuring current price levels. Also, since futures prices reflect information about expected changes in commodity prices, they rise and fall in line with deviations from expected inflation.

Furthermore, investing in commodity futures contracts may provide a hedge against changes in the exchange rate of the dollar. Since most commodities are traded in dollars, commodity prices in dollar terms tend to increase as the dollar depreciates. However, the International Monetary Fund (IMF, 2008: 63) shows that, measured in a currency basket, commodity prices are generally less correlated with the dollar and the sign of the correlation is reversed. This suggests that changes in the value of the dollar against other currencies may partly explain the negative correlation between the prices of dollar-denominated commodities and the dollar.

B.   Financial investment in commodity indexes

Most financial investors in commodities take positions related to a commodity index. The two largest indexes by market share are the Standard & Poor's Goldman Sachs Commodity Index (S&P GSCI) and the Dow Jones-Union Bank of Switzerland Commodity Index (DJ-UBSCI) (previously called the Dow Jones-American International Group Commodity Index).[5] These indexes are composites of futures contracts on a broad range of commodities (including energy products, agricultural products and metals) traded on commodity exchanges.

Financial investment in commodity indexes is undertaken as part of a passive investment strategy (i.e. there is no attempt to distinguish between the good and bad performance of individual commodities). Index investors gain exposure in commodity indexes by entering into a bilateral financial agreement, usually a swap, with a bank or a broker. They purchase parts in a commodity index from the bank or the broker, which in turn hedge their exposure resulting from the swap agreement through commodities futures contracts on a commodity exchange.

Financial investment in commodity indexes involves only "long" positions (i.e. pledges to buy commodities) and relates to forward positions (i.e. no physical ownership of commodities is involved at any time). According to Informa Economics (2009), index funds build forward positions often relating to futures contracts with a remaining maturity of about 75 working days (i.e. roughly three calendar months), which they sell at about 25 working days (or roughly one calendar month) prior to expiry of the contract, and they use the proceeds from this sale to buy forward positions again. This means that investors that own, say, the March maize contract, will sell that contract at the end of February (i.e. before delivery begins on the March contract) and then buy the May contract. Then they will "roll" from May into July, and so on.[6] This process – known as "rolling" – is profitable when the prices of futures contracts are progressively lower in the distant delivery months (i.e. in a "backwardated" market) and negative when the prices of futures contracts with longer maturities are progressively higher (i.e. in a "contango" market).

Four variables determine the total return earned by financial investors in commodity indexes: spot return, roll yield, collateral return, and recomposition yield. The spot return reflects the spot price movements of the underlying commodities, the collateral return is the interest on the collateral[7] that the investors have to set aside as margin for investments in commodity futures positions, the recomposition yield arises from a periodic redefinition of the basket of commodities underlying a portfolio, and the roll yield is obtained from selling futures contracts that have an expiry date the month prior to the delivery month and using the proceeds to buy futures contracts with a longer maturity.

The roll yield is similar to the risk premium that speculators expect to earn by taking an opposite position to that of commodity producers that seek to hedge the price risk of their output. This risk premium corresponds to the difference between the current futures price and the expected future spot price at the time the position is taken. If the futures price is set below the expected future spot price, a purchaser of futures contracts (speculator) will generally earn the risk premium; on the other hand, if the futures price is higher than the expected future spot price, a seller of futures contracts (hedger) will earn the premium. Assuming hedgers outnumber speculators, Keynes (1930) and Hicks (1939) – in their theory of "normal backwardation" – expected that, in general, the futures price would be lower than the expected future spot price, so that the risk premium would normally accrue to speculators.

The roll yield differs slightly from this kind of risk premium because index traders do not hold futures contracts until their expiry. When the price of futures contracts depreciates near the delivery date, the roll yield is negative. Roll returns were positive during much of the 1980s and 1990s, but since 2002 they have mostly been negative. However, given the large spot returns during the commodity price hikes between 2002 and mid-2008, the total return was nonetheless positive during most of this period (figure 3).

The above implies that the total return on investment in commodity indexes partly depends on the intertemporal relationship between futures and spot prices on commodity exchanges. This relationship is known from financial markets, but the difference is that commodity futures markets trade contracts on assets that incur storage and interest costs – often called "cost of carry". This cost implies that in order to induce storage, futures prices and expected future spot prices must increase more than the cost of carry to compensate inventory holders for the costs associated with storage. However, the cost of storage must be weighed against the so-called "convenience yield" (i.e. the a priori unmeasurable utility of physically owning a particular commodity, or the premium when the inventory is sold). Inventory holders have the option to sell commodities on the spot markets when market conditions tighten, or to dispose of a secure supply of the commodity, thus insuring themselves against the costs associated with supply disruption.

The convenience yield tends to be higher when inventories are lower, as tighter market conditions confer greater benefits for the physical ownership of a commodity. It will increase sharply when inventories fall below the level of short-term consumption requirements.

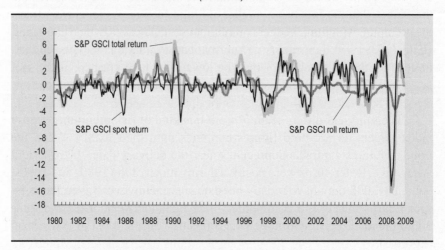

Figure 3

**SPOT AND ROLL RETURNS ON COMMODITY INDEX INVESTMENTS,
JANUARY 1980–DECEMBER 2009**

(Per cent)

Source: Author's calculations, based on Bloomberg.
Note: The roll return is the discount or premium obtained by "rolling" positions in futures contracts
forward as they approach delivery. The numbers shown in the figure approximate the roll return
(calculated as the difference between excess and spot returns of the S&P GSCI) and are expressed
as six-month moving averages. The excess return reflects the return on commodity futures price
movements, while the spot return reflects changes in spot prices.

The above elements can be combined to determine the term structure
of commodity prices. The difference between contemporaneous spot and
futures prices – often called "basis" – depends on the relative size of the
cost of carry and the convenience yield. The negative of the basis can be
expressed as follows:

$$F_{t,T} - S_t = Int_t + w_t - c_t$$

where $F_{t,T}$ is the futures price at date t for delivery at time T, S_t is the spot
price at time t, Int_t is the interest cost, w_t is the storage cost, and c_t is the
convenience yield. An upward sloping futures curve, a phenomenon known
as "contango", implies that inventory holders are rewarded for the cost of
carrying inventories. A downward sloping futures curve, a phenomenon

known as "backwardation", indicates that the convenience yield exceeds the cost of carry.

It should be noted that the notion of backwardation, which relates to the comparison of contemporaneous spot and futures prices, differs from the concept of "normal backwardation" (mentioned above), which compares futures prices with expected future spot prices. From the latter perspective, the basis is determined by a risk premium, $\pi_{t,T}$, which corresponds to the difference between futures prices and expected future spot prices, and the expected appreciation or depreciation of the future spot price, $[E_t(S_T) - S_t]$. It can be expressed as:

$$F_{t,T} - S_t = [E_t(S_T) - S_t] - \pi_{t,T}$$

The risk premium will be positive, thus attracting more speculators to the market, to the extent that hedgers have net short positions and offer a risk premium to speculators with net long positions, and to the extent that hedging demand exceeds the net long positions of speculators. Moreover, the risk premium – and thus the gap between spot and futures prices – can be expected to rise when low inventories heighten the risk of price volatility.[8] Changes in traders' positions will usually indicate changes in expected future spot prices with attendant effects on the term structure of contemporaneous spot and futures prices.

A major purpose of futures contracts traded on commodity exchanges is to provide a way for hedgers to insure themselves against unfavourable movements in the future values of spot prices. To serve this purpose, speculators who take positions opposite to those of hedgers must collect information on the likely future movements of spot prices, so that the value of the futures contract is an unbiased estimate of the value of the spot price on the delivery date specified in the futures contract. Policymakers, especially central bankers, commonly base part of their decisions on this feature, as they use the price of commodity futures contracts as a proxy for the market's expectations of future commodity spot prices (Svensson, 2005; Greenspan, 2004).

However, the value of futures contracts will not serve this price discovery purpose (i) if those taking speculative positions base their activities on information unrelated to the underlying supply and demand fundamentals on commodity markets, or (ii) if the size of their position is substantially larger than that of hedgers, so that the weight of their position determines prices. Empirical evidence generally indicates that futures prices are less accurate forecasts than simple alternative models such as a "random walk without drift" (i.e. expecting no change from current spot prices). Indeed, Bernanke (2008) has highlighted the difficulty in arriving at a reasonable estimate of future commodity price movements based on signals emanating from commodity futures markets. He has therefore emphasized the importance of finding alternative approaches to forecasting commodity market movements. Thus, empirical evidence indicates that mechanisms that would prevent prices from moving away from levels determined by fundamental supply and demand factors – efficient absorption of commodity-related information and sufficiently strong price elasticity of supply and demand – may be relatively weak on commodity markets.

II. The impact of financialization on commodity price developments

As already mentioned, financial investors in commodity markets aim to diversify their asset portfolios and hedge inflation risk. Their decisions to invest in commodities thus depend on broad-based portfolio considerations that also include the risk and return characteristics of other asset classes, such as equities, bonds and exchange rates.

There is substantial historic evidence of the improved risk-return characteristics of portfolios that include commodity futures contracts in addition to equities and bonds. Gorton and Rouwenhorst (2006), for example, provide such evidence for the period 1959–2004. Investment in commodities appears to have been a particularly effective hedge against inflation and dollar depreciation since 2005, as the correlation between these two variables and commodity prices was much higher during the period 2005 to early 2009 than in previous years (figure 4).

Figure 4

CORRELATION BETWEEN MOVEMENTS IN COMMODITY PRICES AND EQUITY PRICES, DOLLAR EXCHANGE RATE AND INFLATION, JANUARY 2002–DECEMBER 2009

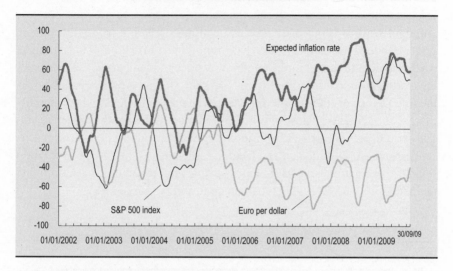

Source: Author's calculations, based on Bloomberg.
Note: The data shown are six-month moving averages of 60-day rolling correlations between the S&P GSCI and the respective financial variable. Expected inflation is the difference between nominal and real United States 10-year bonds.

By contrast, there are indications that commodity prices, equity markets and the exchange rates of currencies affected by carry-trade speculation[9] moved in tandem during much of the period of the commodity price hike in 2005–2008, and in particular during the subsequent sharp correction in the second half of 2008. Commodity and equity prices were largely uncorrelated between 2002 and 2005, but were positively correlated during much of the period 2005–2008 (figure 4). There has also been a strong correlation of commodity prices – particularly since 2004 – with the exchange rate of carry-trade currencies such as the Icelandic krona and the Hungarian forint (figure 5). This correlation was particularly strong during the unwinding of speculative positions in both currency and commodity markets during the second half of 2008 (UNCTAD, 2009: 28). Commodity index traders started unwinding their positions in commodities because their swap agreements with banks began to be exposed to significantly larger counterparty risks,

Figure 5

CORRELATION BETWEEN MOVEMENTS IN COMMODITY PRICES AND SELECTED EXCHANGE RATES, JANUARY 2002–DECEMBER 2009

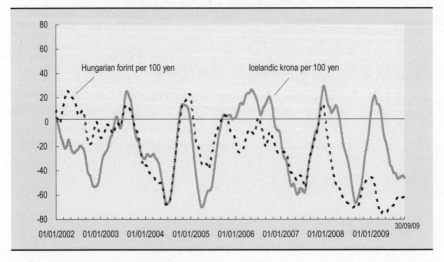

Source: Author's calculations, based on Bloomberg.
  Note: The data shown are six-month moving averages of 60-day rolling correlations between the S&P GSCI and the respective financial variable.

while managed funds started unwinding their exposure in commodities when their leveraged positions faced refinancing difficulties.

Taken together, this evidence for the past few years indicates that, relative to the historic importance of strategic diversification considerations, more recently tactical reasoning may have played a greater role for financial investors in commodities. Indeed, the search for higher yields through commodities trading may have been based on the illusion of risk-free profit maximization, given the historic diversification and hedging characteristics of financial investment in commodities. Financial investors started to unwind their relatively liquid positions in commodities when their investments in other asset classes began to experience increasing difficulties. This strong correlation between commodities and other asset classes during the second half of 2008 suggests that financial investors may have considerably influenced commodity price developments.[10]

III. Commodity price volatility

A. The origin of commodity price volatility

Price volatility is a major feature of commodity markets. Commodities experience far greater price volatility than do manufactures or services. UNCTAD (2008: 40) has demonstrated graphically the higher price volatility of non-fuel commodities and petroleum relative to that of manufactures between 1970 and 2008.

The particular reasons for commodity price volatility differ by commodity, and may change over the course of time. But in general, low short-term elasticities of supply and demand cause any shock to production or consumption to translate into significant price fluctuations. Short-term supply elasticity is low in agriculture because input decisions must be made before new crop prices are known, and in extractive industries because production decisions must be made several months before the mineral product can be sold. Short-term demand elasticity is low because the actual price of an unprocessed agricultural commodity often represents a very small component of the overall value of the final product (for example, cocoa in chocolate), and because price movements for energy and mineral products are closely linked to global industrial and economic activity (Dehn, Gilbert and Varangis, 2005). The impact of shocks on price fluctuations is moderated by stockholding and the maintenance of spare production capacities.

B. Recent developments in commodity price volatility

The sharp changes in commodity prices over the past few years, especially in 2007 and 2008, and the associated potentially adverse effects on economic activity, particularly in poor countries that either depend on a small number of commodities for their export earnings or are net food and

Figure 6

COMMODITY PRICE INSTABILITY INDEX, SELECTED COMMODITIES, 1997–2009

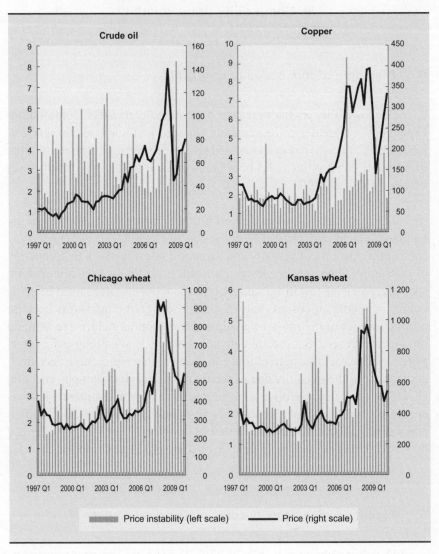

Figure 6 (concluded)

COMMODITY PRICE INSTABILITY INDEX, SELECTED COMMODITIES, 1997–2009

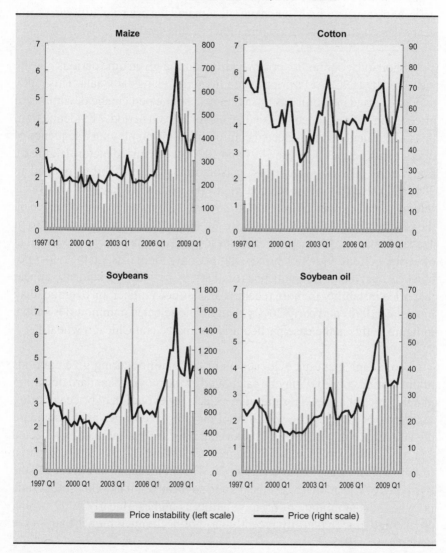

Price instability (left scale)   ——— Price (right scale)

Source: Author's calculations, based on Bloomberg.

Note: Price instability is the average absolute percentage deviation of daily prices from their exponential trend levels for any given quarter. Price refers to end-of-quarter prices in $/barrel for crude oil (West Texas Intermediate), cents/bushel for wheat, maize and soybeans, and cents/lb for copper, cotton and soybean oil.

energy importers, have led to a renewed interest in strategies to manage price volatility. However, in order for such measures to be effective, it is necessary to understand the nature of the problem and the role of new elements in its underlying causes which may have accentuated the price volatility in recent years. This is the focus of the remainder of this section.

Short-run commodity price volatility during given time periods may be measured by UNCTAD's price instability index using daily data. This index expresses price instability as the average absolute percentage deviations of prices from their exponential trend levels for a given period.[11] Evidence from this index calculated for selected commodities and employing a sequence of three-month periods between 1997 and 2009 gives a mixed picture (figure 6). Looking at individual quarters in isolation, price instability peaked in 2008–2009 for most of the selected eight commodities (crude oil (West Texas Intermediate), copper, maize, cotton, soybeans, soybean oil, wheat traded on the Chicago Board of Trade, and wheat traded on the Kansas City Board of Trade). However, the magnitude of these peaks substantially exceeded that of earlier periods with high price volatility only for maize and the two types of wheat. But looking at sequences of quarterly periods, it would also appear that price instability in more recent years has been higher, on average, than in the late 1990s and early 2000s. Among the selected commodities shown in figure 6, this is the case particularly for maize and Chicago wheat.

To complement the evidence on price volatility during given periods of time, price volatility may be calculated as the moving standard deviation of daily price changes. This measure reflects the evolution of price volatility over time. Measuring the volatility of daily price changes as the standard deviation over the preceding 30 working days for the same eight selected commodities clearly indicates higher price volatility in 2008–2009 compared to the 10-year period before (figure 7). This evidence is strongest for the two types of wheat, maize, soybeans and soybean oil. It is weakest for crude oil where the amplitude of price volatility is highest in early 2009, while, on average, price volatility recently has not been much higher than in the period 1998–2003.[12]

Figure 7

MOVING VOLATILITY OF DAILY PRICE CHANGES, SELECTED COMMODITIES, JANUARY 1997–JANUARY 2010

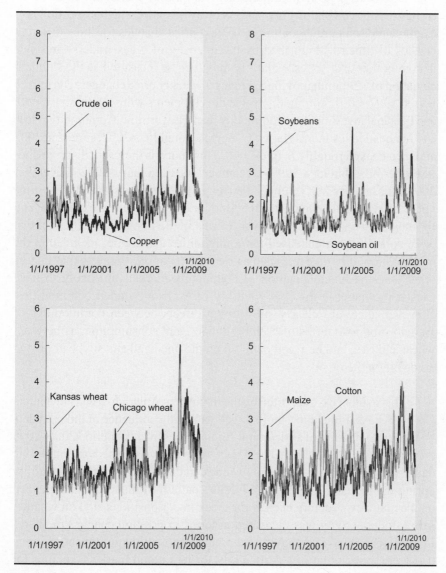

Source: Author's calculations, based on Bloomberg.

Note: Price volatility is calculated as the moving standard deviation of daily price changes over the preceding 30 working days.

C.   Financial investment and commodity price volatility

How has the financialization of commodity exchanges affected commodity price volatility? An indirect way of answering this question is to examine the standard deviation of weekly price changes for three different periods of time, distinguished by the intensity of index traders' presence in commodity exchanges. Volatility may then be measured as the standard deviation of 12-month moving averages of weekly price changes. During the period 1997–2001, commodity price developments were relatively smooth and financial investments in commodity markets were low. Commodity prices and financial investments started to increase roughly in 2002, surged in 2007 and then peaked roughly in mid-2008. This analysis therefore distinguishes three periods: January 1997–December 2001, January 2002–December 2006, and January 2007–June 2008 (figure 8). The figure reveals that price volatility was highest in the third period for all commodities except oil, and for most of the commodities it was lowest in the first period. The fact that price volatility also increased for commodities that are not included in the major commodity indexes, such as rice and palm oil, suggests that factors other than the financialization of commodity markets are likely to have caused the increase in price volatility of exchange-traded commodities. However, there are clearly substitution effects between commodities of the two groups in terms of both production and consumption, as between wheat and rice, and between palm oil on the one hand and soybean oil and crude oil on the other.

This evidence is supported by the findings of Aulerich, Irwin and Garcia (2010), who examined in a more direct manner the influence of index traders on the price volatility of agricultural commodities over the period 2006–2008 compared with 2004–2005. Their regression analysis, based on non-public data, suggests that the presence of index traders increased price volatility during the period 2006–2008. While the pattern of their results depended on the maturity structure chosen for index trader positions, and on whether index trader activity was measured in terms of position changes or shares in total open interest,[13] they found a comparatively large impact of index traders on price volatility, particularly for less liquid markets, such as for cocoa, coffee, cotton, hogs, sugar and Kansas wheat.

Figure 8

COMMODITY PRICE VOLATILITY, SELECTED COMMODITIES AND PERIODS

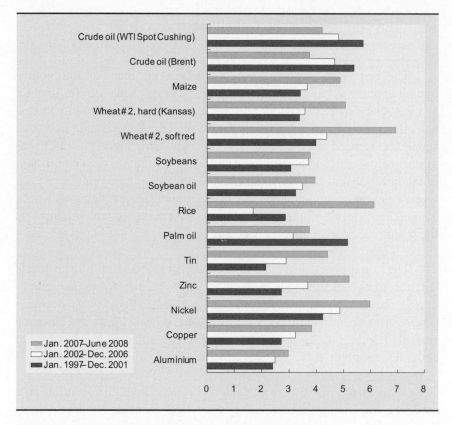

Source: Author's calculations, based on Thomson Financial Datastream.
Note: Volatility is measured as the standard deviation of 12-month moving averages of weekly price changes.

Taken together, this evidence suggests that the financialization of commodity exchanges has led to greater price volatility. This is most probably because the trading strategy of financial investors on commodity exchanges takes account of events in other asset markets, particularly equity and currency markets, so that these investors transmit price volatility from those asset markets onto commodity markets.

IV. Conclusions

The increasing importance of financial investment in commodity trading appears to have caused commodity futures exchanges to function in a way that may have led to a fairly wide deviation in commodity prices, at least in the short run, from levels that would reliably reflect fundamental supply and demand factors. Financial investment undermines the traditional mechanisms – efficient absorption of information and physical adjustment of markets – that normally would prevent prices from moving away from levels determined by fundamental supply and demand factors. As a result, commodity prices become more prone to overshooting, which heightens the risk of speculative bubbles occurring.

The strongest evidence for commodity prices deviating from levels determined by fundamentals is found in the high correlation, particularly during the deleveraging process in the second half of 2008, between commodity prices and prices on other markets, such as equity and currency markets. In the latter, which were particularly affected by carry-trade activities, speculative activity played a major role.

These effects of the financialization of commodity futures trading have made the functioning of commodity exchanges increasingly contentious. They risk reducing the participation of commercial users, because commodity price risk hedging becomes more complex and expensive. They also cause greater uncertainty about the reliability of signals emanating from the commodity exchanges with respect to making storage decisions and managing the price risk of market positions. It has therefore become necessary to consider how the functioning of commodity futures exchanges could be improved so that they can continue to fulfil their role of providing reliable price signals to producers and consumers of primary commodities and contributing to a stable environment for development.

Regulatory changes designed to keep pace with commodity market developments, in particular the participation of new trader categories such as index funds, could play a key role in this respect. It is indispensable to broaden and strengthen the supervisory and regulatory powers of mandated commodity market regulators. In order for them to identify what is moving prices and intervene effectively, regulators must be able to understand the market and collect the required data. Such data are currently not available, particularly for off-exchange derivatives trading. Yet such trading and trading on regulated commodity exchanges have become increasingly interdependent. Hence, comprehensive trading data need to be reported to enable regulators to monitor information about sizeable transactions, including over-the-counter trading, that could have an impact on regulated futures markets. In addition to collecting more comprehensive data, broader regulatory mandates might be required. Supervision and regulation of commodity futures markets may need to be enhanced, particularly with a view to enabling regulators to counter unwarranted impacts from off-exchange trading on commodity exchanges. A substantial part of commodity futures trading is executed on exchanges located in the United States, which the Commodity Futures Trading Commission (CFTC) is mandated to regulate. It is therefore encouraging to observe that the CFTC is making greater efforts to get to grips with futures and options trading in all commodity areas, including agriculture, energy and metals (see, for example, Gensler, 2010).

In addition to regulatory issues, the financialization of commodity futures trading raises the issue of how supply-side measures can address excessive commodity price volatility. This issue is of particular importance for food commodities: despite some recent improvement, grain and oilseed stocks remain very low, which means that any sudden increase in demand or a major shortfall in production, or both, will rapidly cause significant price increases. Hence, physical stocks of food commodities need to be rebuilt urgently to an adequate level in order to moderate temporary shortages and buffer sharp price movements.

It has often been argued that it is difficult to finance and guarantee the accumulation of sufficiently large physical buffer stocks, especially of food commodities. Moreover, holding large inventories around the world has often been judged economically inefficient, leading to the recommendation that net food importing countries should rely on global markets rather than building their own reserves. However, there can be little doubt that newly imposed trade restrictions (particularly for rice) played a role in exacerbating the spiralling increase in food prices in early 2008. This has added to anti-globalization sentiments and to more favourable assessments of the protection that national food reserves can provide.

Partly to counter such anti-globalization sentiments, and in particular as part of efforts to prevent humanitarian crises, von Braun and Torero (2008) – echoed by the G-8 summit in June 2008 – have proposed a new, two-pronged global institutional arrangement: a minimum physical grain reserve for emergency responses and humanitarian assistance, and a virtual reserve and intervention mechanism. The latter would enable intervention in the futures markets if a "global intelligence unit" were to judge market prices as differing significantly from an estimated dynamic price band based on market fundamentals.

However, adopting such a mechanism would commit a public agency to second-guessing market developments. Experience with commodity agreements suggests that this is a difficult task. The impact of the speculative activities of financial investors in commodity markets on price volatility adds to the already complex task of making market forecasts: for one, it becomes more difficult to determine whether, or to what extent, any given price change reflects a change in underlying supply and demand relationships or results from events taking place in other asset markets; in addition, given that the presence of financial investors results in a general increase in commodity price volatility, it becomes more difficult to determine whether a given price movement indicates a change in a long-term trend or whether it is just a short-term episode of price volatility. Moreover, in order to prevent speculative price bubbles, the agency would need to be prepared to sell large amounts of physical commodities. Given the certainty that any accumulated stocks will eventually be exhausted, there is considerable risk that speculators could mobilize significantly more funds than any public agency's capacity to provide physical commodities. Hence it is likely that the funds allocated to such an agency would be an easy target for speculators.

Even if the technical problems could be solved and the political will found to make a virtual reserve and intervention mechanism work satisfactorily, it would not make more physical commodities available on markets, except for emergency situations. Since the historically low level of inventories was one determinant of the abrupt price hike in food commodities in early 2008, the question remains as to how incentives could be provided to increase production and productivity in developing countries, particularly of food commodities. Further research on price stabilization mechanisms and supply support measures is clearly warranted.

Notes

1   A commodity exchange is a market in which multiple buyers and sellers trade commodity-linked contracts according to rules and procedures laid down by the exchange and/or a mandated supervisory and regulatory body. Such exchanges typically act as a platform for trade in futures contracts (i.e. standardized contracts for future delivery).

2   Financial investors can gain exposure on commodity markets also through spot market activities (i.e. buying and accumulating physical commodities in inventories). This strategy mainly aims at hedging against inflation, and is usually confined to the relatively small markets for precious metals such as gold and silver. It is more difficult to adopt this physical market strategy for other commodities, especially because of the greater storage costs they entail. Other financial instruments that enable investors to gain exposure to commodities include exchange-traded funds, which are traded on exchanges like equities, and exchange-traded notes, which permit investors to purchase debt securities linked to a commodity index.

3   The Bank for International Settlements (BIS) is the only source that regularly provides publicly available information about OTC commodity trading. However, commodity-specific disaggregation is not possible with these data. Notional amount refers to the value of the underlying commodity. However, since traders in derivatives markets do not own or purchase the underlying commodity, notional value is merely a reference point based on underlying prices.

4   These salient features are based on data for periods in which few investors were actually following this strategy. Recent studies cast some doubt as to whether these features have continued to prevail in more recent periods (see section II).

5   In the DJ-UBSCI, weights primarily rely on the relative amount of trading activity of a particular commodity, and are limited to 15 per cent for individual commodities and to one third for entire sectors. In the S&P GSCI, on the other hand, weights depend on relative quantities of world production, with energy products usually accounting for about two thirds of the total index. Alternative Investment Analytics (2008) provides a detailed account of the construction of these two indexes, as well as of other smaller indexes operated by other institutions.

6   However, it should be noted that funds have considerable discretion as to when and how they roll, even if they want to replicate an index. For example, they may skip the contract of a specific month if the contract of the following month is more liquid. They may also vary the timing of the roll in relation to market conditions. This kind of variation can reduce the costs of rolling substantially, partly because rolling will become less predictable for other market participants so that their betting against index investors will become more difficult.

7   Collateral is a position set aside by traders to ensure that they are able to fulfil their contractual commitments. During the lifetime of a futures contract, the clearing house of the concerned commodity exchange issues margin calls to adjust the amount of collateral so as to reflect changes in the notional value of traders' contractual commitments.

8   Falling inventories signal the scarcity of the commodity for immediate delivery, which will cause spot prices to increase. Futures prices will also increase, but not by as much, because of expectations that inventories will be restored over time and spot prices will return to normal levels, and perhaps also because the risk premium rises. However, if inventories are slow to adjust, past demand and supply shocks will persist in current inventory levels.

9   For a discussion of carry-trade speculation, see UNCTAD, 2007, chapter I.

10   Recent studies (e.g. Büyükşahin and Robe, 2009; Tang and Xiong, 2009; and Silvennoinen and Thorp, 2010) also indicate that in recent years the link between the risk-return characteristics of commodities and those of equities has become much closer.

11   See also UNCTAD Handbook of Statistics, table 6.2, available at: stats.unctad.org/Handbook/TableViewer/tableView.aspx?ReportId=2057.

12   Time-series evidence based on non-public daily price data for the period January 2005–August 2008 also shows that price volatility increased, except for crude oil (Informa Economics, 2009: part 3).

13   Total open interest equals the total number of contracts in a market that has been entered into and not yet liquidated by an offsetting transaction or fulfilled by delivery.

References

Alternative Investment Analytics (2008). Comparing commodity indices: multiple approaches to return. 14 May. Amherst (Mass), Alternative Investment Analytics LLC. Available at: www.bache.com/media/managed/ComparingCommodityIndicesMultipleApproachestoReturn.pdf.

Aulerich NM, Irwin SH and Garcia P (2010). The price impact of index funds in commodity futures markets: evidence from the CFTC's daily large trader reporting system. Available at: farmdoc.illinois.edu/irwin/research/PriceeImpactIndexFund,%20Jan%20 2010.pdf.

Bernanke B (2008). Outstanding issues in the analysis of inflation. Speech delivered at the Federal Reserve Bank of Boston's 53rd Annual Economic Conference, Chatham, MA, 9 June.

Büyükşahin B and Robe MA (2009). Commodity traders' positions and energy prices: evidence from the recent boom-bust cycle. 29 December. Paper presented at the 2010 Annual Meeting of the American Economic Association in Atlanta. Available at: www.aeaweb.org/aea/conference/program/retrieve.php?pdfid=355.

Dehn J, Gilbert CL and Varangis P (2005). Agricultural commodity price volatility. In: Aizenman J and Pinto B, eds. *Managing Economic Volatility and Crises: A Practitioner's Guide*. Cambridge and New York, Cambridge University Press.

Gensler G (2010). Testimony of Chairman Gary Gensler before the House Committee on Agriculture Subcommittee on General Farm Commodities and Risk Management. 3 March. Available at: www.cftc.gov/ucm/groups/public/@newsroom/documents/speechandtestimony/opagensler-30.pdf.

Gorton G and Rouwenhorst KG (2006). Facts and fantasies about commodity futures. Working Paper No. 10595, National Bureau of Economic Research, Cambridge, MA, March.

Greenspan A (2004). Oil. Remarks to the National Italian American Foundation, Washington, DC, 15 October. Available at: www.federalreserve.gov/boarddocs/speeches/2004/200410152/default.htm.

Hicks JR (1939). *Value and Capital*. Oxford, Oxford University Press.

Informa Economics (2009). An evaluation of the influence of large reporting traders on futures markets performance. Available at: www.informaecon.com/TraderStudy/TraderStudy.htm.

IMF (2008). *Global Financial Stability Report*, Annex 1.2. Washington, DC.

Keynes JM (1930). *A Treatise on Money*, vol. 2. London, Macmillan.

Scherer B and He L (2008). The diversification benefits of commodity futures indexes: a mean-variance spanning test. In: Fabozzi FJ, Füss R and Kaiser DG, eds. *The Handbook of Commodity Investing*. Hoboken, NJ, Wiley: 241–265.

Silvennoinen A and Thorp S (2010). Finanialization, crisis and commodity correlation dynamics. January. Available at: www.business.uts.edu.au/qfrc/research/research_papers/rp267.pdf.

Svensson LEO (2005). Oil prices and ECB monetary policy. Princeton University. Available at: www.princeton.edu/svensson/papers/ep501.pdf.

Tang K and Xiong W (2009). Index investing and the financialization of commodities. September. Available at: www.princeton.edu/~wxiong/papers/commodity.pdf.

UNCTAD (2007). *Trade and Development Report 2007*. United Nations publication, New York and Geneva.

UNCTAD (2008). *Trade and Development Report 2008*. United Nations publication, New York and Geneva.

UNCTAD (2009). The Global Economic Crisis: Systemic Failures and Multilateral Remedies. United Nations publication, New York and Geneva.

von Braun J and Torero M (2008). Physical and virtual global food reserves to protect the poor and prevent market failure. Policy Brief 4, International Food Policy Research Institute, Washington, DC, June.

RISK FACTORS IN INTERNATIONAL FINANCIAL CRISES: EARLY LESSONS FROM THE 2008-2009 TURMOIL

Sebastian Dullien

Abstract

This paper analyses the global transmission of the recent economic and financial crisis as a function of macroeconomic factors such as per capita gross domestic product, current-account positions prior to the crisis, exchange-rate regimes, inflation prior to the crisis and financial openness. It finds that large current-account imbalances (both surpluses and deficits) were a risk factor in the current global economic turmoil. It also finds that countries that use currency boards have suffered much more from the crisis than countries with other exchange-rate regimes. Financial openness appears to have increased the risk of experiencing a deep recession, while higher inflation prior to the crisis seems to have mitigated its impact.

Introduction

There is a growing body of literature on the various impacts of the economic and financial crisis on countries around the world. Much has been written on its impacts on world trade, on commodity producing countries, on countries which have close trade linkages with the United States, and on countries which rely heavily on remittance flows from developed countries.[1] This paper aims to shed light on the spreading financial turmoil from a different angle: it attempts to examine the international transmission of the subprime crisis in the United States to determine which macroeconomic characteristics, beyond sectoral specialization and trade specialization, make countries more vulnerable to the contagion effects of a global financial and economic crisis. It looks at economic aspects which can be influenced by policymakers, such as the exchange-rate regime, inflation, the current-account balance and capital-account openness. In so doing, it adds to the debate on the choice of exchange-rate regimes, on macroeconomic management, including under- or overvaluation of a currency, and on capital account convertibility.

The paper is structured as follows. After a brief discussion on measuring the impact of the crisis on individual countries, it provides a quantitative description of the most important stylized facts of the global spread of the crisis, building on economic data for 181 countries covered by the *World Economic Outlook* of the International Monetary Fund (IMF).[2] It then uses econometric techniques to determine which macroeconomic features helped some countries to be more resilient to the financial and economic crisis than others. This section also looks at the factors that might have played a role in determining whether a country should turn to the IMF to cover financing needs in the recent crisis. The final section seeks to offer tentative explanations for the empirical observations. Other contributions in this book dwell on the wider implications of the findings, though these will also require further research as more data become available.

I. Empirical analysis of the crisis

For determining the negative impact of the crisis, the following three criteria have been used throughout the paper:

1. The change of trend in the GDP growth rate from the average of the years prior to the crisis (2003–2007) to the average of the crisis years 2008–2009. This measure has been chosen because the crisis hit different countries at different points in time. World trade was already

severely affected in the last quarter of 2008, and some countries already had trouble financing their foreign deficit that year. However, due to the base effect, this drop is partly reflected in the annual GDP growth rate in 2008 and partly in 2009. Looking only at the growth rate of one of these two years would have distorted the picture.

2. The simple average growth rate of GDP for the years 2008 and 2009. Again, looking at both years together gives a better picture than looking only at 2009 when most of the decline occurred.

3. The fact that a country had to turn to the IMF for borrowing. Especially after the huge wave of criticism of the IMF's policies during the East Asian crisis of 1997–1998, borrowing from the IMF has come to be seen not only as a national humiliation, but also, increasingly, as an economic evil best avoided. Thus, being forced to accept IMF lending can be viewed as a sign that a country has been severely affected by a crisis.

Of course, there are other important negative economic and social consequences of the crisis, such as rising unemployment and poverty, and increasing government debt. However, limited availability of up-to-date data on these aspects constrains the analysis here. Unemployment data are often not comparable between countries, and recording of unemployment figures, especially for developing countries and emerging-market economies, are often inexact, as employment in the informal sector is not always well covered. Moreover, the impact of the crisis on the labour market may exhibit different time lags in different countries. In some countries, retrenchment of workers is an easy and quick process, while in others it takes much longer due to the legal regime or conventions. In addition, some countries have passed measures temporarily stabilizing labour markets. Thus data currently available on labour market performance are not an adequate indicator for measuring the impact of the crisis at this particular point in time; its full impact can only be evaluated later.

Reporting of government debt and government budget deficits outside the OECD countries is also not very exact and up-to-date, and the IMF's *World Economic Outlook* therefore provides such data for only a limited number of countries. Similarly, due to the lack of reliable, up-to-date statistics for the incidence of poverty across countries, it is difficult to assess to what extent poverty has increased as a result of the crisis. While there have been a number of estimates (i.e. Chen and Ravallion, 2009), these are necessarily only very rough. These indicators have therefore been omitted from this paper; instead, the paper focuses on the drop in GDP and the extent of IMF involvement.

The analysis in this paper is based on data assembled from various sources. Data on GDP, inflation and current accounts have been taken from the IMF's *World Economic Outlook* database (January 2010). Data on capital-account openness have been derived from Chinn and Ito (2008). And data on exchange-rate regimes have been taken from the IMF's classification of exchange-rate regimes (IMF, 2009) and modified to include an additional group of countries in the European Monetary Union (EMU).[3] Altogether, the sample comprises 179 countries.

A. *Descriptive statistics*

Before we turn to a rigorous econometric analysis, it is useful to take a brief look at the data. At the beginning of the crisis, it was often argued by the IMF and financial sector analysts that the emerging-market economies and developing countries might be decoupled from developed economies, particularly the United States, and may therefore be able to cope with the turmoil more effectively. While this hope proved to be illusory, at least some emerging-market economies have performed much better than other parts of the world. Asian countries, in particular, have managed to recover very quickly and briskly from the crisis, with parts of Latin America following. In contrast, economic data for most of the members of the Commonwealth of Independent States (CIS) and the new member States of the European Union (EU) have shown few real improvements. Also the United States and the Western European industrialized economies have proved to be laggards, with vulnerable economic recovery (IMF, 2010).

Beyond these regional features, however, the impact of the crisis has clearly varied with the state of development of the economies in question.[4] On examining the different categories of countries, namely low-income countries (GDP per capita below $975), lower middle-income countries (GDP per capita between $976 and $3,855), upper middle-income countries (GDP between $3,858 and $11,905) and high-income countries, we found fairly large variations in the fall in the growth between the years 2003–2007 and 2008–2009: high-income countries experienced a drop in the growth rate of 5.2 percentage points,[5] upper middle- income countries saw an almost equally large drop of 4.9 percentage points, while lower middle-income countries saw growth decline by 2.7 percentage points and lower income countries by only 1.2 percentage points. The group of high-income countries was the only category which recorded an average annual negative growth rate for the years 2008 and 2009 of minus 0.7 per cent. This group therefore was solely responsible for the contraction of world GDP in 2009.

The crisis has also seen a resurgence of borrowing from the IMF. After years of not being able to find borrowers, the IMF has started to lend again, supported by a pledge by its shareholders to provide more funding as part of internationally coordinated crisis-fighting efforts. Net disbursements by the Fund have been higher than at any time since the mid-1980s, with net payouts totalling more than 20 billion in Special Drawing Rights (SDRs) (about US$ 30 billion) in 2009 (figure 1). Also, the number of countries borrowing from the IMF has risen sharply: out of 179 countries in our sample, 53 received IMF funding in 2009 – a share of almost 30 per cent.

The impact of the crisis has clearly varied with the size of the external imbalances of individual countries. Dividing the sample into four country groups according to their current-account positions prior to the crisis (those with a high current-account surplus of more than 5 per cent of GDP, those with a current-account surpluses of less than 5 per cent of GDP, those with a current-account deficit of more than 5 per cent of GDP and those with a current-account deficit of less than 5 per cent of GDP), it can be observed that countries with large-current account imbalances – surpluses or deficits – have been hit harder than those with moderate imbalances. The group with very high surpluses experienced a drop in the growth trend by 4.2 percentage points, followed by an only slightly smaller drop in the growth trend of 3.9 percentage points for the group with very high deficits. In contrast, countries with moderate deficits and those with moderate surpluses experienced a decline of only 2.2 percentage points and 3.1 percentage points respectively (figure 2).

Figure 1

NET IMF LOAN DISBURSEMENTS, 1984–2009

(SDR billion)

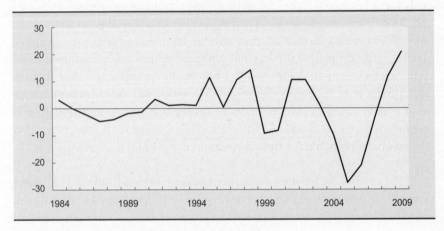

Source: Author's calculations, based on IMF data.

Figure 2

CHANGE IN GDP GROWTH BETWEEN 2003–2007 AND 2008–2009 BY CURRENT-ACCOUNT POSITION OF COUNTRIES

(Percentage points)

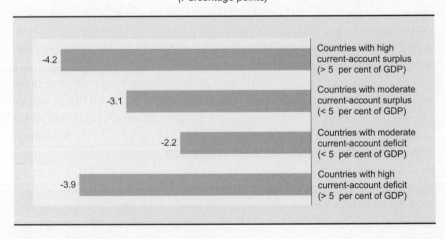

Source: Author's calculations, based on IMF data.

The exchange-rate regime also seems to have an impact on the vulnerability of a country to the contagion effects of a crisis. After the Asian crisis in the 1990s, the notion of the stable corner solutions ("corner solution paradigm") came into vogue. According to this proposition, in the long run only two currency regimes would be stable: the completely fixed or the completely flexible exchange rate.[6] Proponents of this hypothesis understood by "completely fixed" any regime which was then seen as providing an irrevocably fixed exchange rate, thereby providing no room for speculation. In addition to dollarization, currency boards and monetary union were also seen as belonging to this category of exchange-rate regimes, because, in principle, under these regimes the authorities have the necessary means in the form of reserves to prevent any crack in the exchange-rate peg.[7]

In order to get an idea of the initial impact of the exchange-rate regime on the vulnerability of countries, the sample was divided into nine groups, using the IMF's classification of exchange-rate regimes plus a separate group for countries in the EMU.[8] Again, the results are quite revealing. The (small) group of dollarized economies, including countries such as Ecuador, Montenegro and Panama,[9] managed the crisis relatively well: their GDP growth fell by only 0.6 percentage points, and growth continued at an average rate of 3.7 per cent in 2008–2009 – above average in the overall sample. None of these countries had to seek IMF support. However, before taking this result as a strong endorsement of dollarization, it must be borne in mind that the countries which lacked a legal tender of their own had been growing less rapidly in the years prior to the crisis than other countries of similar income levels (see annex table). In addition, abandoning the national currency deprives policy makers of the possibility of domestic financing of investment, as noted in Dullien (2009). Countries having the other types of exchange-rate regimes originally considered as "completely fixed" have performed comparatively badly during the crisis. The group of currency board countries, including Bulgaria and Estonia, but also some smaller Caribbean countries, have been the worst affected. GDP growth there declined, on average, by a whopping 6 percentage points. In addition, these countries experienced a contraction in average annual GDP of 1 per cent in 2008 and 2009.

Interestingly, the exchange-rate regimes that, on average, produced the best outcome during the crisis are those in the "middle ground" which were

Table 1

IMPACT OF THE CRISIS ON GDP GROWTH
BY EXCHANGE-RATE REGIME OF COUNTRIES

	Change in GDP growth, 2008–2009 compared to 2003–2007	Average annual GDP growth, 2008–2009	Average annual GDP growth 2003–2007
	(Percentage points)	*(Per cent)*	
Dollarized economies	-0.6	3.7	4.3
Currency board arrangements	-6.0	-1.0	5.1
Free floating	-4.2	-0.1	4.1
Managed floating	-3.2	3.0	6.2
European Monetary Union	-4.3	-1.3	3.0
Others ("middle ground")[a]	-3.0	3.0	5.9

Source: Author's calculations, based on IMF, *World Economic Outlook* database (accessed in January 2010); and IMF, 2009.
  a Other conventional fixed peg arrangements, pegged exchange rate within horizontal bands, crawling peg, crawling band.

once seen as not sustainable. Countries which had exchange-rate regimes classified as "conventional fixed peg" (except currency boards, monetary union and dollarization), "pegged exchange rate within horizontal bands", "crawling pegs" or "crawling bands" saw their GDP growth rates decline by an average of only 3 percentage points, and they achieved an average annual GDP growth rate of 3 per cent in 2008 and 2009, while those with exchange-rate regimes closer to the "corners" saw their GDP growth rate decline by 3.8 percentage points and recorded an average annual GDP growth rate of only 1.2 per cent.

B.   Econometric estimates

Descriptive statistics like those above can be misleading. For example, currency board countries as a group also usually have high current-account deficits. The question is therefore whether the factors analysed above have a direct influence on their own, or only an indirect influence. This can only be answered by means of rigorous econometric testing. Thus, as a first step, a regression was run with the change in GDP growth between 2003–2007 and 2008–2009 as the dependent variable, and the current-account balance prior to the crisis (2007), the inflation rate prior to the crisis (2007), GDP per capita, the variable for capital-account openness, a dummy for an IMF programme in 2009 and dummies for the different types of exchange-rate regimes as independent variables. In a general-to-specific-approach, variables that were not significant, at least at a 10 per cent level, were eliminated. In addition, both the current-account balance and the absolute value of the current-account balance were alternatively included in order to allow for the possibility that large surpluses also make a country vulnerable. The final equation for the change in the growth trend during the crisis reads as follows:

$$\Delta growth = -2.27 - 0.428 GDP_{capita} - 0.07 |CurrentAccount_{2007}|,$$

where $\Delta growth$ is the percentage point change in the average annual growth rate between 2003–2007 and 2008–2009, GDP_{capita} is GDP per capita in current US\$ 1,000, and $|CurrentAccount_{2007}|$ is the absolute value of the current account in 2007 as a per cent of GDP.

From this it can be observed that only per capita GDP levels and current-account imbalances had a clearly negative influence on the way a country was affected by the crisis (both coefficients are significant at the 5 per cent level), where the impact was measured as a change in the trend growth rate. Countries with higher per capita incomes have been hit significantly harder by the crisis than those with lower incomes. Interestingly, the current-account balance as a per cent of GDP was insignificant in explaining the change in GDP growth, while the *absolute* value of the current-account balance as a per cent of GDP turned out to be highly significant. Hence, not only current-account deficits appear to have contributed to the propagation of the crisis, but also current-account surpluses.

In a second step, a regression analysis was undertaken of the current-account balance prior to the crisis (2007), the inflation rate prior to the crisis (2007), GDP growth rate prior to the crisis (2003 to 2007), GDP per capita, the variable for capital-account openness, a dummy for an IMF programme in 2009 and dummies for the different types of exchange-rate regimes as possible factors influencing the average annual rate of GDP growth in 2008–2009. As before, variables which turned out to be statistically insignificant were eliminated, and both the current-account balance and the absolute value of the current-account balance were tested. The resulting equation reads:

$$growth_{2008\_9} = 1.69 + 0.16growth_{2003\_7} + 0.05CurrentAccount_{2007}$$
$$- 0.74GDP_{capita} + 0.08inf_{2007} - 2.01cb$$

Where $growth_{2008\_9}$ is the average annual growth rate of GDP in 2008 and 2009, $growth_{2003\_7}$ is the average annual growth rate of GDP during the period 2003–2007, $CurrentAccount_{2007}$ is the current account position as a per cent of GDP in the year 2007, inf_{2007} is the rate of inflation in 2007 and cb is a dummy for the country using a currency board.

All variables were significant at the 5 per cent level, except inflation and the GDP growth rate for the period 2003–2007 which were significant at 10 per cent.

A few of the results are notable. First, again GDP per capita turned out to be a very strong predictor of lower growth in the crisis years, even when controlling for growth prior to the crisis. One reason might be that the crisis originated in some of the most developed countries. Second, the current-account *deficit,* not the absolute value, seems to be a significant variable. A larger deficit prior to the crisis led to lower growth during the crisis years. Third, countries with a currency board in place had a significantly lower growth rate in 2008–2009 (by an annual two percentage points on average), even after controlling for the effects of the huge current-account deficits some of the currency board countries such as Lithuania and Estonia were running prior to the crisis. Third, inflation prior to the crisis seems to have influenced the impact of the crisis, but not in the way that would be predicted by standard theory. In actual fact, a higher rate of inflation prior to the crisis was correlated with a higher growth rate during the crisis (even when controlling for GDP growth prior to the crisis).

Another interesting feature seems to be the lack of any correlation between the depth of the crisis in a country and its request for IMF support. This result would mean first that countries seem to have sought IMF support regardless of the scale of their economic downturn, and second, that the

IMF programmes do not appear to have significantly influenced the growth outcomes of those countries compared with other countries having similar characteristics.

In a third step, a probit approach was used to test which characteristics increased the probability of a country seeking IMF support. Again, all variables were initially included and subsequently eliminated. In the end, the probit model for the probability of an IMF programme was estimated (table 2).

Table 2

PROBIT MODEL: PROBABILITY OF IMF INTERVENTION

Variable	Coefficient	Standard error
Constant	-0.575	0.151 (***)
CurrentAccount$_{2007}$	-0.056	0.011 (***)
GDP$_{capita}$	-0.392	0.118 (***)

*** Significant, at 1 per cent level.

Only two variables are significant for explaining the need for an IMF programme: the current-account balance and the GDP per capita. The larger the current-account deficit prior to the crisis, the larger was the probability of a country seeking IMF assistance in response to the crisis. In fact, looking at the descriptive statistics, it can be seen that only 2 out of the 53 countries which borrowed from the IMF in 2009 had a current-account surplus prior to the crisis. In addition, the richer a country in per capita terms, the less likely it was to seek IMF intervention. This is an interesting result, as IMF intervention was considered most likely for emerging-market economies. During the crisis, however, the Fund has lent strongly also to lower income countries. None of the exchange-rate regime dummies proved to be significant.[10]

Finally, the group of worst performers during the crisis was selected and another probit estimation run on the characteristics of this group. To this end, a threshold of an annual contraction by more than 3 per cent for 2008–2009 was chosen (a total contraction of more than 6 per cent), which produced 12 countries: Armenia, Botswana, Estonia, Hungary, Iceland, Ireland, Italy, Japan, Latvia, Lithuania, Seychelles and Ukraine. The probit estimation for these countries yielded the results presented in table 3, with *KOpen* referring to capital-account openness as measured by the Chinn/ Ito index.

Table 3

PROBIT MODEL: PROBABILITY OF A DEEP RECESSION

Variable	Coefficient	Standard error
Constant	-2.671	-2.671 (***)
$CurrentAccount_{2007}$	-0.028	0.013 (**)
GDP_{capita}	0.154	0.857 (*)
$growth_{2003\_7}$	0.092	0.055 (*)
KOpen	0.262	0.122 (**)

***   Significant at 1 per cent level.
 **   Significant at 5 per cent level.
  *   Significant at 10 per cent level.

Thus again, having a higher GDP per capita generally increases the risk of experiencing a severe recession. A large current-account deficit prior to the crisis is also an important risk factor. Having a relatively open capital account seems to be another risk factor for suffering severe consequences of a global financial and economic crisis. Our regression analysis revealed yet another factor: experiencing very strong growth in the years 2003–2007 (i.e. just prior to the crisis) also seemed to have increased the risk of the crisis plunging a country into a deep recession. This finding hints that a boom prior to the crisis might have led to imbalances, which made the economy in question more vulnerable (as it might have been part of a boom-and-bust cycle). Finally, having a very open capital account, as measured by the Chinn/Ito index, significantly increased the risk of experiencing a very deep recession as a consequence of the United States subprime crisis.

C.   Summing up the empirical evidence

Thus, the findings may be summarized as follows:

1. In terms of impact on GDP and GDP growth, the crisis appears to have affected high- and upper middle-income countries more than poorer countries, even though there may have been greater suffering in lower income countries, as a drop in GDP growth might be more severe in an environment without social safety nets and widespread poverty as a result of the crisis.

2. Large current-account imbalances – not only deficits – seem to be an important risk factor for vulnerability to crisis transmission.

3. Currency boards seem to be an additional risk factor, in addition to the impact a currency board might have on the external balance by increasing the current-account deficit.

4. An open capital account appears to exacerbate vulnerability.

5. Inflation, long seen as a prime concern for macroeconomic stability and an important factor in increasing countries' vulnerability to financial and currency crises, does not seem to be as significant a factor as was previously thought.

6. Higher per capita incomes make IMF intervention less likely.

7. IMF programmes cannot be shown to have significant positive or negative effects on the depth of a crisis

II. Tentative explanations and conclusions

From a theoretical point of view, and against the background of the Washington Consensus, these results provide the basis for considerable rethinking. First, the benefits of free global capital flows are very difficult to detect in this data set. Economic textbook theory tells us that open capital accounts can do two things. First, they can help countries which lack capital to import capital to grow faster. They can borrow from abroad, invest and hence boost growth. As marginal productivity of capital is higher than in countries which are capital-abundant, they can easily use the proceeds from their investments to service their debt. Second, open capital accounts can help countries weather asymmetric shocks. If an unexpected shock lowers national income, borrowing from abroad can be used to smooth national consumption, thus increasing welfare.[11] As long as domestic consumption has an influence on domestic output, this should also help reduce the volatility of overall output. Countries which are more financially open can more easily borrow from abroad, and therefore should be able to withstand a crisis – such as the recent one – better.

However, the data presented in this paper do not confirm this story. Whether importing capital is a sensible strategy for sustainably accelerating economic growth has been disputed for a number of years (see, for example, Prasad, Rajan and Subramanian, 2007). The data set used in this paper raises doubts about the ability of capital inflows to smooth the economic cycle. While an open capital account per se does not seem to have a significant influence on the depth of a crisis for the whole sample, it seems to increase the probability that a global economic and financial crisis can push a country with such an account into a deep recession. Moreover, using the possibility of global capital flows, either as an exporter or an importer of large amounts of capital (as reflected in a large current-account imbalance) clearly and strongly adds to a country's vulnerability to a crisis. One plausible explanation would be that in a financial crisis, such as the current one, access to foreign finance might not be possible due to a sudden increase in risk aversion among investors, thereby hurting countries that have relied on external capital inflows. The significant impact on countries with large surpluses might be explained by the fact that the large surpluses possibly hint at macroeconomic imbalances in these countries prior to the crisis in the form of permanently insufficient domestic demand. With borrowers being cut off from the global financial markets during the current crisis, countries that relied on other countries' demand growth for their own economic growth were hit disproportionally, due to the lack of internal demand growth momentum to make up for the loss of external demand.

The probability of entering a very deep recession might increase in proportion to the openness of the capital account. This is because capital controls are usually geared more towards short-term capital flows, and hence a more open capital account means a larger share of volatile short-term inflows in the overall capital inflows of a country. Given that the benefits of free capital flows do not seem to materialize as promised to the countries which – at least in the textbook model – should profit most from them (because they have made most use of international capital flows), there might be a case for introducing controls and limits on global capital flows.

Of course it may seem somewhat inappropriate to use the recent crisis as evidence against the textbook argument of the cushioning effects of global capital flows. After all, the textbook argument is in general about supply-side shocks to national output, while the origin of the latest crisis has clearly been a financial one. However, given the magnitude of the crisis and the fact that most of the economic crises of the past few decades arguably had financial origins, one has to question the relevance of the argument in favour of insuring against national supply shocks compared to potential shocks created by international capital flows for an individual economy.

If one agrees with the necessity of proactive macroeconomic management to limit current- account imbalances, and the need for bold policy action to counteract potential crises, the other results are rather easy to explain: moderate rates of inflation (instead of low rates) are not necessarily a problem, but might provide more space for monetary policy to implement rate cuts before the zero bound limits further actions. Such a stance could be considered as supporting the conclusions drawn by a recent IMF paper on the optimum rate of inflation (Blanchard, Dell'Ariccia and Mauro, 2010). Currency boards are a danger as they create a false sense of security and make proper macroeconomic management aimed at limiting current-account imbalances virtually impossible.

More puzzling is the fact that IMF involvement does not seem to have any explanatory power for the depth of a recession or a slowdown in growth. This result might be uncomfortable both for the IMF itself as well as its critics. If it turns out to be robust, it would mean that IMF involvement does not necessarily stabilize economic growth (as measured in GDP terms), nor does the conditionality attached to IMF programmes exacerbate the short-term impact of a crisis, as was repeatedly claimed for IMF programmes during the Asian crisis (Stiglitz, 2002). It might also indicate that there has been a change in the way the IMF designs its adjustment programmes so as to reduce their negative short-term impact on GDP growth compared with the IMF programmes of previous decades, as some observers claim (Schieritz, 2010). Turning this evidence against the IMF would imply that its programmes, while not exacerbating the economic situation, have not contributed much towards economic stabilization in the latest crisis.

From an economic policy perspective, this means that emerging-market economies and developing countries should think twice about opening up their capital accounts. Should they decide to open their capital accounts, countries should undertake active macroeconomic management to prevent the emergence of large current-account imbalances, even if this comes at the price of higher inflation. Finally, the results are a clear warning against creating a currency-board framework. Far from providing a stable macroeconomic environment, as some proponents have long argued, empirically such a framework seems to amplify shocks.

Notes

1   For a recent overview of a number of these issues, see Ocampo et al., 2010.
2   For this study, Zimbabwe has been excluded from the data set as it is an outlier for a number of the data points considered, and the country's recession is by most accounts largely independent of the global crisis.
3   The IMF classifies EMU countries as "independently floating". While this might be an appropriate description of EMU as a whole, it is misleading when looking at the performance of individual member countries such as Greece, as that country has a fixed exchange rate with its main trading partners.
4   For descriptive statistics on the impact of the crisis on different economies, see the table in the annex.
5   All data for each country group refer to simple, unweighted averages for the country group in question.
6   Early proponents include Eichengreen, 1994, and Obstfeld and Rogoff, 1995.
7   Of course, the Argentine crisis of 2001-2002, which resulted in its exit from a currency board, showed that such a regime is certainly not an "irrevocably fixed" exchange-rate regime.
8   The IMF classifies EMU countries as "independently floating". While this might be an appropriate description of EMU as a whole, it is certainly misleading when looking at the performance of a single member country such as Greece as that country has a fixed exchange rate with its main trading partners.
9   Countries are counted as "dollarized" if they have adopted a foreign currency. Thus, Montenegro is considered as having a "dollarized" economy even though it uses the euro.
10   However, some of the exchange-rate regime dummies showed a 100 per cent correlation with no IMF programmes. For example, no dollarized country turned to the IMF in the latest crisis. However, interpreting this fact in economic terms is not straightforward. While proponents of dollarization might claim that this shows the greater stability of dollarized economies, it is just as plausible that dollarized economies lack the channels for intervention through an IMF loan, or that the number of dollarized economies was too small (5 out of 179) to enable a reliable conclusion to be drawn.
11   For a typical detailed explanation, see Feenstra and Taylor, 2008, chap. 17.

References

Blanchard O, Dell'Ariccia G and Mauro P (2010). Rethinking macroeconomic policy. IMF Staff Position Note 10/03, Washington, DC.

Chen S and Ravallion M (2009). The impact of the global financial crisis on the world's poorest. VoxEU. Available at: http://www.voxeu.org/index.php?q=node/3520.

Chinn MD and Ito H (2008). A new measure of financial openness. *Journal of Comparative Policy Analysis*, 10 (3): 307–320.

Dullien S (2009) Central banking, financial institutions and credit creation in developing countries. UNCTAD Discussion Papers 193, United Nations Conference on Trade and Development, Geneva.

Eichengreen B (1994). International monetary arrangements for the 21st century. Washington, DC, Brookings Institution.

Feenstra RC and Taylor AM (2008). *International Economics*. New York, Worth Publishers.

IMF (2009). De facto classification of exchange rate regimes and monetary policy frameworks (as of April 31, 2008). Available at: http://www.imf.org/external/np/mfd/er/2008/eng/0408.htm.

IMF (2010), World Economic Outlook. Washington, DC, April.

Obstfeld M and Rogoff K (1995). The mirage of fixed exchange rates. *Journal of Economic Perspectives*, 9 (4): 73–96.

Ocampo JA et al. (2010). The great recession and the developing world. Initative for Policy Dialogue Working Paper. Available at: http://www0.gsb.columbia.edu/ipd/pub/Crisis_Complutense%5B1%5D_Great_Recession.pdf.

Prasad ES, Rajan R and Subramanian A (2007). Foreign capital and economic growth. *Brookings Papers on Economic Activity*, 38: 153–230.

Schieritz M (2010). Waschlappen aus Washington. *DIE ZEIT* Nr. 14/2010: 16.

Stiglitz J (2002). *Globalization and its Discontents*. New York, W.W. Norton & Co. Inc.

Annex table A.1

IMPACT OF THE CRISIS, BY COUNTRY CATEGORIES

	Number of countries	Number of countries receiving IMF credit in 2009	Change in GDP growth, 2008–2009 vs. 2003–2007 (Percentage points)	Average annual GDP growth, 2008–2009 (Per cent)	Average current-account position, 2007 (Per cent of GDP)	Absolute average current-account position in 2007	Average rate of inflation, 2007 (Per cent)	Average annual GDP growth, 2003–2007 (Per cent)	Average Chinn/Ito index for capital-account openness
Total sample	**179**	**53**	**-3.5**	**2.0**	**-3.1**	**10.7**	**6.1**	**5.4**	**0.5**
Countries with									
Per capita GDP of									
less than $976	44	26	-1.2	4.3	-7.0	8.8	8.4	5.4	-0.5
between $975 and $3 855	45	14	-2.7	3.3	-3.5	9.4	6.8	6.1	0.3
between $3 856 and $11 905	42	10	-4.9	1.0	-5.0	13.0	6.3	5.9	0.2
more than $11 905	48	3	-5.2	-0.7	2.4	11.7	3.3	4.5	1.8
Current-account surplus of									
less than 5 per cent of GDP	21	0	-3.1	1.8	2.2	2.2	3.8	5.0	1.2
more than 5 per cent of GDP	40	2	-4.2	2.6	15.8	15.8	7.5	6.8	0.4
Current-account deficit of									
less than 5 per cent of GDP	34	14	-2.2	2.6	-2.4	2.4	6.6	4.8	0.1
more than 5 per cent of GDP	84	37	-3.9	1.3	-13.8	13.8	5.9	5.2	0.5
Severe recession	12	6	-11.5	-5.4	-8.6	11.7	5.8	6.1	1.8
IMF credit in 2009	53	53	-2.9	2.2	-12.3	12.9	6.8	5.1	0.1
Dollarized economies	5	0	-0.6	3.7	-7.9	9.3	3.7	4.3	1.4
Currency boards	13	7	-6.0	-1.0	-18.2	27.9	3.9	5.1	0.8
Managed floating regimes	43	17	-3.2	3.0	-5.0	9.8	8.3	6.2	0.6
Freely floating currencies	23	4	-4.2	-0.1	-1.4	6.1	3.5	4.1	1.3
"Middle ground" exchange rate regimes	78	24	-3.0	3.0	-0.1	10.8	6.9	5.9	-0.2
European Monetary Union	15	0	-4.3	-1.3	-2.1	6.6	2.2	3.0	2.1

Source: Author's calculations, based on IMF, 2009; and IMF, *World Economic Outlook* database (accessed January 2010).

THE CRISIS

COUNTRY AND REGIONAL STUDIES

CHINA'S ECONOMY IN THE GLOBAL ECONOMIC CRISIS: IMPACT AND POLICY RESPONSES

Laike Yang and Cornelius Huizenga

Abstract

The global economic and financial crisis has affected China differently from other countries, in that its impact has been felt more by the real economy than by the Chinese financial system. The global crisis caused a dramatic fall in China's foreign trade and foreign direct investment (FDI) inflows, higher unemployment rates and strong price fluctuations. Regarding China's foreign trade, its exports of capital- and technology-intensive products were affected more than its exports of labour-intensive products. Foreign-invested enterprises (FIEs) and State-owned enterprises (SOEs) were affected more than domestic private enterprises, and China's processing trade was affected more than its ordinary trade. The Chinese Government responded quickly to tackle the adverse effects of the crisis through a sizeable stimulus package. This stimulus package has had some positive effects, but also some negative effects, and some difficulties persist.

Introduction

The Chinese economy is heavily dependent on foreign trade and foreign direct investment (FDI). In 2007, China overtook the United States to become the world's second largest exporter of merchandise goods after the European Union (EU). The share of exports of goods and services in China's GDP rose from 9.1 per cent in 1985 to 37.8 per cent in 2008 (figure 1) and net exports accounted for about 9 per cent of China's GDP in 2008.[1] The Chinese Government estimates that export-oriented industries provide employment to more than 80 million people, of whom 28 million are employed in foreign-invested enterprises (FIEs). FDI flows to China have been a major factor contributing to China's rapid economic growth and productivity gains. In 2007, such flows totalled US$ 75 billion, making China the largest FDI recipient among developing and emerging-market economies and the third largest overall, after the EU and the United States.

Initially, China was less affected by the global financial and economic crisis than many other countries. Although the country's financial sector did not suffer from the impacts of the global shock waves resulting from the collapse of the United States investment bank, Lehman Brothers, in September 2008, its economic development, particularly export-oriented industries, suffered a setback. How serious has this impact been, especially on China's foreign trade? How did China respond to the financial crisis and what have been the results? What can China learn from this current crisis? In this paper, we discuss these questions and present policy recommendations for Chinese policymakers.

The paper is structured in four sections as follows: section I analyses the general impact of the global financial and economic crisis on the Chinese economy; section II provides an in-depth analysis of the impact of the crisis on China's foreign trade; section III describes the various responses of the Government and industry to tackle the crisis, and the economic impacts of those responses. In the last part, section IV, concluding remarks and policy recommendations are presented.

Figure 1

CHINA: RATIO OF EXPORTS TO GDP, 1985–2008

(Per cent)

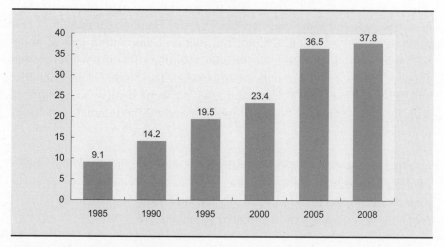

Source: Authors' calculations, based on data for exports from the Ministry of Commerce of China (www.
mofcom.gov.cn); and GDP data from the National Bureau of Statistics of China (www.stats.gov.cn).

I. Impacts of the global economic crisis
on the Chinese economy

A.   *Relatively small impact on Chinese financial institutions*

Compared to the banking systems of developed countries, Chinese banks generally have very little exposure to risks on international financial markets, particularly the risks associated with complex financial instruments. China's strict restrictions on capital inflows and outflows limit the ability of individual Chinese citizens and firms to invest their savings overseas. Most Chinese investment flows are controlled by government entities such as State-owned banks, the China National Investment Corporation and State-owned enterprises (SOEs). Such entities have maintained relatively conservative investment strategies on international financial markets. As a result, Chinese financial institutions have suffered relatively small losses in the ongoing global financial turmoil. The biggest loss reported was by the Bank of China, of about US$ 2 billion, as a result of the subprime crisis. Other Chinese financial institutions that reported relatively large losses include the Industrial and Commercial Bank of China with a loss of about US$ 1.8 billion, China Construction Bank with a loss of about US$ 673 million, and Ping An Insurance Group of China with a loss of about 1 billion euros through investments in the Fortis Group (Schüller and Schüler-Zhou, 2009).[2] These figures are very small when compared with losses of about US$ 4.1 trillion incurred by the international banks (Landler, 2009).

However, the Chinese economy has not been immune to the effects of the global economic and financial crisis. The crisis has affected the manufacturing sector significantly, and has been unexpectedly severe, particularly for many export-oriented industries.

B.   Impact on economic growth

There is a broad consensus among China's key economic policymakers over the country's growth strategy: they believe China must maintain its high growth rate for the sake of social stability and to build a "harmonious society". Also, China needs to maintain a GDP growth rate of at least a 9 per cent to be able to absorb the growing labour force and provide jobs in the urban sector for migrants from rural areas. Many economists believe that China could face a recession if its growth rate were to slow down to 5–6 per cent (Roubini, 2008). China enjoyed a high GDP growth rate of almost 10 per cent per annum over the past three decades, but this has slowed down since the middle of 2008 (figures 2 and 3). In March 2009, China's GDP growth rate reached a 10-year low of 6.1 per cent, leading many economists and international institutions to forecast that Chinese economic growth could fall to 5–6 per cent in the period 2009–2010. Concern over this possibility led the Chinese Government to take various measures to secure a GDP growth rate of 8 per cent in 2009. Because of very large government tax revenues and foreign exchange reserves, China was able to put in place a huge stimulus package that resulted in a growth rate of 8.7 per cent in 2009.[3] This was

Figure 2

CHINA: GDP GROWTH, MARCH 2006–SEPTEMBER 2009

(Per cent)

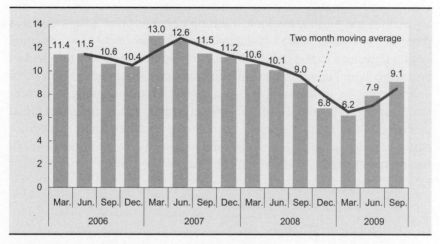

Source: National Bureau of Statistics of China (www.stats.gov.cn).

Figure 3

CHINA: GDP, 1. QUARTER 2006–2. QUARTER 2009

(RMB billion)

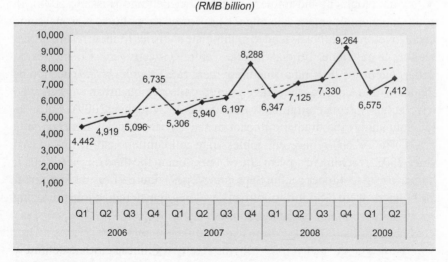

Source: National Bureau of Statistics of China (www.stats.gov.cn).

much higher than what was forecast for most economies of the world, and high enough to generate new jobs for millions of laid-off workers and young unemployed graduates.

China has finished the industrialization, but its urbanization is still in process. This is a time of considerable social transformation, which could result in greater social instability. Chinese policymakers attach the greatest priority to maintaining a "peaceful", "harmonious" environment for further development. With the number of protests in China mounting, it is clear that Chinese leaders will use whatever economic policy measures are at their disposal to try to maintain a sufficient level of economic growth for ensuring social stability, just as they did in response to the Asian financial crisis a decade ago.

C.   Impact on employment

It is difficult to determine the exact unemployment rate in China. Poor and incomplete collection of data and flaws in the statistical system – such as the lack of nationally accepted and implemented definitions and standards – not only hamper academic research, but, more importantly, they affect labour policy development and implementation (Duckett and Hussain, 2008). In addition, unemployment data might be distorted for political reasons: some local government officials tend to manipulate statistics to show results which would please higher officials or the Central Government. Consequently, data concerning the official unemployment rate (*dengji shiyelü*) need to be treated with caution, as they merely refer to the eligible urban workers who have actually registered to seek employment (Schucher, 2009). But even this rate shows the dramatic impact of the global financial and economic crisis. The urban "registered" jobless rate fell continuously for five years since 2002, reaching its lowest rate of 4 per cent in the third quarter of 2007, before rising to 4.6 per cent in September 2009 (figure 4). By 31 December 2009, there were 8.86 million urban residents registered as jobless, rising by 560,000 in the fourth quarter alone.

However, the actual unemployment rate in Chinese cities is definitely higher than is indicated in the official unemployment rate. A survey

Figure 4

CHINA: QUARTERLY UNEMPLOYMENT RATE, MARCH 2006–SEPT. 2009

(Per cent)

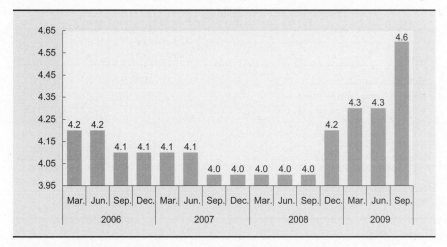

Source: National Bureau of Statistics of China (www.stats.gov.cn).

conducted by the Chinese Academy of Social Sciences (CASS, 2008) estimated that the urban unemployment rate was 9.4 per cent if migrant workers were included. In medium-sized and large cities the unemployment rate was even higher, reaching as much as 10.1 per cent (CASS, 2008; Li, 2009). Zhou Tianyong, a researcher at the China Central Party's School, estimates that the real rate of urban joblessness was 12 per cent in 2008, and this could climb to 14 per cent in 2009 (Zhou, 2008). A study by Schucher (2009) estimates that in 2009 there were 32.7–45.7 million urban laid-off and unemployed workers in China, and 36.8–41.8 million non-agricultural job seekers (table 1).

Those worst affected by the global financial and economic crisis in China have been migrant workers and new university graduates. According to the Ministry of Human Resources and Social Security (2010), by the end of 2008 China had 132 million migrant workers, most of whom were employed in the coastal area, and 60–70 per cent were active in labour-intensive manufacturing, trade and services. In February 2009, the Ministry

Table 1

CHINA: URBAN UNEMPLOYMENT AND NON-AGRICULTURAL JOB SEEKERS, BY CATEGORY OF WORKERS, 2009

(Million)

	Laid-off or unemployed	Job seekers
Migrant workers	20–30	11
Newly arriving rural migrants	–	5–9
Registered urban unemployed	8.9	8.9
Laid-off workers, unpaid leave	2–5	0
Demobilized soldiers	0.3	0.3
College graduates, 2008	1.5	1.5
New college graduates, 2009	–	6.1
New entrants to labour force	–	4–5
Total	32.7–45.7	36.8–41.8

Source: Schucher, 2009.

of Agriculture revealed that 20 million migrant workers had lost their jobs shortly before the Spring Festival (in February 2010). In Guangdong Province, China's biggest export hub, thousands of export-oriented factories were closed, which left about 6 million migrant workers without jobs. Many of these peasant workers are second-generation migrants, 60–70 per cent of whom are under 28 years of age and lack basic agricultural skills (Tan and Xin, 2009). They are not willing to return to country life, but they are not entitled to urban social security or medical care and have no access to education.

In 1999, the Chinese Ministry of Education launched a large-scale higher education expansion plan. Apart from improving the education level of average Chinese citizens, this plan also aimed to alleviate the immediate pressure on the labour market. Since then, the number of students enrolled in universities and colleges has been growing by about 20 per cent a year, or from about 1.08 million newly enrolled students in the late 1990s to about 6.51 million in 2008.[4] When the global financial crisis spread to China, most of the FIEs and all foreign banks stopped recruiting new employees. This left millions of university graduates without jobs: about 1.5 million and 2 million university graduates in 2008 and 2009, respectively, were unable to find a job. The unemployment rate for these young people was higher than 12 per cent – three times the official urban unemployment rate (Lawrence, 2008; Zhan, 2009).

D.   Impact on FDI inflows

FDI has been the main driving force behind Chinese economic growth over the past decade. FIEs have not only provided China with physical and financial capital; they have also created numerous jobs and brought in new technologies and know-how. As much as 90 per cent of China's FDI inflows have gone to the manufacturing sector, and mostly to export-oriented industries. Moreover, FIEs account for more than 50 per cent of China's foreign trade. Until mid-2008, China's FDI inflows had been growing rapidly, but since August of that year, they declined sharply by 20 per cent or more (figure 5). This fall in FDI was an important warning signal that the global crisis had spread to the Chinese economy. It is believed that a large amount of

Figure 5

CHINA: MONTHLY GROWTH RATES OF FDI INFLOWS, JAN. 2007–NOV. 2009

(Per cent)

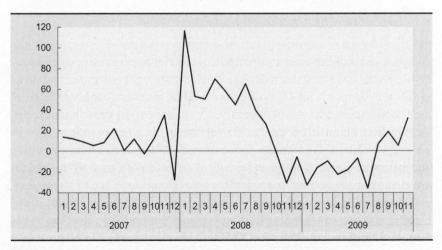

Source: Ministry of Commerce database (http://zhs.mofcom.gov.cn/tongji.shtml).

speculative money, included under FDI in Chinese statistics, has flowed into China's real estate sector in recent years. This makes it difficult to identify the impact of the global crisis on FDI in manufacturing. However, the shrinking number of investment projects are an indication of how strongly China's manufacturing and exports have been affected by the global crisis.

E.   Inflation

The Chinese economy depends heavily on external energy supply and imported raw materials. The dramatic rise in prices of crude oil and commodities in the last few years has had a strong impact on China's domestic prices. From mid-2006 to mid-2007, China's consumer price index (CPI) soared from just above 1 per cent to almost 9 per cent.[5] Thereafter, it declined rapidly, converting to deflation by February 2009. To cope with the high price volatility, the Chinese monetary authority increased overnight interest rates seven times from September 2006 to January 2008. Subsequently, the interest rates were cut four times from September to December 2008 (figure 6). This was the first time in Chinese history that the Government took this kind of dramatic monetary policy stance.

F.   Impact on China's foreign trade

Undoubtedly, the strongest impact of the global financial and economic crisis on China was the sharp decline in its foreign trade. As the crisis spread to the real economy of China's major trading partners especially that of the United States and the EU countries, Chinese export growth contracted sharply, from about 20 per cent to -25 per cent in just a few months (figure 7). This shocked both the Chinese Government as well as those scholars who had believed China was an independent growth pole that would not be affected by crises in other parts of the world (Dong He, Cheung and Chang, 2007; Huang, 2008; Pisani-Ferry and Santos, 2009). Throughout 2009, Chinese exports to its major trading partners continued to decline. It has been estimated that the fall in exports will have cut China's GDP growth in 2008 by more than 5 percentage points (Yu, 2010).

Figure 6

CHINA: INFLATION AND THE OFFICIAL INTEREST RATE, 2006–2009

(Per cent)

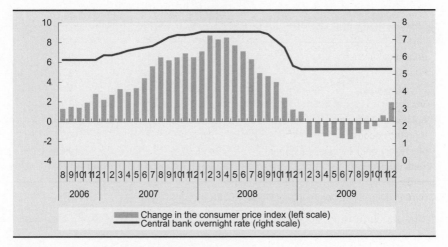

Change in the consumer price index (left scale)
Central bank overnight rate (right scale)

Source: http://www.tradingeconomics.com.

Figure 7

CHINA: MONTHLY GROWTH RATE OF EXPORT (YEAR-ON-YEAR), NOVEMBER 2006–AUGUST 2009

(Per cent)

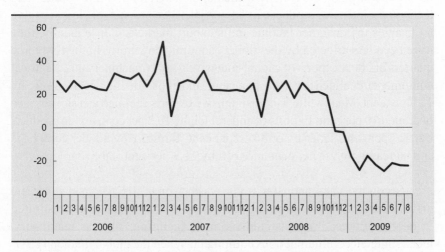

Source: Ministry of Commerce of China (www.mofcom.gov.cn/tongji.shtml).

Table 2

CHINA'S MAIN MERCHANDISE EXPORTS, BY CATEGORY, JAN.–SEPT. 2009

Commodities	Value (US$ 100 million)	Percentage change
Toys	56.0	-11.3
Bags and suitcases	91.5	-9.7
Furniture	177.3	-8.5
Shoes	208.9	-5.6
Textiles	431.0	-13.7
Apparel and accessories	785.4	-10.2
High-tech goods	2 558.4	-17.7
Machinery and electrical equipment	4 963.7	-19.6
Total	8 466.5	-21.3

Source: Ministry of Commerce of China, 2009a.

Although the general impact on exports was severe, it was not evenly distributed among sectors, regions and types of enterprise. Firstly, exports of labour-intensive products were less affected than those of capital- and technology-intensive products. China's labour-intensive products, such as textiles and apparel, leather and shoes, furniture and paper products, have a lower income elasticity of demand.[6] Therefore, unlike capital- and technology-intensive products, its labour-intensive products are less sensitive to changes in consumer income in its export markets. Consequently, they have been less affected by the global economic downturn. In the first three quarters of 2009, exports of capital-intensive goods (machinery and electrical equipment) declined by 19.6 per cent, and those of high-tech goods by 17.7 per cent. Meanwhile, labour-intensive exports declined at a slower pace of around 10 per cent. Exports of apparel fell by 10.2 per cent, textile products by 13.7 per cent, shoes by only 5.6 per cent, furniture by 8.5 per cent, bags and suitcases by 9.7 per cent and toys by 11.3 per cent (table 2).

Secondly, FIEs and SOEs have been worse affected than domestic private enterprises. A large proportion of China's FDI is concentrated in export-oriented, capital-intensive manufacturing, such as machinery, metals and telecommunications equipment. When the global financial crisis developed into a worldwide recession, many FIEs withdrew investments

Table 3

CHINA'S FOREIGN TRADE, BY TYPE OF ENTERPRISE, 2009[a]

	Export		Import	
Type of enterprise	Value (US$ 100 million)	Percentage change	Value (US$ 100 million)	Percentage change
State-owned enterprises	1 375.2	-30.2	2 044.9	-28.0
Foreign invested enterprises	4 701.8	-21.1	3 841.9	-20.6
Privately owned enterprises	2 389.5	-15.5	1 225.0	-2.1

Source: Ministry of Commerce of China, 2009a.
   a Data refer to the first three quarters of 2009.

from China due to financial difficulties in their home countries. Consequently, both exports and imports by these firms fell dramatically in 2009, by 21.1 per cent and 20.6 per cent respectively (table 3).

Chinese SOEs are the biggest contributor to China's technology and capital-intensive exports. As mentioned, these products are more vulnerable in times of recession because consumers tend to switch to cheaper, more labour-intensive products. During the current global crisis, they were first hit by the higher prices of raw materials and then by sharply declining demand abroad. In the first three quarters of 2009, the exports and imports of SOEs fell by 30.2 per cent and 28 per cent respectively. As a result, many SOEs are still suffering from huge losses due to lower exports.

Privately owned domestic companies in China are mostly small and medium-sized enterprises (SMEs). Unlike SOEs, which are mostly financed by bank loans and the capital market, most privately owned domestic enterprises are self-financed. Since their exports consist mainly of low-cost, labour-intensive products, they have been less affected by the crisis. In 2009, their exports declined by 15.5 per cent and imports by only 2.1 per cent, which is much smaller than the declines suffered by the large SOEs and the FIEs (table 3).

Thirdly, the impact on trade between China and the developed world was not as strong as that between China and developing countries. At the

Table 4

**CHINA: GROWTH OF EXPORTS TO MAIN DESTINATIONS,
2007–AUGUST 2009**

(Per cent)

	2007	2008	2009
EU-27	34.7	19.5	-19.3
United States	14.4	8.4	-12.5
Hong Kong (China)	18.7	3.4	-12.8
Japan	6.3	19.2	-15.7
ASEAN	32.1	21.2	-6.9
Republic of Korea	26.1	31.8	-27.5
Russian Federation	80.0	15.8	-46.9
India	64.7	31.2	-5.8
Taiwan Province of China	13.1	10.3	-20.7
Canada	25.0	12.3	-18.9
Total	18.1	24.9	-15.9

Source: Ministry of Commerce of China (www.mofcom.gov.cn/tongji.shtml).

beginning of the economic and financial crisis, China's trade with major developed economies fell very rapidly, but it has stabilized since mid-2009. On the other hand, China's trade with its developing-country trade partners deteriorated more. While in the first nine months of 2009, exports from China to Japan, the United States and Australia declined by 18.8 per cent, 16.9 per cent and 12.7 per cent, respectively, exports to the Russian Federation, Brazil, and the Republic of Korea shrank by 49.4 per cent, 37.3 per cent and 34 per cent respectively (table 4). The main reason for this considerable difference in impact is that a large proportion of exports to developed economies are labour-intensive products which are not easily substituted by local products. But the goods exported to developing countries are similar to products made in those countries and can be replaced easily by local supply.

II. Responses of the Chinese Government and their outcomes

A.   *Responses of the Chinese Government to the global crisis*

To cope with the negative impacts of the global financial and economic crisis on the Chinese economy, particularly on exports, the Chinese Government took swift action. In November 2008, the Government announced a 4 trillion renminbi (RMB) (US$ 586 billion) fiscal stimulus package for 2009 and 2010 – equivalent to 13.3 per cent of China's nominal GDP in 2008. The package is mainly intended to drive demand in following areas: (i) development of public transport infrastructure (including railways, subways, highways, airports and ports); (ii) post-earthquake reconstruction in Sichuan Province; (iii) creation of affordable public housing in urban areas; (iv) development of rural infrastructure (including irrigation, drinking water, electricity and transport); (v) environmental projects; (vi) technology development and innovation; (vii) health care and social security; and (viii) education. The largest share of the stimulus package (37.5 per cent) has been allocated to the development of transport infrastructure, and the second largest share – about 25 per cent – to post-earthquake reconstruction of Wenchuan County in Sichuan Province. Rural area infrastructure and the construction of affordable housing in urban areas have received shares of 9.3 per cent and 10 per cent respectively. Since the fund to support post-earthquake reconstruction is intended mainly for infrastructure development, the total amount of money allocated to infrastructure accounts for more than 70 per cent of the total stimulus package (table 5). The stimulus plan includes many very ambitious projects. For example, the Government plans to spend RMB 400 billion to build 50 new airports and to expand 90 existing airports by the end of 2010. An additional RMB 600 billion is designated for upgrading the railway system, and another RMB 1,000 billion for expansion of the network of roads, local transit systems and seaways (Schüller and Schüler-Zhou, 2009). Not long after the Central Government announced its stimulus package, numerous local government officials announced their own

Table 5

SECTORAL DISTRIBUTION OF CHINA'S STIMULUS PACKAGE

	RMB	US$	Share in total stimulus package	Share in China's GDP, 2008
Sector	(Billion)		(Per cent)	
Transport infrastructure	1 500	220	37.5	5.0
Post-earthquake reconstruction	1 000	146	25.0	3.3
Public housing	400	59	10.0	1.3
Rural infrastructure	370	54	9.3	1.2
Innovation and technology	370	54	9.3	1.2
Environmental protection	210	31	5.3	0.7
Health care and education	150	22	3.8	0.5
Total	4 000	586	100.0	13.3

Source: China National Development and Reform Commission (www.NDRC.gov.cn).

stimulus plans which were estimated to total as much as RMB 18 trillion or US$ 2.64 trillion (Yu Yongding, 2009).[7]

The main source of funding for the RMB 4-trillion stimulus package is the Central Government, which is financing 25 per cent of the package. Bank credits are the second most important source of finance. To fund the local governments' stimulus packages, the Central Government authorized the local governments to issue RMB 200 billion in government bonds, while the remainder of their packages was also expected to be financed by loans from commercial banks.

Shortly after its announcement of the RMB 4-trillion stimulus package, China also launched industrial revitalization plans to promote the long-term competitiveness of the so-called 10 pillar industries: vehicle manufacture, steel, shipbuilding, textiles and clothing, machinery, electronics and information technology, light industries, petrochemicals, non-ferrous metals and logistics. Government support policies for these 10 industries include tax cuts and incentives, industrial subsidies, government procurement, special funds to support technology upgrade, foreign investment promotion and development of domestic brands.

To support the troubled export-oriented industries, the Chinese Government also sought to expand domestic consumption, especially in unexploited rural markets. For example, the Government launched the Home Appliance Subsidy Programme in Rural Areas in December 2007, first in Shandong, Henan and Sichuan provinces, and in Qingdao City, and later extending this to the whole country. Since February 2009, an estimated 900 million Chinese rural residents have been eligible to receive a 13 per cent discount on their purchase of certain brands of home appliances. In March 2009, the Government expanded this subsidy scheme to auto products, offering an average 10 per cent subsidy for various automotive products. The Government plans to spend RMB 5.43 billion over a four-year period on this scheme (Ministry of Commerce, 2009b). In the beginning of 2010, the Chinese Government again expanded its consumer subsidy scheme, this time to construction-related products and materials to support the rural housing industry.

In April 2009, the Chinese Government announced another plan to spend US$ 124 billion over the next three years to create a universal health care system. The plan aims to extend basic health-care coverage to most of the population by 2011, and to invest in public hospitals and training for rural doctors.

One important measure aimed especially at promoting exports is the tax rebate policy for various products. Related to the value added tax (VAT), China's tax rebate policy has been used for many years as an effective tool to promote exports of manufactured products. Introduced in 1994, it has been adjusted several times since then. Due to the widening trade surplus and increasing trade conflicts with its main trading partners, in 2005 the Chinese Government started to cut the tax rebate rates for labour- and resource-intensive products as well as for products that are highly polluting. But as the global financial crisis severely affected Chinese exports, the Government revised this policy again in August 2008, particularly for labour-intensive products. By the end of 2009, the Chinese tax authority had raised the VAT rebate rates seven times (table 6), and the highest tax rebate rate has now risen to 17 per cent. In 2009 alone, tax rebates cost China RMB 648.7 billion – slightly less than US$ 100 billion.

Apart from the VAT rebate policy, the Chinese Government took several other measures to support its export industries. In 2009, the Government

Table 6

CHINA'S TAX REBATE RATE ADJUSTMENTS DURING THE GLOBAL CRISIS

	Industry	Revision of tax rebate rate (Per cent)
1 Aug. 2008	Textile and apparel	From 11 to 13
1 Nov. 2008	Textile and apparel	From 13 to 14
	Toys	From 13 to 14
	High-tech products (e.g. HIV/AIDS drugs)	From 9 to 13
12 Dec. 2008	Rubber products	From 5 to 9
	Glasses	From 5 to 11
	Frozen seafood products	From 5 to 13
	Bags, shoes, furniture, lights, clocks, bedding	From 11 to 13
	Metal products	From 9 to 11
	Motors, bicycles, home appliances	From 9, 11 and 13 to 11,13 and 14, respectively
1 Jan. 2009	Aviation products, industrial robots	From 13 and 14, respectively, to both 17 for each
	Sewing machines, motor cycle products	From 11 and 13, respectively, to 14 for each
2 Feb. 2009	Textiles and apparel	From 14 to15
1 April 2009	Colour television sets	From 14 to 17
	Textiles and apparel	From 15 to 16
	Metal products	From 11 to 13
	Automobile parts	From 9 to 11
	Locks	From 7 to 9
1 June 2009	Canned food, juices	From 13 to15
	Corn products, alcohol	From 0 to 5
	Steel products (including scissors)	From 5 to 9
	Bags, shoes, furniture, lights, clocks and bedding	From 13 to 15
	Plastic products, glasses, porcelain and ceramic products	From 11 to 13

Source: Various announcements by the Ministry of Finance and the China National Tax Bureau.

cut the premium rates for export insurance. Consequently, export credit insurance rose to US$ 90 billion – more than double the 2008 value. To help SMEs, the Government established an export financing guarantee system, which greatly increased export-related loans to these companies. To reduce exporting enterprises' foreign exchange risks, in April 2009 China's State Council announced a pilot programme to allow exporters and importers in five Chinese cities (Shanghai, Guangzhou, Shenzhen, Zhuhai and Dongguan) to settle cross-border trade deals in renminbi. This pilot programme involved 365 trading companies.

In order to diversify China's export market, the Government has sought to promote exports to developing countries over the past few years by becoming very active in negotiating and signing free trade agreements (FTAs). China has signed FTAs with the Association of Southeast Asia Nations (ASEAN), Pakistan, Peru and Singapore, and has initiated free trade negotiations with Chile, Colombia, Costa Rica, the Gulf Cooperation Council, the Republic of Korea and South Africa. The FTAs have helped Chinese enterprises to expand their market in the countries that have signed up to these agreements.

B.   Outcomes of China's expansionary policies and stimulus package

The Chinese Government's expansionary policies have had positive effects on the country's exports and macroeconomic stability. China's GDP growth rates were 9 per cent in 2008 and 8.7 per cent in 2009 – the highest among the major economies of the world. China's exports, after a drop to a 36-month low in March 2009 (with export values down to US$ 64.89 billion), experienced a turnaround for the first time since the start of the economic and financial crisis in December 2009, with a year-on year increase of 17.7 per cent (figure 7). At the same time, China's imports soared by 55.9 per cent due to a sharp rebound in prices of oil and other raw materials in international markets. Crude-oil shipments surged to a record monthly high of 21.26 million tons in December. Iron-ore imports jumped to 62.16 million tons – an increase of more than 80 per cent over the previous year. The increase in imports of raw materials and oil contributed to narrowing China's trade surplus, which in December 2009 shrank to US$ 18.43 billion

Figure 8

CHINA'S TRADE BALANCE, JANUARY 2008–DECEMBER 2009

(US$ billion)

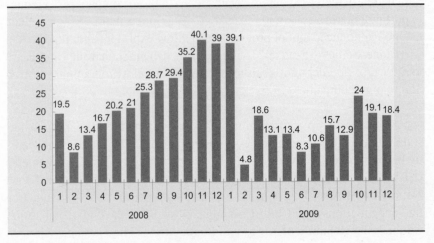

Source: Ministry of Commerce of China, *Foreign Trade* database.

from US$ 19.1 billion the previous month. This represented less than half of China's trade surplus of a year earlier (figure 8).

The massive stimulus package also pushed China's budget deficit to a historical high, to reach 2.8 per cent of GDP in 2009. This was much higher than in previous years, and the Government expects a similar deficit in 2010, amounting to RMB 1,050 billion (table 7). Total governmental debt in 2008 and 2009 was RMB 5,327.2 billion and RMB 6,023.8 billion respectively, while the ratio of national debt to total GDP was 17 per cent and 18 per cent respectively. Comparing the figures in many other major economies, for instance Japan (198.6 per cent), Italy (104.3 per cent), France (65.2 per cent) Germany (76.4 per cent), India (59.6 per cent) and the United States (61.5 per cent), the national debt in China is quite low.[8]

Thanks to the Government's efforts to diversify China's export markets, exports to some "new markets" such as Central Asia and Middle East have increased even during the crisis. In the first half of 2009, exports to Afghanistan, Kyrgyzstan, Tajikistan, Turkmenistan and Uzbekistan increased

Table 7

CHINA: CENTRAL GOVERNMENT BUDGET DEFICIT, 2001–2010[a]

	Central Government budget deficit (RMB billion)	Budget deficit/GDP (Per cent)
2001	259.8	2.7
2002	309.6	2.6
2003	319.8	2.4
2004	319.2	2.0
2005	300.0	1.6
2006	274.9	1.3
2007	200.0	0.8
2008	180.0	0.6
2009	950.0	2.8
2010	1 050.0	2.8

Source: Ministry of Finance of China (http://yss.mof.gov.cn/2010zhongyangyusuan/201003/t20100325_280110.html).
a Figures for 2010 are projections.

40.6 per cent, 30.4 per cent, 29.8 per cent , 76.5 per cent and 70.5 per cent respectively (table 8). Exports to China's South-East Asian neighbours have also risen. For example, exports to Viet Nam increased by 7.8 per cent, to Myanmar by 14.3 per cent and to the Lao People's Democratic Republic

Table 8

CHINA'S TRADE WITH SELECTED CENTRAL ASIAN COUNTRIES, JANUARY–JUNE 2009

Country	Exports + Imports	Exports	Imports	Exports + Imports	Exports	Imports
	Value (US$ 10 000)			Percentage change		
Uzbekistan	106 294	85 566	20 728	49.4	70.5	-1.0
Turkmenistan	67 578	65 742	1 835	77.9	76.5	149.1
Kyrgyzstan	47 399	35 525	11 874	67.7	29.8	1243.5
Tajikistan	4 199	3 880	320	4.2	30.4	-69.7
Afghanistan	21 500	21 300	100	39.0	40.6	-48.9

Source: Ministry of Commerce of China, 2009a.

Table 9

CHINA'S TRADE WITH SELECTED COUNTRIES IN EAST AND SOUTH ASIA, 2009

	Total trade		Exports		Imports	
	Value (US$ 100 million)	Percentage change	Value (US$ 100 million)	Percentage change	Value (US$ 100 million)	Percentage change
Democratic People's Rep. of Korea	26.81	-4.0	18.88	-7.1	7.93	4.3
Mongolia	23.97	-1.7	10.58	16.7	13.39	-12.6
Brunei Darussalam	4.23	93.5	1.40	8.4	2.82	217.5
Myanmar	29.07	10.7	22.61	14.3	6.46	-0.2
Lao PDR	7.44	79.0	3.77	40.5	3.67	149.2
Viet Nam	210.48	8.1	163.01	7.8	47.47	9.3
Nepal	4.14	8.7	4.09	9.0	0.05	-11.6

Source: Ministry of Commerce of China, 2009a.

by 40.5 per cent (table 9). Although the volume of trade between China and these countries is still relatively small, the speed of its expansion has been quite notable.

III. Concluding remarks and policy proposals

The Chinese economy was affected by the global economic and financial crisis in a very different way from other major economic powers. China follows an export-led development strategy similar to that adopted by small and open economies such as Hong Kong (China), Malaysia and Singapore. Therefore the global crisis did not affect the Chinese economy through the financial channel, but through the real economy, in particular its export-oriented industries. The Chinese Government's policy response to the crisis was also quite different from that of most of the other economic powers. Most of the bail-out plans in developed countries aimed at stabilizing the financial system and generating more jobs. But in China, the stimulus package is being spent largely on the real economy to promote exports and stimulate domestic demand. Although there are signs that the Chinese economy is back on a fast-growth track, it is still too early to conclude that China has achieved a level of sustainable recovery. The country still faces many difficulties.

First, given its high dependence on external markets and the high market concentration of its exports, the Chinese economy will not fully recover as long as the EU, Japan and the United States continue to be in recession or continue to have very low growth rates. China's five largest trading partners account for 70 per cent of its exports. It has been estimated that if the GDP growth rate in the United States declines by 1 per cent, the growth rate of China's exports will fall by 5–6 percentage points. Although it is not likely that the world economy will experience a double-dip recession, growth over the next few years is likely to be slow. The IMF's *World Economic Outlook* (updated in August 2009) forecasts that the economy of the euro zone will contract by 0.3 per cent in 2010, and that the Japanese and United States economies will grow at 1.7 per cent and 0.8 per cent respectively (figure 9). China's export will therefore continue to struggle in 2010 and 2011.

Secondly, the global financial and economic crisis has triggered renewed trade protectionism. China is now facing more trade disputes with its main trading partners than at any time in its history. Since 2008, 17 of the G-20 countries have adopted more than 100 trade-related measures to protect their domestic market. In 2009, there were over 100 trade protection measures against Chinese products – double the number in 2008 – amounting to more than US$ 12 billion worth of goods.[9] The EU initiated 7 anti-dumping investigations against Chinese textiles, metallic and electronic products, which accounted for 58 per cent of the EU's new anti-dumping investigations. The United States initiated 11 anti-dumping and 7 countervailing trade measures against Chinese products, more than in any year since China's accession to the WTO.[10] Some developing countries, particularly Brazil, India and Mexico, have also initiated trade protection measures against Chinese exports.

Thirdly, notwithstanding the Chinese Government's efforts to stimulate domestic consumption, there remain considerable challenges. For example, in 2008, China's domestic consumption contributed to about 50 per cent of

Figure 9

GDP GROWTH RATES OF THE EU, JAPAN AND THE UNITED STATES, 1st QUARTER 2007–4th QUARTER 2010[a]

(Per cent)

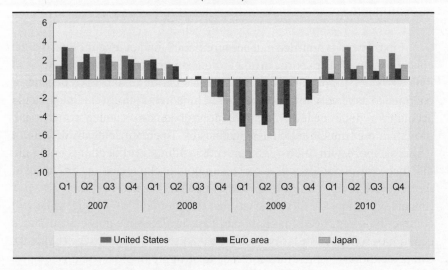

Source: IMF, *World Economic Outlook, 2009.*
  a GDP growth rates for 2009 and 2010 are projections

GDP, which translates to a market size of US$ 2.2 trillion. However, China's net exports, or trade surplus, amounted to US$ 297.1 billion, which accounts for about 6.8 per cent of China's GDP. In 2009, China's trade surplus declined to US$ 198 billion. To compensate for the fall in its net exports, China had to generate US$ 100 billion worth of extra domestic demand, which was no easy task. The widening income disparities, the lack of an efficient social security network, and soaring real estate prices are all obstacles to boosting private consumption in China.

Fourthly, many scholars are concerned about the medium- and long-term negative effects of China's expansionary policies. Chinese economic growth is based on a highly investment-driven economy. As a result of the large stimulus package, the investment rate increased from 43 per cent in 2007 to 50 per cent by the end of 2009. This poses a risk of overcapacity, overheating and low efficiency. Moreover, the overenthusiasm of local governments for local investment may worsen China's fiscal balance in the future in an unexpected and dramatic way (Yu, 2010).

What can China learn from the global crisis, and what are the policy implications for Chinese policymakers? First of all, China needs to rethink its economic development strategy and change its economic structure. The country has been pursuing an open-door policy since the late 1970s, which has helped it to become the world's biggest exporter of commodities and created millions of jobs. However, this has also made China highly dependent on external demand and vulnerable to external economic crises. China should gradually reduce its level of preference for export-oriented policies and provide more support to domestic industries. To create domestic demand, a comprehensive social security system, an affordable education system and affordable housing are needed. The stimulus package and tax revenues of RMB 5.42 trillion can play a bigger role in this regard.

China's heavy dependence on exports and its huge trade surplus have also drawn considerable international attention to its foreign exchange policy. We believe that a moderate appreciation of the renminbi would be helpful for China, not only for calming the trade disputes but also for economic transformation. Although this might reduce the country's trade surplus in the short term, it will definitely lead to benefits in the long term.

Secondly, China should change the commodity composition of its exports by reducing resource-intensive exports and encouraging exports of services and high-technology goods. It is not only because of the global financial and economic crisis that demand for China's resource-intensive goods declined sharply, but also because of the extreme price volatility of energy and raw materials. China's natural resource reserves cannot support its massive exports of capital-intensive products. Increased exports of steel, machinery and metal products have made China highly dependent on imports of energy and raw materials, not to mention the adverse environmental effects and their contribution to climate change. In response to the economic downturn, the Chinese Government increased export subsidies and tax rebates for labour- and resource-intensive commodity exports, but their effect has been limited.[11] Instead of spending billions of dollars on tax rebates, China could offer more subsidies or VAT refunds for exports of high-tech products and services.

Thirdly, China should rethink its policies towards FDI. After 30 years of development, with more than US$ 2 trillion in foreign reserves and more than RMB 25 trillion in bank deposits, China is no longer short of capital. Most of the FIEs are engaged in low-cost, export-oriented manufacturing and processing. Half of China's exports and 60–70 per cent of its trade surplus are generated by FIEs. FDI has helped create jobs and increase GDP, but it has also crowded out domestic investment, and has a lock-in effect on industrialization and technology development. China must therefore be more selective with regard to the FDI it attracts.

Fourthly, regarding the stimulus package, there are two areas that need to be improved. One is the fiscal expenditure system. Traditionally, China's fiscal spending is through government agencies that are characterized by low transparency, and this has resulted in many cases of corruption. To improve the efficiency of fiscal policy and reduce the risk of overcapacity and overheating, the Chinese Government should introduce more market mechanisms in government spending and allow private institutions to be involved in the financial market. Furthermore, China should and could improve the composition of its stimulus package: a larger share of that package should be directed to innovation and technology development, education and culture, and health care. It should also support creativity and entrepreneurship in the domestic private sector.

Fifthly, to avoid being the target of the new protectionism, China should import more to reduce its trade surplus, particularly high-tech products, environmental goods and services, educational facilities and services, energy and mining products. Chinese policymakers should abandon the new mercantilist view of "the more surplus, the better". Indeed, the huge trade surplus not only triggers intense trade conflicts but also puts strong pressure on China's monetary policy. Instead of buying United States Treasury bonds, the Chinese Government should use its sovereign funds to support science and education, technology and innovation, and environmental protection. In addition, China should enhance the development of its national reserves of energy and strategic resources, which would benefit Chinese manufacturing and help to stabilize prices in world energy and commodity markets.

Notes

1   There are scholars who question the extent of China's dependence on exports: Anderson (2007) has argued that the Chinese economy is not export-led, and Leong (2009) notes that China is less dependent on foreign demand than is commonly believed.

2   Neither Chinese banks nor the Chinese Government have disclosed official losses as a result of the subprime crisis; therefore all the data presented here are estimates.

3   Source: National Bureau of Statistics of China, Statistical Communiqué of the People's Republic of China on the 2009 National Economic and Social Development; available at: http://www.stats.gov.cn/english/newsandcomingevents/t20100226_402623115.htm.

4   Source: National Bureau of Statistics of China, at: ww.stats.gov.cn.

5   It should be pointed out that China does not include housing prices in its CPI statistics; if these were to be included, the inflation rate in China would be much higher.

6   Income elasticity of demand measures the responsiveness of the demand for a good to a change in income. It is calculated as the ratio of the percentage change in demand to the percentage change in income.

7   There are various opinions about the local governments' stimulus plans. Some believe the figure to be inflated; others argue that it could end up overheating the economy and creating overcapacity which had already occurred by early 2010. The Chinese Central Government has refused to announce the real amount of local stimulus spending. This sound a little strong. Could one tone it down and say: data on the actual amount of the local stimulus packages were not available from official sources?

8   Source: http://en.wikipedia.org/wiki/List_of_countries_by_public_debt. Figures for all these countries except India are estimates by the IMF (2008), while the figure for India is provided by the CIA World Factbook, 2009.

9   People's Daily online at: http://english.peopledaily.com.cn/90001/90778/90861/6849816.html.

10   Ministry of Commerce of China, Bureau of Fair Trade, at: http://gpj.mofcom.gov.cn/aarticle/subject/mymcyd/subjectff/201001/20100106739921.html.

11   This is because such a policy has only been able to help the companies which had orders for their products, and not the companies that had lost orders.

References

Anderson J (2007). Is China export-led? UBS Investment Research. Available at: http://www.allroadsleadtochina.com/reports/prc_270907.pdf.

CASS (2008). *China Social Blue Paper 2009*. Beijing, China Social Science Literature Press.

Dong He, Lillian Cheung, and Jian Chang (2007). Sense and nonsense on Asia's export dependency and the decoupling thesis. Working Paper 03/2007, Hong Kong Monetary Authority, Research Department, Hong Kong.

Duckett J and Hussain A (2008). Tackling unemployment in China: State capacity and governance issues. *The Pacific Review*, 21(2), May: 211–229.

Huang Yiping (2008). China not immune from the US financial crisis. *East Asia Forum,* 6 October. Available at: http://www.eastasiaforum.org/2008/10/06/china-not-immune-from-the-us-financial-crisis.

IMF (2009). World Economic Outlook: Crisis and Recovery. IMF publication, 2009 April, Washington D.C.

Landler M (2009). IMF puts bank losses from global financial crisis at $ 4.1 trillion. *The New York Times*, 21 April. Available at: http://www.nytimes.com/2009/04/22/business/global/22fund.html.

Lawrence D (2008). Chinese graduates recruited for rural work. *International Herald Tribune*, 16 December.

Leong H Liew (2009). Dealing with the inharmonious world: China and the global financial crisis. The Griffith-Lowy Institute Project on the Future of China. The Griffith University, Australia, February. Available at: http://www.griffith.edu.au/business/griffith-asia-institute/pdf/Liew,-Dealing-final-draft.pdf.

Li Li (2009). Unemployment blues. *Beijing Review*, 4 January. Available at: http://www.bjreview.com.cn/print/txt/2009-01/18/content_175396.htm (accessed, 4 March 2009).

Ministry of Commerce of China (2009a). *China Foreign Trade Situation and Outlook Report 2009* (Fall). Available at: http://zhs.mofcom.gov.cn/aarticle/cbw/200910/20091006592536.html.

Ministry of Commerce of China (2009b). Policy Explanation on "Home Appliance Subsidy Program in Rural Areas". Available at: http://jjs.mof.gov.cn/zhengwuxinxi/zhengcefagui/200812/t20081209_96760.html.

Ministry of Human Resource and Social Security (2007). *China Labor and Social Security Development Bulletin.*

Ministry of Human Resource and Social Security (2010). *China Labor and Social Security Development Bulletin.*

Pisani-Ferry J and Santos I (2009). Reshaping the global economy. *Finance and Development*, March: 8-12.

Roubini N (2008). The rising risk of a hard landing in China: The two engines of global growth – U.S. and China – are stalling. Available at: http://www.japanfocus.org/-Nouriel-Roubini/2940.

Schucher G (2009). China's employment crisis: A stimulus for policy change? *Journal of Current Chinese Affairs*, 38(2): 121–144.

Schüller M and Schüler-Zhou Y (2009). China's economic policy in the time of the global financial crisis: Which way out? *Journal of Current Chinese Affairs*, 3: 165–181.

Tan Yingzi and Xin Dingding (2009). 20 million migrants lost jobs: Survey. *China Daily*, 3 February. Available at: http://www.chinadaily.com.cn/china/2009-02/03/content_7440106.htm.

Yu Yongding (2010). China's policy responses to the global financial crisis. *Journal of Globalization and Development*, Vol. 1 : Iss. 1, Article 12. DOI: 10.2202/1948-1837.1044.

Zhan Lisheng (2009). Graduating this year? Bad luck. *China Daily*, 16 January. Available at: http://www.chinadaily.com.cn/china/2009-01/16/content_7403142.htm.

Zhou Tianyong (2008). Dui jingji xingshi kunju yu hongguan tiaokong chulu de sikao he jianyi (Considerations and suggestions regarding economic difficulties and for macro control). *ZhongguoJingji Shibao* (*China Economic Times*), 5 December.

SUSTAINING GROWTH IN A PERIOD OF GLOBAL DOWNTURN: THE CASE OF INDIA

Abhijit Sen Gupta

Abstract

Despite boasting a financial system that was largely insulated from toxic assets, India's growth prospects have been significantly hampered by the current global financial crisis due to its increased trade and financial linkages with the countries at the epicentre of the crisis. The impact has been exacerbated by the fact that India was already facing an autonomous downturn when the crisis reached its shores. Fortunately, a proactive policy stance, including a sufficiently large stimulus, helped to arrest the dip in the growth rate. This policy stance, aided by robust domestic demand, offset the decline in the growth rate to a certain extent, revealing signs of an incipient recovery in mid-2009. However, it has raised a number of policy challenges that will have to be addressed in the medium term.

Introduction

The ongoing global financial and economic crisis has significantly dented growth prospects in India, largely negating the decoupling theory that was propounded during the onset of the crisis in the developed world in 2007. According to the decoupling theory, cited by Akin and Kose (2007) and The Economist (2008), owing to the rapid expansion of intraregional trade over the past few decades, high savings ratios and a burgeoning stockpile of international reserves, business cycles in a number of emerging-market economies had become decoupled from those of the developed economies. However, this was clearly not the case: a number of emerging-market economies, including China and India, were strongly affected by the crisis, resulting in a sharp drop in their gross domestic product (GDP) growth rates and a rise in unemployment rates.

Like other countries, India was hit by the spillover effects of the crisis due to its increased integration into the global economy. The overall GDP growth rate almost halved, from a peak of 10.6 per cent in the third quarter of 2006 to 5.8 per cent in the fourth quarter of 2008. As pointed out by Subbarao (2009), the share of total external transactions, including gross trade flows and gross financial flows, in India's GDP more than doubled, from 47 per cent in 1997-98 to 117 per cent in 2007-08. Consequently, India was affected by the global crisis through both the trade and the financial channel. However, it would be incorrect to attribute the entire drop in annual growth rate, from a peak of 9.8 per cent in 2006-07 to 6.7 per cent in 2008-09, to the global crisis. India was already in the midst of a domestic downturn in September 2008 when the effects of the financial crisis began to take their toll. The situation on the eve of the crisis was worsened by the adverse effects of a severe terms-of-trade shock that resulted from a sharp rise in global food and oil prices. Although India's reliance on food commodities is relatively low, an overwhelming proportion of the country's petroleum and fertilizer needs is met by imports.

The overall adverse impact of the global financial crisis was mitigated by a series of proactive policy measures. While India's monetary policy largely aimed at enhancing domestic liquidity, which had shrunk considerably since the collapse of the United States investment bank, Lehman Brothers, its fiscal policy sought to boost aggregate demand. A number of policy measures were also initiated to attract foreign capital back into the country. All these measures were able to curb the decline in the growth rate to a certain extent, and there have been several signs of an incipient recovery since April 2009. However, they have also raised a number of policy challenges for the medium term.

The remainder of this paper is organized as follows. Section I describes some key macroeconomic developments in India prior to the advent of the crisis. Section II outlines the main channels through which the global crisis affected the Indian economy, and discusses the impact of the crisis on the economy. Section III highlights the various policy measures used to counter the global crisis and analyses their impact. Section IV presents some of the medium-term challenges facing the economy as a result of the crisis and the resultant policy measures, and section V concludes.

I. India's growth slowdown prior to the financial and economic crisis

Prior to the transmission of the global financial and economic crisis to India in September 2008, the country was in the midst of a period of sustained high growth. Between 2003-04 and 2006-07, the Indian economy grew at an impressive average annual rate of 8.8 per cent, compared to only 4.7 per cent during the period 2000-01 to 2002-03. This near doubling of the annual GDP growth rate was largely due to the impressive performance of certain sectors such as agriculture, manufacturing, construction, trade and communication, finance and real estate services. In addition, the rise in GDP growth during the period 2003-04 to 2007-08 was associated with a sharp surge in investment, especially private sector investment which recorded growth rates of over 20 per cent. Consequently, the share of investment in GDP jumped from 22.8 per cent in 2001-02 to 39.1 per cent in 2007-08, and the contribution of investment to overall GDP growth more than quadrupled, from 1 per cent in 2000-01 to 2002-03 to 4.4 per cent in the period 2003-04 to 2006-07 (figure 1). Also, private consumption nearly doubled during the high growth period, from 3.8 per cent to 7.4 per cent. Finally, as pointed out by Rakshit (2009), rising exports also contributed to the higher GDP growth rate. They increased by 18.5 per cent between 2003-04 and 2006-07 compared to 15.2 per cent between 2000-01 and 2002-03, thereby raising their contribution to overall GDP growth to 2.6 per cent from 1.9 per cent.

As a result of the sustained growth of over 8.5 per cent for over four years, the Indian economy started exhibiting some unmistakable signs of overheating from late 2006 onwards. According to a survey conducted by

Figure 1

DECOMPOSITION OF GDP GROWTH

(Per cent)

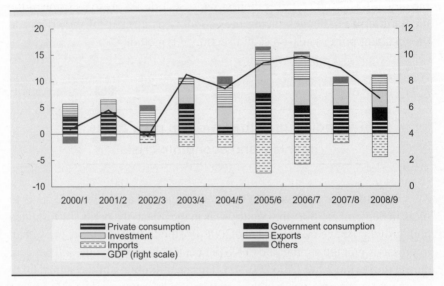

Source: Reserve Bank of India, *Handbook of Statistics on Indian Economy 2008/09.*

the National Council of Applied Economic Research (NCAER), 99 per cent of respondents reported operating at or close to full capacity in November 2006, compared with only 75 per cent in January 2002. Overall inflation had risen to over 6.5 per cent in April 2007, well over the comfort level of 5 per cent set by India's central bank, the Reserve Bank of India (RBI), and significantly higher than the April 2006 level of 3.8 per cent. Domestic credit growth surged to over 23 per cent in March 2007 from 15 per cent in March 2006. The trade deficit worsened from 2.1 per cent of GDP in 2002-03 to 6.8 per cent in 2006-07, while the current-account position switched from a surplus of 1.2 per cent of GDP to a deficit of 1.1 per cent of GDP during the same period. There was also a sharp rise in asset prices. According to the National Housing Bank's Residex, while housing prices in Delhi doubled between 2004 and 2007, in Mumbai and Kolkata they increased by more than 65 per cent. Equity markets were in the midst of a strong rally and the BSE Sensex doubled between June 2005 and February 2007.

The rapid rate of growth meant that various sectors began to encounter infrastructural bottlenecks, which constrained growth across various sectors. The aviation sector was plagued by a scarcity of skilled crew and inadequate airport facilities, for example, while the maritime sector suffered from a high average ship turnaround time and lack of rail and road connectivity of the ports. Industrial infrastructure was also becoming overstretched as a result of the rush for creation of special economic zones (SEZs) leading to escalating land prices. The dearth of coal, natural gas and power generating equipment resulted in power shortages, while a lack of trained and skilled human resources led to wage escalation, which adversely affected the information technology sector. The GDP growth was further dented by a decline in the growth rate of exports in 2007, partly as a result of the beginning of the economic downturn in the United States and a sharp appreciation of the Indian rupee (Rs). With the real effective exchange rate (REER) appreciating by 11 per cent between July 2006 and July 2007 and the rupee strengthening by 15 per cent against the United States dollar, there was an erosion of the net profit margins of low-import-intensity sectors such as textiles and leather. Exporters in these sectors lost their advantage in price-sensitive global markets.

Furthermore, in response to rising inflation and the increasing growth rate of money supply due to the incomplete sterilization of foreign capital inflows, the RBI adopted a relatively strict monetary stance. It raised the cash reserve ratio (CRR) by 250 basis points between November 2005 and November 2007. During this period the repo rate and the reverse repo rate were raised by 100 basis points and 175 basis points respectively, thereby increasing the cost of credit for the private sector. Consequently, as can be seen from figure 2, India's economy started experiencing a slowdown from early 2007, more than 18 months before the collapse of Lehman Brothers in September 2008.

India's vulnerability on the eve of the crisis was accentuated by a sharp increase in commodity prices globally from the second half of 2007, and a resulting worsening of its terms of trade. With the transmission of globally high prices to domestic markets, inflation, based on the Wholesale Price Index, surged to nearly 13 per cent in August 2008 from 3.1 per cent in October 2007. The current-account deficit was also expected to widen to around 4 per cent of GDP on account of high import bills. As the Government

Figure 2

QUARTERLY GROWTH RATES

(Year on year real growth rate, per cent)

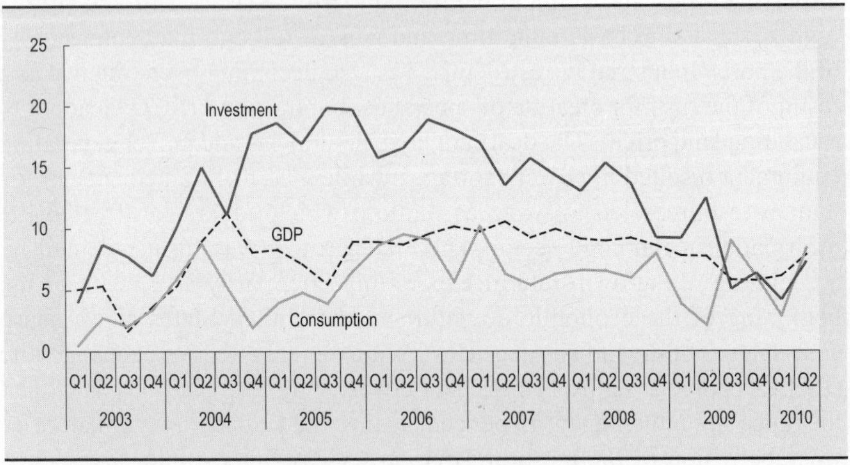

Source: Reserve Bank of India, *Handbook of Statistics on Indian Economy 2008/09.*

intervened to prevent the transmission of the increase in global prices of crude oil and fertilizer to the domestic retail markets through off- and on-budget subsidies, the fiscal deficit sharply worsened. In addition, as the sub-prime crisis deepened in the United States and spread to other developed countries, there was a "flight to safety" of capital from emerging- market economies. In India, there was a net outflow of investments by foreign institutional investors (FIIs) of $6.8 billion during January-August 2008, and a significant slowdown in external commercial borrowings (ECBs).

India's policymakers undertook a range of actions to moderate the impact of these shocks and achieve a soft landing with some degree of moderation in both GDP growth and inflation. The RBI further tightened monetary policy by raising key policy rates in an attempt to control inflationary pressures. Retail prices of petroleum products were increased by 15–20 per cent to ease the burden on the exchequer. Foreign capital outflow was accommodated by a drawdown of reserves and a managed depreciation of the Indian rupee. Finally, a number of trade measures, including a reduction in import duties, export taxes and export bans, were introduced to counter the impact of imported inflation. As a result of these policy measures, on the eve of the crisis most estimates still expected the Indian economy to grow by 7.5–8 per cent in 2008-09.[1]

II. Transmission and impact of the crisis

The current global financial crisis has affected India more significantly than the Asian financial crisis in 1997, despite the fact that the current crisis originated in the financial markets of geographically distant developed countries whereas the Asian crisis primarily affected countries in India's vicinity. The primary reason for the greater impact is India's increased integration with the rest of the world.

As is evident from figures 3 and 4, India's industrial and trade cycles have become increasingly correlated with those of the OECD countries over the past two decades. Moreover, while the share of trade in GDP increased from 23 per cent in 1996-97 to close to 50 per cent in 2007-08, over the same period the ratio of gross capital flows to GDP more than tripled, from 17 per cent to 56 per cent. Hence the global financial crisis was transmitted to India through both the current and capital accounts.

In recent years there has been an increase in the share of Asian emerging-market economies in Indian exports, but the largest share of India's merchandise, and especially services exports still go to developed countries. Even in 2007-08, the major OECD countries accounted for 37 per cent of Indian exports. As a result, the sharp economic slowdown in these countries has adversely affected Indian exports. Merchandise exports from October to March 2008-09 shrunk by 19 per cent compared to 2007-08 (figure 5).

Some of the major commodities which experienced a contraction in exports in the second half of 2008-09 included cotton yarn and fabric (22 per cent), iron ore (40 per cent), non-ferrous metals (52 per cent) and primary and semi-finished steel (17 per cent). The decline in exports was partly due

Figure 3

INTERNATIONAL TRADE CYCLE

(Year on year real growth rate and correlation)

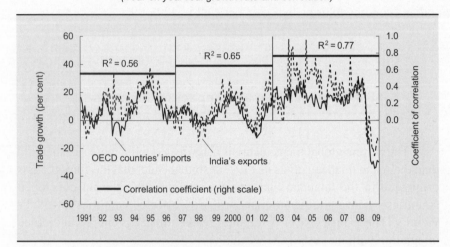

Source: World Bank, *Global Economic Monitor Database.*

Figure 4

INTERNATIONAL INDUSTRIAL CYCLE

(Year on year real growth rate and correlation)

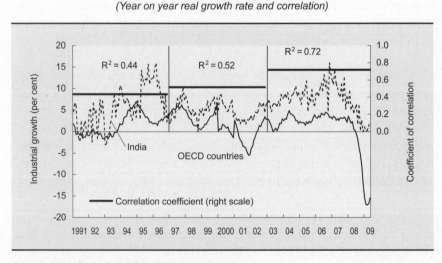

Source: World Bank, *Global Economic Monitor Database.*

Figure 5

MERCHANDISE TRADE AND EFFECTIVE EXCHANGE RATES

(Year on year real growth rate and indices)

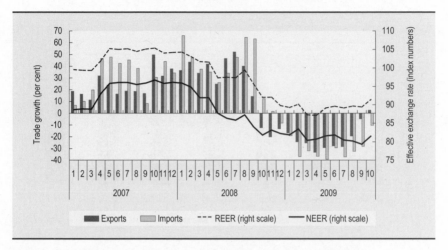

Source: Reserve Bank of India, *Handbook of Statistics on Indian Economy 2008/09.*

to a fall in commodity prices in the second half of 2008-09, but mainly to a slump in demand in developed countries. Moreover, even though India's services exports showed greater resilience, they too were adversely affected (Borchert and Mattoo, 2009). Exports of software services grew by less than 1 per cent in the second half of 2008-09 compared to the previous year, while business, financial and communication services witnessed declines of 13.8 per cent, 6.4 per cent and 28.2 per cent. Overall, exports of services declined by 0.53 per cent compared to the previous year.

Remittance inflows, which are an important source of foreign exchange earnings for India, grew strongly in 2008, despite the global crisis, to reach $51.6 billion in 2008, compared to $37.2 billion in 2007. However, according to the World Bank (2009), these flows are set to decline to $47 billion in 2009 due to expectations of a shallow and jobless recovery in developed countries, tighter immigration controls and unpredictable exchange rate movements that could affect the United States dollar value of remittances as well the motivation for the remittances.

Figure 6

REMITTANCE INFLOWS, 2003–2009

(Billions of dollars)

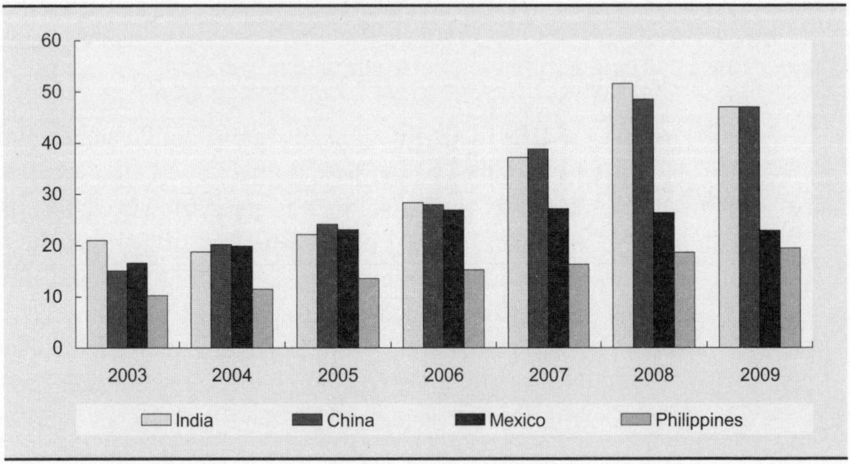

Source: World Bank, 2009.

Indian financial institutions were largely insulated from the shocks emanating from the sub-prime crisis in the United States due to their low exposure to toxic assets. However, in the immediate aftermath of the collapse of Lehman Brothers there were apprehensions regarding the exposure of some Indian banks. Given their strong capital-to-risk (-weighted) assets ratio (CRAR) the banks were able to absorb these losses. In the insurance sector, the American International Group (AIG) has two joint ventures in India with a minority holding of 26 per cent. Again, these corporations enjoyed adequate solvency margins. The non-bank financial companies (NBFCs) and mutual funds, however, came under some pressure. The mutual funds are largely dependent on corporations for their funding. With the increase in liquidity needs of the corporate sector, there was a rise in the redemption pressure on mutual funds, which, as an important source of funds for NBFCs, led to liquidity problems for some of the NBFCs.

The financial sector suffered also from the indirect effects of the global financial crisis. The initial impact was felt in the money market, which tightened sharply, resulting in call money rates increasing to 20 per cent in

October 2008. Uncertainty about the exposures of the various Indian banks to toxic United States assets contributed to the spiking of the call money rates. Patnaik and Shah (2010) suggest that since Indian multinationals that were using the global money market were short of dollars after the collapse of Lehman Brothers, they borrowed in India and took capital out of the country, thereby tightening the money market.

At this point the RBI reversed its tight monetary policy stance and started injecting liquidity into the economy through a variety of measures, which resulted in a moderation of the call money rates. However, despite these measures, which included lowering policy rates, relaxing provisioning norms and reducing risk weights on exposures, the credit growth rate declined from 30 per cent in October 2008 to less than 17 per cent in March 2009, and to 10 per cent in October 2009. Non-food bank credit declined by nearly 5 per cent in 2008-09 compared to the previous year, while non-bank resource flows to the commercial sector fell by more than 20 per cent. In particular, there has been a sharp decline in public issues by non-financial entities, and net issuance of commercial paper and net credit by housing finance companies.

Apart from the domestic liquidity crunch, the global financial crisis resulted in a sharp decline in foreign capital inflows. Net capital inflows fell from $108 billion in 2007-08 to $9.1 billion in 2008-09 as a result of increased risk averseness. Net FDI inflows remained robust despite the global crisis, and actually increased from $15.4 billion to $17.5 billion in 2008-09, but other components of the capital account witnessed a sharp decline. There was a reversal of portfolio investment flows from a net inflow of $29.6 billion in 2007-08 to a net outflow of $14 billion in 2008-09. A large part of this reversal was due to a drop in FII flows, which experienced a net outflow of $15 billion in 2008-09. Foreign capital raised through American Depository Receipts or Global Depository Receipts also shrank from $8.8 billion in 2007-08 to $1.2 billion in 2008-09. Finally, over the high growth period, the Indian corporate sector had been increasingly resorting to ECBs due to attractive rates of borrowing. Net ECB inflows into India stood at $16.1 billion in 2006-07, increasing to $22.6 billion in 2007-08. However, as conditions worsened in the developed world there was a scramble for global liquidity. and ECB inflows into India dropped to $8.2 billion. As a result, overall resource flows to the commercial sector from foreign sources declined by 49 per cent in rupee terms in 2008-09, despite the rupee depreciating by by 13 per cent in 2008-09 compared to the previous year.

The transmission of the global crisis through both the current and capital account channels had a deep impact on the Indian economy. At the broadest level, the overall GDP growth rate dropped from 7.8 per cent during April–September 2008 to 5.8 per cent during October–March 2008-09 (table 1). The manufacturing sector was the worst affected, shrinking by 0.3 per cent in the second half of 2008-09. A high base, a relatively tight monetary policy in the pre-crisis period, the rising cost of capital and adverse global developments contributed to the slowdown in the manufacturing sector. The Index of Industrial Production data shows that some of the worst affected sectors included cotton textiles, jute fibre, wood products, leather products, metal and metal products. Investment growth nearly halved, from 10.9 per cent to less than 5.7 per cent during October–March 2008-09, while private consumption growth declined from 3.3 per cent to 2.5 per cent. The slowdown in the investment growth rate led to lower purchases of capital goods. Both production and import of capital goods shrunk considerably in the second half of 2008-09.

The slowdown in the real estate sector and the liquidity crunch also adversely affected the construction industry. In the services sector, the growth rate in trade, hotels, transport and communications more than halved in the second half of 2008-09. On the other hand, the growth rate of community, personal and social services doubled, largely due to measures taken by the Government to stimulate aggregate demand, including pay revision for government employees, increased developmental expenditure and other fiscal stimulus measures. This was also evident from the 35.9 per cent increase in government consumption during the second half of 2008-09.

Given that parts of the manufacturing and services sectors that witnessed a slowdown in growth were highly labour-intensive, there has been an adverse impact on employment. While there is a long time lag in the provision of accurate data on employment, several surveys have nevertheless indicated that the ongoing crisis has significantly affected employment. A Ministry of Labour survey revealed that over 0.5 million jobs were lost between October and December 2008 as a result of the economic slowdown.

Table 1

SECTORAL DECOMPOSITION OF INDIA'S GDP GROWTH RATE

(Per cent)

	April–September 2008-09	October–March 2008-09	April–September 2009-10
Agriculture and allied activities	2.9	0.7	1.7
Mining and quarrying	4.2	3.2	8.7
Manufacturing	5.3	-0.3	6.3
Electricity, gas and water supply	3.3	3.5	6.8
Construction	9.0	5.5	6.8
Trade, hotels, transport and communication	12.5	6.1	8.3
Finance, insurance, real estate and business services	6.6	8.9	7.9
Community, social and personal services	8.6	17.1	9.9
Gross domestic product at factor cost	**7.8**	**5.8**	**7.0**

Source: Reserve Bank of India, *Handbook of Statistics on Indian Economy 2008/09,* .

Most of these job losses were in export-oriented sectors such as gems and jewellery, automobiles and textiles. Subsequent surveys by the Labour Ministry in January-March and April-June 2009 show a continuing declining trend in employment, with export-oriented industries accounting for the bulk of job losses. These surveys estimate that about 167,000 workers in export industries lost their jobs during the period April-June 2009.

A number of industry associations have also indicated job losses in their respective industries. In December 2008, the Federation of Indian Micro, Small and Medium Enterprises reported that nearly 4,000 ancillary units were on the brink of a shutdown, which would affect the livelihoods of 200,000 people. The Auto Components Manufacturers Association also reported job losses of around 70,000 between September and December 2008, mostly involving casual workers. With the economic slowdown hitting the engineering industry, about 50,000 workers are estimated to have been laid off in the South Indian town of Coimbatore alone. Similarly, about 200,000 workers are estimated to have lost their jobs in the diamond sector in the town of Surat.

III. Policy response to the crisis

Indian policymakers acted swiftly and decisively to contain the negative impacts of the crisis. As liquidity constraints led to tightness in the money market and the spiking of call money rates, the RBI introduced a series of measures aimed at injecting liquidity. Between August 2008 and January 2009, the cash reserve ratio was lowered from 9 per cent to 5 per cent. This move resulted in a rise in the money multiplier from 4.3 in March 2008 to 5.3 in April 2009, thereby ensuring an increase in broad money supply. Over the past few years the RBI had issued a large amount of Market Stabilization Scheme (MSS) bonds to sterilize the impact of foreign capital inflows.[2] In the post-crisis period, the RBI injected liquidity by unwinding these bonds. As a result, the RBI's balance sheet did not show an unusual increase, in contrast to the global trend. Other measures initiated by the RBI included a reduction in the statutory liquidity ratio (SLR), which aimed at enabling banks to expand their credit operations.

The RBI also sharply cut back various policy rates to encourage credit expansion. While the repo rate was lowered from 9 per cent to 4.75 per cent, the reverse repo rate was reduced from 6 per cent to 3.25 per cent. The RBI also resorted to conventional open market operations (OMOs) involving an outright purchase of government securities in the secondary market as well as provision of liquidity through repos under its daily liquidity adjustment facility. However, owing to a weak transmission mechanism and heightened risk averseness, the lowering of policy rates did not fully translate into a reduction in retail rates. As pointed out by Mohanty (2009), the weighted average benchmark prime lending rate of public sector banks fell by only two percentage points: from 14 per cent in March 2008 to 12.1 per cent in June 2009 while the average lending rates of the public sector banks declined by only 1.5 percentage points over this period.

Finally, a number of refinance windows were opened to allow easy access to credit for some of the troubled sectors such as real estate, small and medium-sized enterprises (SMEs) and exporters. There was also a reduction of prudential norms relating to provisioning and risk weights. Mohanty (2009) estimates that the actual/potential injection of liquidity as a result of these measures was Rs 5.6 trillion, or 10.5 per cent of GDP.

While most of the monetary policy measures were aimed at ensuring adequate liquidity, the fiscal measures endeavoured to boost aggregate demand. Fortunately in India a number of fiscal measures had been announced and implemented prior to the transmission of the crisis. These included a complete waiver of existing farm loans for small and marginal farmers, an increase in civil servants' salaries in conformity with the recommendations of the Sixth Pay Commission, and extending the National Rural Employment Guarantee Scheme to cover the entire country.[3]

In addition, to ensure against transmission of the sharp rise in international commodity prices in the first half of 2008 to domestic retail prices, the Government issued a large food and fertilizer subsidy. While the food subsidy bill increased from an originally estimated Rs 327 billion to Rs 436 billion (0.82 per cent of GDP), the fertilizer subsidy bill more than doubled, from Rs 310 billion to Rs 758 billion (1.43 per cent of GDP). In addition the Government issued a large number of oil bonds to mitigate the transmission of global crude oil prices.

With the transmission of the crisis, India, like many other countries, initiated a slew of fiscal measures to increase aggregate demand. Most of the measures took the form of tax relief to boost demand and increased expenditure on public projects to create employment and public assets. These measures were introduced in three tranches: in early December 2008, and early January and late February 2009. The measures included a general reduction of four percentage points in excise duties on non-petroleum products, reduction of the service tax by two percentage points, and approval for additional expenditure of Rs 200 billion in 2008-09. Furthermore, the Government relaxed the Debt Consolidation and Relief Facility (DCRF) guidelines for 2008-09, thereby allowing various States in the country to borrow an additional Rs 300 billion for undertaking capital expenditure. In addition, the DCRF requirement to eliminate the revenue deficit was also relaxed for 2008-09 and 2009-10.

The Government also introduced some measures that were aimed at selected industries that were adversely impacted by the crisis. For example, labour-intensive export industries such as handlooms, carpets and handicrafts, textiles, gems and jewellery, marine products and SMEs were provided with an interest subvention of 2 per cent up to 31 March 2009 subject to a minimum rate of interest of 7 per cent per annum for pre-shipment and post-shipment export credit. In addition, a fund of Rs 1.1 billion to ensure full refund of terminal excise duty/Central Sales Tax was set up, and various export incentive schemes of Rs 3.5 billion were also introduced. An additional Rs 1.4 billion was allocated to the textile sector to clear the entire backlog of the Technology Up-gradation Fund (TUF) Scheme. The India Infrastructure Finance Company Limited (IIFCL) was allowed to raise Rs 100 billion through the issuance of tax-free bonds to support its infrastructure schemes under a public private partnership mode.

India's policymakers also undertook a series of steps to offset the downward pressure on the Indian rupee stemming from a sudden stop in capital flows. The rupee was allowed to depreciate in a controlled manner, thereby ensuring against a speculative run on the currency that would have had disastrous consequences for the external debt and balance of payments. Part of the outflow of capital was met by drawing down reserves. Between September 2008 and March 2009, the RBI sold reserves worth $29 billion. In addition, to attract foreign capital, interest rates on non-resident Indian (NRI) deposits were progressively raised by 100 to 175 basis points. Furthermore, the cap on foreign investment in corporate bonds was raised from $3 billion to $15 billion, while norms for FIIs and ECBs were relaxed.

In response to the proactive policymaking, the Indian economy began to exhibit distinct signs of recovery from April 2009. As can be seen from table 1, the economy grew by 7 per cent in the first half of 2009, despite a poor monsoon that dampened agriculture growth. The manufacturing sector posted a strong recovery, growing at 6.3 per cent compared to a contraction of 0.3 per cent in the second half of 2008-09. The tax cuts and civil servants' salary hikes succeeded in increasing demand for consumer durables, which grew by 21.7 per cent between March and December 2009 compared to 1.8 per cent in the second half of 2008-09. Increased plan spending also accelerated the demand for capital and intermediate goods, which grew by 6.4 per cent and 11.6 per cent. Merchandise exports, after contracting for

13 months, experienced a positive upturn in November and December 2009. Imports also experienced growth in December 2009, for the first time since the onset of the crisis.

A number of expectation surveys confirmed a revival of consumer and business confidence. While NCAER's Business Confidence Index recorded a growth of 21.2 per cent in the second quarter of 2009-10 over the previous quarter, the Federation of Indian Chamber of Commerce and Industry's (FICCI) Overall Business Confidence Index rose by 7.7 per cent. Confederation of Indian Industries' Business Confidence Index for the second half of 2009-10 rose by 7.4 per cent compared with the first half of the year. The HSBC Markit Purchasing Managers' Index for manufacturing and services also indicated a sharp improvement. The 48th round of the RBI's Industrial Outlook Survey conducted during October-December 2009 also indicated a further improvement in sentiment of the manufacturing sector.

IV. Medium-term policy challenges

The proactive policy interventions succeeded in arresting the declining growth rate and the economy started exhibiting nascent signs of recovery from March 2009. However, the global financial crisis and the subsequent policy measures introduced to counter it have raised a number of serious policy challenges that will need to be addressed in the near future.

An important challenge is to make the nascent recovery broad-based and not limited to certain sectors only. So far, the recent industrial recovery has been skewed: industries such as machinery and equipment, chemicals, rubbers and plastics grew by more than 10 per cent during April to November 2009, while food, beverages and tobacco, and jute textiles witnessed a contraction (figure 7). The growth rate in the production of consumer durables soared from 7.7 per cent in 2008-09 to 18.9 per cent in 2009-10, while the growth rate in the production of consumer non-durables plummeted from 7.7 per cent to -0.5 per cent during the period – evidence of the skewed trend in industrial growth. Similarly, during the same period,

Figure 7

INDUSTRIAL PRODUCTION, BY SECTOR

(Year-on-year real growth rate, April–November 2009)

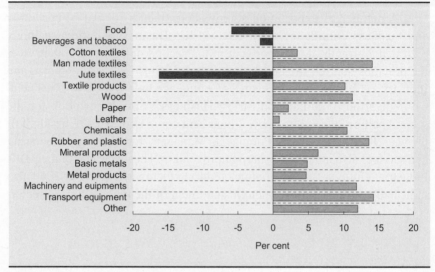

Source: Reserve Bank of India Bulletin, January 2010.

the growth of basic goods production rose from 3.9 per cent to 6.7 per cent, that of intermediate goods soared from 0.4 per cent to 9.5 per cent, but that of capital goods production declined from 10.7 per cent to 5.3 per cent, and consumer goods production fell from 7.6 per cent to 4.3 per cent.

Secondly, the pre- and post-crisis fiscal stimulus measures have significantly reduced the fiscal space, with the consolidated government deficit being close to 11 per cent of GDP in 2008-09 – more than double its 2007-08 level. Higher government expenditure and continued tax cuts have meant that the fiscal deficit is budgeted to be even higher in 2009-10, with the Central Government deficit estimated at 6.8 per cent, compared with 6.1 per cent in 2008-09. While increased government spending has strongly contributed to the overall growth rate in recent quarters (1.02 percentage points in the first quarter of 2009-10 and 2.65 percentage points in the second quarter of 2009-10), it is evident that such high levels of deficit cannot be sustained. In India, government borrowing is largely domestically financed, and a large borrowing programme crowds out private investment. Moreover, large borrowings result in pre-empting a major portion of revenues for servicing the debt. The interest payment on government debt in 2009-10 is estimated to constitute 36.6 per cent of the Central Government's revenues and 19 per cent of its expenditures. Thus it is evident that the accommodative stance needs to be rolled back. However, the timing and magnitude of the rollback is likely to be a thorny issue: it has to be done in a way that does not disrupt the country's nascent economic recovery.

Apart from the magnitude of the fiscal deficit, another challenge concerns the financing of that deficit. The second quarter review of the annual monetary policy estimates that net borrowings by the Central and State Governments during 2009-10 will amount to about Rs 5.4 trillion (9.2 per cent of GDP), of which the Central Government is set to borrow Rs 3.9 trillion. To achieve this goal, till October 2009 the Central Government had de-sequestered MSS securities worth Rs 280 billion and redeemed another Rs 420 billion.[4] It also resorted to the purchase of securities through OMOs totalling about Rs 575 billion, while net issuance of fresh securities amounted to Rs 2.84 trillion. Thus a large proportion of the borrowing was financed by monetizing the deficit, but this is likely to incite inflationary expectations.

Thirdly, easy liquidity conditions – indicated by the call money rate hovering at around the reverse repo rate – rising inflation and a narrowing output gap indicate the need for exiting an excessively accommodative monetary stance sooner rather than later. In the latest monetary policy statement in January 2010, the RBI raised the reserve ratio by 75 basis points, thereby sucking liquidity to the tune of Rs 380 billion from the banking system. Further interest rate hikes are expected in the current year. However, the timing of the hikes will be a critical issue for the RBI so as not to jeopardize the recovery process. In addition, for the reversal of monetary accommodation to achieve its goal the Government will need to return to a path of fiscal consolidation.

Fourthly, the return of foreign capital inflows will require India to find a way of managing these flows, which tend to be much higher than India's absorptive capacity. India, like many other emerging-market economies, has been grappling with various alternatives of the 'impossible trinity'.[5] Capital flows create a pressure on the currency to appreciate, which the RBI is keen to avoid as it leads to a loss of competitiveness of India's exports.

Consequently, it intervenes in the foreign exchange market to accumulate reserves. However, unsterilized intervention runs the risk of increasing the money supply and fuelling inflationary pressure. On the other hand, sterilized intervention carries an associated fiscal cost, as government bonds issued to keep the money supply in check tend to have a higher yield than the return earned on the foreign assets.

Finally, a deficient and irregular south-west monsoon has had a significantly adverse impact on agricultural production. The summer (*kharif*) production of foodgrains and oilseeds is estimated to have declined by 15.9 per cent compared to the previous year. The winter (rabi) crop, which depends crucially on the soil's moisture retention may also be adversely affected due to a poor monsoon. Although agriculture contributes only about 17 per cent to GDP, nearly 65 per cent of the population still depends on this sector for a living, implying strong demand-side impacts. This in turn will affect industry and services, albeit with a time lag. As the Government introduces a host of measures to mitigate the impact, such as an increase in calamity funding, an interest waiver and rescheduling of loans, the fiscal space will be further constrained. The decline in agricultural production will generate greater demand for work under the National Rural Employment Guarantee Scheme, which will further exacerbate the fiscal pressure.

V. Conclusion

The transmission of the global financial crisis to India has clearly demonstrated that the country has become integrated into the global business cycle. While undoubtedly this opening up has helped India achieve robust growth rates in recent years, it has also made the country prone to shocks originating in other parts of the world. Consequently, there is a need to create policy space in good times that can be utilized during periods of crisis. This would imply moving to a path of fiscal consolidation, regulating the availability of liquidity in the economy and ensuring the availability of foreign exchange liquidity through the accumulation of sufficient reserves.

Notes

1   While the Prime Minister's Economic Advisory Council estimated a growth rate of 7.7 per cent in mid-2008, RBI, in its August 2008 Bulletin, estimated a growth rate of 8 per cent.

2   MSS bonds are short-term government securities introduced in April 2004 to sterilize the expansionary effects of surges in capital inflows. The amount sterilized through MSS bonds remained immobilized in the Central Government's account with the RBI. As at end-September 2008, the MSS amount was more than 1.7 trillion rupees.

3   Under this scheme, an adult member of any rural household willing to do public works-related unskilled manual work at the statutory minimum wage of Rs 100 per day is guaranteed 100 days of employment in every financial year.

4   Typically, the MSS borrowings are held in a separate account than normal government borrowings. However, the government signed a Memorandum of Understanding with the RBI in 2008-09 to transfer some of the MSS amount to normal cash account of the government, which is called desequestering of MSS bonds. By doing so, the government does not need to go for additional borrowing.

5   The theorem of impossible trinity argues that a country can simultaneously only achieve two of the following three objectives: stable exchange rate, independent monetary policy and an open capital account.

References

Akin C and Kose MA (2007). Changing nature of north-south linkages: stylized facts and explanations. *IMF Working Paper No. 07/280*. Washington, DC, International Monetary Fund.

Borchert I and Mattoo A (2009). The crisis resilience of services trade. *Policy Research Working Paper Series No. 4917*. Washington, DC, World Bank.

The Economist (2008). The decoupling debate, 6 March.

Mohanty D (2009). Global financial crisis and monetary policy response in India. Speech delivered at the 3rd ICRIER-InWEnt Annual Conference in New Delhi, 12 November. Available at: http://rbidocs.rbi.org.in/rdocs/Speeches/PDFs/FCMP12112009.pdf (accessed 31 January 2010).

Patnaik I and Shah A (forthcoming). Why India choked when Lehman Broke. In: Bery S, Bosworth B and Panagariya A, eds., *India Policy Forum 2009-10*. New Delhi, Sage Publications.

Rakshit M (2009). India amidst the global crisis. *Economic and Political Weekly*, 44 (13): 94–106.

Subbarao D (2009). Impact of the global financial crisis on India: Collateral damage and response. Speech delivered at the Symposium on The Global Economic Crisis and Challenges for the Asian Economy in a Changing World. Organized by the Institute for International Monetary Affairs, Tokyo, 18 February.

World Bank (2009). Migration and development. Brief No. 11, prepared by Dilip Ratha, Sanket Mohapatra and Ani Silawal, Washington, DC.

BRAZIL AND INDIA IN THE GLOBAL ECONOMIC CRISIS: IMMEDIATE IMPACTS AND ECONOMIC POLICY RESPONSES

*André Nassif**

Rather than an economic tsunami like in the U.S., the financial crisis in Brazil will be a little wave.
Brazil´s President Luiz Inácio Lula da Silva. O Globo, 4 October 2008.

A crisis of this magnitude was bound to affect our economy and it has.
India´s Prime Minister Manmohan Singh. Thaindian News, 3 November 2008.

Abstract

In an economic environment in which depression, or the risk of depression, is global, the timeliness and intensity of economic policy responses matter. In September 2008, when Brazil and India faced the first adverse impacts of the global crisis through the financial channels, it might have been expected that both countries would be negatively affected in very similar ways. However, while the Brazilian economy fell into recession and registered a real GDP contraction of -0.2 per cent in 2009, India's real GDP grew by over 6 per cent (with an estimated growth rate of 6.9 per cent for its fiscal year from April 2009 to March 2010). This remarkable performance meant that India was the second least adversely affected country by the global crisis, after China. This chapter shows that the monetary and fiscal policy response to the global crisis by Indian policymakers was both quicker and more far-reaching than that of Brazil, which not only helped save the Indian economy from recession, but also set it on a path of rapid growth.

* This chapter is a revised version of a paper originally presented at the International Conference on The World Economy in Crisis: The Return of Keynesianism? The Conference was organized by the Hans Böckler Stiftung, Berlin, Germany, on 30–31 October 2009. This work benefited from interviews carried out in government, academic and corporate institutions in New Delhi and Mumbai from 12 to 22 January 2009. This technical mission was supported by BNDES with competent assistance from the Brazilian diplomatic service in India. The opinions are the author's responsibility and do not reflect those of the Brazilian Government or BNDES. The author wishes to thank Luiz Carlos Bresser-Pereira, Carmem Feijó, José Luis Oreiro and Jan Priewe for their careful reading and suggestions. The errors are, as usual, the author's exclusive responsibility.

Introduction

In September 2008, the damaging effects of the simultaneous reduction in credit, trade and global gross domestic product (GDP) turned the financial crash into the most serious downturn since the Great Depression of the 1930s. Both Keynes (1936; 1937) and Minsky (1986) were aware that depression can only be avoided if policymakers take immediate measures to provide liquidity to revive the credit channels (monetary policy) and boost growth in income and private spending (fiscal policy). Indeed, Minsky had identified several episodes of severe economic recession in the United States, which had all the traits of becoming a major global depression. He found that depression was only avoided because of the immediate actions and coordinated efforts of the United States Federal Reserve and because the United States Treasury managed to stabilize the negative impacts of economic agents' broken expectations and restore adequate levels of effective demand to the economy.[1]

This chapter compares the impacts of the global economic crisis on the Brazilian and Indian economies, as well as the economic policies that those countries immediately implemented to restore the regular credit channels and reduce the negative effects of the crisis on economic growth. There are several reasons to compare Brazil with India, a major one being that, although the initial financial impacts occurred through similar transmission channels in both countries, their different economic policy responses produced distinct effects on their real economies.

By September/October 2008, most economists were already identifying, or at least identifying the beginning of the financial crash as a likely depression rather than an ordinary economic fluctuation. In this context, our hypothesis is that for preventing recession in a country the speed and intensity of monetary and fiscal policy responses matter. The following sections attempt to support this hypothesis by showing that the quicker and more aggressive monetary and fiscal countercyclical response to the global crisis by policymakers in India than in Brazil explains why the Indian economy was able to avoid a recession in 2009.

Figure 1

BRAZIL AND INDIA: REAL GDP GROWTH RATES, 2005–2009

(Per cent)

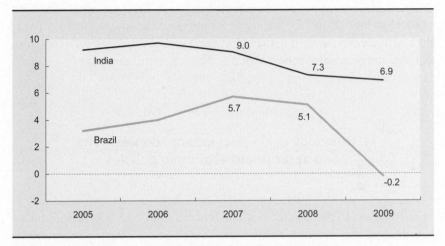

Source: Instituto Brasileiro de Geografia e Estatística; and Reserve Bank of India.
Note: The data for India refer fiscal year to the respective (April–March). The data for India in 2008 and
2009 refer to the real GDP at factor prices. Real GDP growth for India in 2009 is an estimate.

In India, notwithstanding high real GDP growth rates prior to the eruption of the 2008 global crisis (figure 1), the economy had been decelerating since 2006 due to the priority given by India's central bank, the Reserve Bank of India (RBI), to reducing inflation. However, since September 2008, the RBI has radically shifted its priority in order to safeguard India's economic growth. Thus, because of swifter and more intense monetary and fiscal policy responses than Brazil between September 2008 and January 2009, Indian policymakers were not only more successful at saving the economy from recession, but also at setting it on a path of rapid recovery and growth. Unlike Brazil, which fell into recession in 2009, India was the second least adversely affected country by the global crisis, after China.

To address these issues, this chapter is divided into the following sections. Section I discusses some theoretical concepts of short-term business cycle fluctuations and their different implications for the appropriate instruments of macroeconomic policy for dealing with either recession or the threat of depression. Section II examines the macroeconomic situation in Brazil and India before the September 2008 financial crash. Section III compares the economic policy responses of both countries and the immediate impacts on them from the global crisis. Section IV briefly analyses the main challenges faced by policymakers from both countries to sustain growth over the coming years, assuming that the current global economic recovery does not lose momentum. Section V draws the main conclusions.

I. Business cycle fluctuations, depressions and appropriate economic policies

Business cycle fluctuations are generally defined as a period during which capitalist economies alternate, with some rhythm and regularity, between a period of expansion, on the one hand, and a relatively strong deceleration or even a recession, on the other. This well-known concept of business cycle fluctuations is consistent with Keynes' original notion (1936: 314) stated thus: "We do not, however, merely mean by a cyclical movement that upward and downward tendencies, once started, do not persist forever in the same direction but are ultimately reversed. We also mean that there is some recognizable degree of regularity in the time-sequence and duration of the upward and downward movements." In this sense, consistent with Keynes' ideas, it could be said that most short-term business cycle fluctuations are caused by a reversal of expectations, monetary policy reaction against inflationary pressures, inadequate economic policy or other occasional factors which might provoke a drop in effective demand in such a way that the economy either decelerates or enters into a temporary recession.

Another concept of business cycle fluctuations, also stressed by Keynes but not often presented in mainstream macroeconomic theories, is related to situations in which capitalist economies are suddenly and violently assaulted by a general deterioration of expectations. In Keynes' words: "There is, however, another characteristic of what we call the trade cycle which our explanation must cover if it is to be adequate; namely, the phenomenon of the *crisis*, the fact that the substitution of a downward for an upward tendency often takes place suddenly and violently, whereas there is, as a rule, no such sharp turning-point when an upward is substituted for a downward tendency" (Keynes, 1936: 314).

This latter kind of business cycle fluctuation is not characterized by rhythm and regularity. However, rather than analysing whether or not this abrupt rupture of the business cycle is characterized by any regularity, it is necessary to understand that the nature of the capitalist system evolves in a non-deterministic, uncertain way. In this sense, uncertainty about the future is one of the main features in a monetary economy, and as such it is permanently present in varying degrees. Minsky (1982: 62) reminds us that "in Keynes's theory, 'time' is calendar time and the future is always uncertain." In such a theoretical context, an abrupt rupture of the business cycle is a possibility, and subsequent recovery is not necessarily guaranteed by market forces alone.

As soon as an expansive period within a business cycle is suddenly and violently broken by changing views about the future, investment, aggregate demand and employment are also dramatically and negatively affected (Keynes, 1937). Once this process has started, the role of macroeconomic policies in dealing with the fluctuations of business cycles becomes an important issue. This makes it necessary for policymakers to identify what kind of rupture has occurred in the business cycle. A fluctuation caused by either a normal reversal of expectations or by occasional factors that tend to appear throughout an expansive cycle can be handled by means of "fine adjustments" such as conventional instruments of monetary policy. Indeed, even if effective demand decreases in such a way that the economy either decelerates or enters into a temporary recession, monetary policy, such as a lowering of the basic interest rate or a credit stimulus, may constitute an efficient countercyclical policy.[2] If so, an expansive fiscal policy could be discarded.

However, if the kind of rupture is what Keynes (1936) called "the phenomenon of *crisis*" (i.e. a sudden and violent rupture that provokes a general lowering of expectations), macroeconomic policy requires a much more complex set of mechanisms. In fact, this rupture is usually preceded by a boom cycle during which economic agents generally take speculative positions (Minskyan "Ponzi" finance) that are so wide-ranging that the financial system ends up facing a liquidity crisis and a credit crunch. Consequently, the first-round effects on the real side of the economy are characterized by a dramatic downturn of investment and consumption.[3] As the Keynesian-Minskyan concept of crisis is characterized by a high level of uncertainty about the future and a strong liquidity preference, the mechanisms of monetary stimulus are hardly enough either to restore confidence or to boost investment and household consumption. Indeed, when the economy falls into a liquidity trap, monetary policy must be complemented by fiscal stimulus measures.

In such an environment, the speed and intensity of economic policy responses matter. Furthermore, if a depression (or the risk of a depression) is global, countercyclical policies must be applied quickly and intensively both in countries considered as being at the epicentre of the crisis (generally the developed countries) and elsewhere, regardless of whether or not they have entered into recession. With regard to the global economic crisis that erupted in September 2008, all developing countries which were showing significant year-on-year real GDP growth in the third quarter of 2008 should have been diagnosed as if they had fallen into depression, and should therefore have initiated the appropriate economic policy response. This was the case in both Brazil and India, among others, which in the immediate aftermath of September 2008 were in a situation aptly described by Krugman (2009: 181) when referring to the global crisis of 2008: "but while depression itself has not returned, depression economics – the kinds of problems that characterized much of the world economy in the 1930s but have not since – has staged a stunning comeback."

Monetary and fiscal responses by the economic authorities of countries entering into a depression must be immediate. In addition, fiscal policy must give priority to public investment and tax exemptions (in that order of priority) of such magnitude that they can at least partially offset the sharp fall in private spending generally observed in these kinds of cyclical contractions. This recommendation was supported by Keynes (1942) who, in his response to James Meade's comment, surprisingly, expressed his opposition to the use of fiscal policy as a (very) short-term countercyclical instrument, but defended it as the most effective measure for fighting the trends of chronic recession or depression: "Organized public works, at home and abroad, may be the right cure for a chronic tendency to a deficiency of effective demand. But they are not capable of sufficiently rapid organization (and above all cannot be reversed or undone at a later date) to be the most serviceable instrument for the prevention of the trade cycle" (Keynes, 1942: 22).

Krugman (2009: 188) also recognizes this problem, but adds that "as long as public spending is pushed along with reasonable speed, it should arrive in plenty of time to help a weak economy from plunging into an actual depression." He also mentions two advantages of public spending over fiscal cutbacks: the first is that "money would actually be spent", and the second is that "something of value (e.g. bridges that don't fall down) would be created."

Another advantage of increasing the fiscal deficit through public investment in order to overcome the risk of recession is that the large spending on infrastructure, for example, generates backward and forward linkages among other sectors, which has multiplier effects on income and employment. Our hypothesis, therefore, is that some developing countries which in the third quarter of 2008 were characterized by a large internal market, sound macroeconomic indicators (mainly fiscal and external accounts) and real GDP growth that was driven by private domestic demand (investment and consumption) were able to avoid the recession relatively well. This was because their policymakers reacted to the global crisis, both in a timely manner and with intensity, as if their countries were in (or facing a high risk of) depression. This was the situation in both Brazil and India in September 2008. Without minimizing the importance of monetary and credit stimuli, and considering the impact of the economic crisis on expectations of private agents that increased their preference for liquidity, the main instrument to prevent both countries from a recession was the use of fiscal policy. Such a policy should give preference to augmenting public investment rather than cutting fiscal taxes. Needless to say, active and timely fiscal action tends to yield fiscal imbalances and increases the gross public debt. However, two reasons support the argument that fiscal deterioration is transitory and can be remedied once a crisis is over: first, deficits that governments run during an economic downturn can be reversed as soon as the economy recovers; and second, even if the gross public debt grows significantly during a crisis, governments should pursue immediate fiscal adjustment when the economy shows clear signs of a recovery to sustained growth.

II. The macroeconomic environment in Brazil and India before the global crisis of 2008

In 2007, when few economists in the world believed that the subprime crisis in the United States could become a global economic crisis, macroeconomic indicators in Brazil and India could be considered as being reasonable to very good.[4] Both economies were characterized by low and very similar indicators of external financial fragility (table 1), and the total stock and servicing (cost of amortization and interest) of the external debt were low by emerging country standards. The available stock of international reserves covered around 15 months of imports in both countries. Although the short-term external debt had grown significantly in Brazil and India in 2007, it did not indicate any risk of insolvency, given the low annual costs for servicing the external debt (3.9 per cent of GDP in Brazil, and 5.4 per cent in India). On the other hand, Brazil, unlike India, had low domestic savings and investment (private and public).

With respect to fiscal indicators, both countries were undergoing strong fiscal adjustment until mid-2008. In fact, in 2007 the nominal fiscal deficit (including interest payments) fell to 2.3 per cent of GDP in Brazil and to 2.7 per cent in India, after having reached 3.2 per cent and 6.7 per cent, respectively, in 2005. In 2007, India's gross public debt was much higher than that of Brazil. However, the longer maturity of Indian treasury bonds gave Indian policymakers not only more room to sustain much lower nominal interest rates than those in Brazil, but also more freedom to avoid the high primary fiscal surplus, much as Brazil had been obliged to do throughout the last decade.[5]

In addition, India's much higher real GDP growth rate was a major factor that distinguished its recent economic performance from that of Brazil. Between 2000 and 2007 India managed to maintain very high economic growth rates (figure 2), entering a phase of accelerated growth between 2005 and 2007 with an average annual real GDP growth rate exceeding 9 per cent. In contrast, Brazil's relatively lower average annual real GDP growth

Table 1

BRAZIL AND INDIA: BASIC MACROECONOMIC INDICATORS, 2005–2007

(Per cent of GDP, unless otherwise indicated)

Macroeconomic indicators	Brazil			India[a]		
	2005	2006	2007	2005	2006	2007
Total gross savings	17.3	17.6	18.1	34.3	34.8	n.a.
Total gross investment	15.9	16.4	17.5	28.7	30.3	31.8
Central government investment	0.8	0.7	0.9	2.4	2.4	3.1
Gross foreign debt	19.2	15.8	14.5	17.2	18.0	19.1
Primary fiscal balance	3.9	3.2	3.5	-1.0	0.0	0.9
Nominal fiscal balance[b]	-3.2	-3.5	-2.3	-6.7	-5.6	-2.7
Gross public debt	67.4	65.2	63.6	84.0	80.8	78.3
Short-term external debt/ total external debt (per cent)	11.1	11.8	20.1	14.1	15.6	20.9
External debt service	7.5	5.2	3.9	10.1	4.8	5.4
International reserves (in import months)	8.8	11.3	17.9	11.6	12.5	15.0

Source: IPEA data; Central Bank of Brazil; and Reserve Bank of India.
  Note: n.a.: not available.
    a Data for India refer to the fiscal year (April-March).
    b Including interest payments.

rate reflected the country's difficulty in breaking away from its long-lasting semi-stagnant growth since the early 1980s.[6]

In India inflation was initially lower than in Brazil, but since 2003 it has been continuously increasing, while Brazil succeeded in rapidly reducing its consumer price index (IPCA) from its peak of 12.5 per cent in 2002 (figure 3). By the second half of 2008, the consumer price index in India had reached worrying levels in a country where inflation has historically remained low.

To reduce inflation, between January 2005 and September 2008, the RBI steadily increased the annual basic interest rate (repo rate)[7] from 6 per cent to 9 per cent. However, in real terms, the basic interest rate in India did not exceed 2.5 per cent per annum and, shortly before the worsening of the crisis in September 2008, it was at a negative level (table 2). In Brazil,

Figure 2

BRAZIL AND INDIA: REAL GDP GROWTH RATES, 2000–2008

(Per cent)

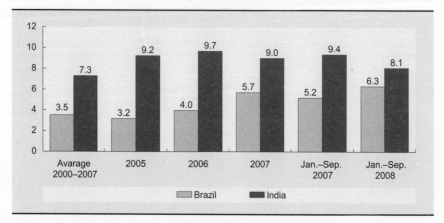

Source: Central Bank of Brazil; Instituto Brasileiro de Geografia e Estatística; and Reserve Bank of India.
Note: Data for the period 2000–2007 refer to real GDP at market prices; data for the periods January–September 2007 and January–September 2008 refer to real GDP at factor costs. Data for India for the period 2000–2007 are for the fiscal year (April-March).

Figure 3

BRAZIL AND INDIA: CONSUMER PRICE INFLATION, 2000–2009

(Per cent)

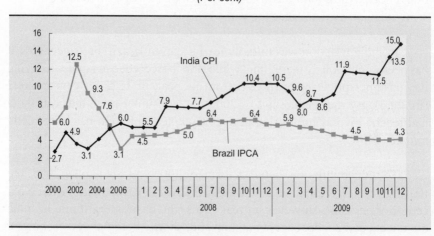

Source: Central Bank of Brazil; and Reserve Bank of India.

Table 2

BRAZIL AND INDIA: CENTRAL BANK INTEREST RATES, 2005–2010

(Per cent)

Period	Brazil		India	
	SELIC rate[a]	Real SELIC rate[b]	Repo rate	Real repo rate[b]
January 2005	18.25	8.35	6.00	0.51
April 2005	19.50	8.23	6.00	0.29
July 2005	19.75	10.69	6.00	1.52
October 2005	19.00	11.79	6.25	1.74
January 2006	17.25	12.68	6.50	1.64
April 2006	15.75	13.25	6.50	1.49
July 2006	14.75	12.90	6.75	0.00
October 2006	13.75	12.37	7.00	-0.35
January 2007	13.00	11.36	7.25	0.03
February 2007	13.00	11.02	7.50	-0.68
April 2007	12.50	10.49	7.75	0.35
July 2007	11.50	8.91	7.75	0.85
October 2007	11.25	7.79	7.75	1.96
January 2008	11.25	6.83	7.75	2.10
February 2008	11.25	6.71	7.75	2.16
March 2008	11.25	6.37	7.75	-0.11
April 2008	11.75	6.01	7.75	-0.06
May 2008	11.75	5.31	7.75	0.00
June 2008	12.25	4.88	8.00	0.11
July 2008	13.00	4.68	8.50	-0.39
August 2008	13.00	4.91	9.00	-0.92
September 2008	13.75	5.13	9.00	-1.50
October 2008	13.75	5.24	8.00	-2.09
November 2008	13.75	5.44	7.50	-2.10
December 2008	13.75	6.22	6.50	-1.53
January 2009	12.75	6.40	5.50	-2.37
February 2009	12.75	6.40	5.50	-1.82
March 2009	11.25	6.80	5.00	-0.55
April 2009	11.25	6.80	4.75	-1.80
May 2009	10.25	5.40	4.75	-1.59
June 2009	9.25	4.80	4.75	-2.47
July 2009	8.75	4.00	4.75	-5.05
January 2010	8.75	n.a.	4.75	n.a.
March 2010	8.75	n.a.	5.00	n.a.

Source: Central Bank of Brazil; and Reserve Bank of India.
Note: n.a: not available.
  a SELIC is the overnight lending rate of the Central Bank of Brazil.
  b Real rates are based on the monthly inflation throughout the period.

real interest rates only started to decline more consistently after July 2006 (when the nominal Special Settlement and Custody System (SELIC) was at 14.75 per cent) to reach 4.7 per cent in July 2008.[8] By August 2008, following successive SELIC increases, and once inflationary pressure had been relieved, real interest rates in Brazil began increasing once more, reaching approximately 6.2 per cent per annum in December 2008 – a level still considered high both by international standards and in the context of global deflationary trends.

Monetary policy in both countries has been marked by at least two different aspects. Firstly, unlike Brazil, India has no explicit inflation target policy.[9] Besides use of the two basic interest rates (repo rate and reverse repo rate),[10] the RBI operates monetary policy by combining a compulsory reserve requirement (or the cash reserve ratio (CRR)) with the statutory liquidity ratio (SLR), a mandatory percentage of government securities that banks must hold in their portfolios. Between July 2006 and August 2008, the CRR increased almost continuously, from 5 per cent to 9 per cent. Secondly, in an attempt to restore price stability without compromising economic growth, Indian policymakers have adopted an anti-inflation strategy since the early 1990s that is much more gradualist than Brazil's (Nassif, 2007).[11] In comparison, although Brazil's Central Bank had kept the compulsory reserve ratio on cash deposits practically unchanged before September 2008, the CR in early July 2008 was approximately 45 per cent, against only 8.75 per cent in India.[12]

III. Impacts of the global crisis on Brazil and India and their economic policy responses

A. Lessons from economic policy responses in Brazil and India: Timeliness and intensity matter

The bankruptcy of the United States investment bank, Lehman Brothers, on 15 September 2008 was a milestone in the 2008 financial crisis. Initially the crisis was limited to the financial markets of the United States, subsequently reaching European countries and Japan, but thereafter quickly spreading to financial markets worldwide. Brazil and India, much like most other developing countries, suffered the immediate impacts of the global economic crisis. Since September and more intensely in October 2008, both countries have suffered from a sudden stopping of foreign capital (especially short-term capital and foreign capital for trade finance), nominal exchange rate depreciation and a strong credit squeeze.

By comparing the behaviour of the nominal exchange rate depreciation between September 2008 and December 2008, it can be concluded that India was more successful than Brazil in stabilizing its foreign exchange market. The Brazilian real depreciated to a much greater extent than the Indian rupee (figure 4). In December 2008, the Brazilian real reported a nominal depreciation of 42.9 per cent compared with the August 2008 level, against a depreciation of 10.9 per cent for the Indian rupee.

There are two reasons why negative expectations were stabilized quicker in India than in Brazil: (i) India is currently open to foreign capital inflows for direct investment and the stock market, but it still imposes high restrictions on foreign investment in treasury bonds and fixed income assets; and (ii) although derivative transactions in India before the 2008 crisis were allowed, since April 2007 all derivative contracts (especially exchange rate and interest rate derivatives) have been tightly regulated by the RBI. The RBI defines and manages the permissible derivative instruments, risk management and eligibility criteria in order "to safeguard the interests of the

Figure 4

**NOMINAL DEPRECIATION OF THE BRAZILIAN REAL AND INDIAN RUPEE
VIS-À-VIS THE DOLLAR, AUGUST 2008–DECEMBER 2008**

(Per cent)

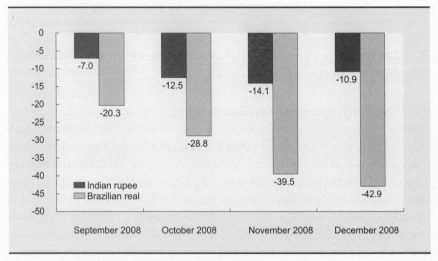

Source: Central Bank of Brazil; and Reserve Bank of India.
 Note: (-) Depreciation of the Brazilian real or the Indian rupee.

system as well as the players in the market" (RBI, 2010a: 9–10). With a lower degree of external financial liberalization than Brazil, Indian policymakers could avoid the effects of the sudden stopping of financial flows in the interbank lending market, notwithstanding the fact that initially overall credit was strongly affected. In contrast, in Brazil the existence of a large foreign exchange market, as well as equity and credit derivative markets connected to domestic and global markets, was not only responsible for deeply worsening the financial health of banks and companies, but also caused a sudden and lengthened halt to both interbank lending and final credit.

As the Commission on Growth and Development (2010)[13] recently recognized, to minimize the negative effects from the financial and confidence crisis on the real sector, both monetary and fiscal policy responses should be quick: "Time matters. Countries need to relieve credit constraints quickly, otherwise viable businesses will fail (...). Fiscal expansion is meant to limit the drop in aggregate demand and employment, partly by restoring confidence, so that the collective fears of consumers do not become a self-fulfilling prophecy. Here again the speed of the response matters" (Commission on Growth and Development, 2010: 30).

Throughout the last quarter of 2008, strong adverse effects of the global crisis on economic activity were already widely acknowledged in both countries. In the first round of measures taken between September 2008 and January 2009, both Brazil and India introduced monetary and fiscal stimuli. The main differences refer to the speed and intensity with which both instruments were implemented. In this respect, the reaction of the Indian authorities was much more aggressive than that of Brazil's authorities.

As in India, the Brazilian economic team was quick to provide liquidity to the financial system to offset the tight private credit squeeze by granting additional resources so that government-owned export-import banks (EX-IM banks) and State development banks would be able to finance trade, companies and households. Yet in September 2008, while the Brazilian Development Bank (BNDES) – traditionally oriented to financing investment in industry and infrastructure – was allowed to provide credit lines to finance working capital, the Banco do Brasil and Caixa Economica Federal acted as "quasi lenders of last resort" by purchasing portfolios from small and medium-sized private banks that were facing serious liquidity problems. Another important decision was taken in January 2009, when the Brazilian Treasury announced an additional credit facility of R$ 100 billion (3.3 per cent of GDP) to BNDES, which aimed at augmenting its credit for working capital and for small and medium-sized enterprises as well as for boosting private investment in sectors with high income multiplier effects, especially infrastructure. However, it took some time until BNDES actually created the special Programme for Sustaining Investment (PSI), in July 2009. This additional fund helped to restore investment demand in Brazil, but only from mid-2009 onwards.

In India, the RBI acted firmly on monetary policy to signal to markets that its previous priority of fighting inflation would be replaced by that of preventing the economy from going into recession. Yet in October 2008, in spite of facing a yearly consumer inflation rate of around 10 per cent (figure 3), the RBI immediately cut the basic interest rate (i.e. the repo rate, see table 2).[14] Between October 2008 and January 2009, successive cuts reduced the yearly repo rate from 9 per cent to 5.5 per cent (i.e. by 350 basis points). In contrast, Brazil's central bank only started to cut the basic interest rate (SELIC) in January 2009 – a delay of about three months after the worsening of the global crisis (table 2). Given the recessionary environment, Brazil's low inflation rate and the actual deflationary trend of the global crisis, this delay could be considered a mistake in economic policy.[15]

As for fiscal policy, the first round of measures implemented in India between September 2008 and January 2009 required additional public spending of approximately 3 per cent of GDP in the 2008-2009 fiscal year (April to March). Most of this involved government guaranteed funds for infrastructure, cuts in indirect taxes, expanded guaranteed cover for credit to micro and small enterprises and additional support to exporters (RBI, 2009: 12; and Subbarao, 2009: 4). This is a considerable countercyclical package, considering that the total investment of the Indian Central Government had been 3.1 per cent of GDP in the previous fiscal year, against 0.9 per cent in Brazil (see table 1).

In contrast, in Brazil in February 2009, the Ministry of Finance estimated a total federal government investment of about 1.2 per cent of GDP for 2009 – an addition of only 0.2 percentage points to the 1 per cent of GDP in 2008 (Ministry of Finance, 2009).[16] Even adding to this the cuts in indirect taxes (of 0.3 per cent of GDP), in view of the sharp slowdown in consumption, private investment and exports in the last quarter of 2008, that total amount would be insufficient to partially offset the drastic drop in aggregate demand and prevent the economy from entering into recession.[17]

The RBI's report on the 2008-2009 fiscal year suggests that in India the aim was to give priority to a countercyclical policy to deter economic deceleration. The report states that "implementing the fiscal stimulus packages required that the government defer the stipulated deficit targets under the Fiscal Responsibility and Budget Management Act, 2003" (RBI, 2009: ii). Indeed, for a nominal fiscal deficit originally budgeted at 2.5 per cent of GDP for the fiscal year, the same document states that the Indian Government revised the results upwards to 6 per cent of GDP in the same period.[18] In Brazil, even taking into account the immediate impacts from the global crisis on the real side of the economy in the last quarter of 2008, the public sector registered a primary surplus of 3.5 per cent of GDP in 2008, the same as the previous year.[19] In practical terms, these indicators suggest that the high risk of depression did not initially induce Brazilian policymakers to turn away from a procyclical fiscal policy.

The slowness of the monetary policy reaction in Brazil, and the hesitation over introducing a more expansionary fiscal package in the last quarter of 2008, suggest that the main political and economic leaders in Brazil were still influenced by the decoupling hypothesis.[20] For instance, in October 2008, President Lula da Silva declared that "rather than an economic tsunami like in the U.S., the financial crisis in Brazil will be a little wave."[21] In the same optimistic vein, in November 2008 the chairman of the Central Bank of Brazil, Henrique Meirelles, still believed a real GDP growth of 3 per cent in 2009 would be possible: "Even in this moment of a serious world crisis, the greatest since 1929, Brazil will have a growth greater than the yearly average growth shown in the period 1980-2003."[22] This belief was expressed despite an environment of rapid deceleration of monthly manufacturing production, as discussed later in this chapter.

In India, politicians and policymakers seemed more realistic about the extent to which the global crisis would affect the Indian economy. Indeed, since the beginning of the crisis, the Indian authorities believed the country would be severely affected. For instance, in early November 2008, Prime Minister Manmohan Singh declared in the press that "a crisis of this magnitude was bound to affect our economy, and it has."[23] In January 2009, he admitted, "our problems will not be overcome this year. Difficulties will persist throughout the (fiscal) year 2009-2010." He concluded, "although the government has little room to act on the fiscal side, the country will need to endure a high fiscal deficit next year (2009-2010), so that the increase in public spending acts as a stimulus to the economy."[24]

In Brazil, only when it became clear that there would be a sharp drop in real GDP in the last quarter of 2008 compared to the immediately preceding quarter (-3.6 per cent) did the economic authorities start to react with a more expansionary monetary and fiscal policy in March 2009. While the Central Bank of Brazil reduced the basic interest rate (SELIC) to 11.25 per cent (a cut of 150 basis points), policymakers recognized the urgency of increasing the resources allocated to public investment programmes, of creating mechanisms to boost private investment and of reducing the primary fiscal surplus target.[25] Two measures were taken in this direction: first, a new housing programme (*Minha Casa, Minha Vida* Program) was adopted with the aim of building 1 million homes by 2010, financed by additional public subsidies amounting to R$ 34 billion (approximately 1.2 per cent of GDP); and second, by July 2009, BNDES began to implement the Programme for Sustaining Investment (PSI), which granted loans with favourable interest rates for the production and purchase of capital goods and for innovation projects. This latter measure played an important role in restoring investment demand in Brazil from mid-2009 onwards. Through PSI, the interest rate on Finame loans (a BNDES programme for promoting the purchase of machinery and equipment) was reduced by 0.6 percentage points, reaching 4.5 per cent per annum. At the time PSI was implemented (in July 2009), daily disbursements from Finame reached their lowest level (R$ 60 million, or US$ 33 million). In December 2009, they had already recovered and reached R$ 182 million (US$ 101 million), an amount superior to that posted in September 2008.

In summary, since the first round of countercyclical fiscal measures adopted between September 2008 and January 2009 had very low impacts on the real side, it is hard to agree with Barbosa (2010), a Deputy Secretary of Macroeconomic Policy at the Brazilian Ministry of Finance, who believed that "the delay in monetary policy to stimulate economic growth immediately after the 2008 crash had to be compensated by fiscal policy." As noted in the next subsection, having perceived that the timing and intensity of monetary and fiscal policy responses matter when economic growth is unexpectedly interrupted by a hard external shock and the economy is under high risk of depression, Indian policymakers were much more successful than Brazil's in preventing the country from sinking into recession in 2009.

B.   *Impact on the real economy*

One of the first transmission channels of the international financial crisis was foreign trade financing and the rapid drop in world trade. In India, as in most countries that are reasonably integrated into the global economy, the first adverse impact of the crisis on the real economy was on

Figure 5

**BRAZIL AND INDIA: EXPORT GROWTH RATES,
JANUARY 2008–DECEMBER 2009**

(Percentage year-on-year growth)

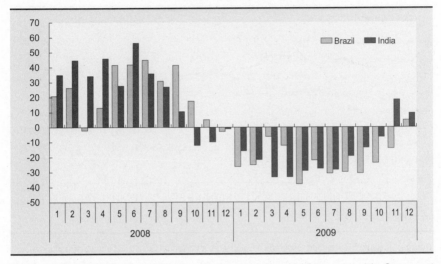

Source: Bureau of Foreign Trade (SECEX) of Brazil; and Department of Commerce and the Government of India.

its exports, which experienced a decline in October 2008 (figure 5). After showing an average monthly drop of -15.1 per cent between October 2008 and October 2009, growth of Indian merchandise exports only began to resume in November 2009.

By comparison, Brazilian exports only began to post negative growth rates in December 2008.[26] Nevertheless, the impact could be considered modest compared to the negative impact caused by the sharp fall in commodity prices, as commodities account for a considerable share of Brazilian exports. However, from December 2008 to November 2009, Brazilian exports experienced an average monthly fall of -18.1 per cent, and they only resumed growth in December 2009.

Regarding the immediate impacts of the global crisis on economic activity in both countries, between the beginning of 2007 and September 2008 while India experienced a slowdown in industrial production, Brazil

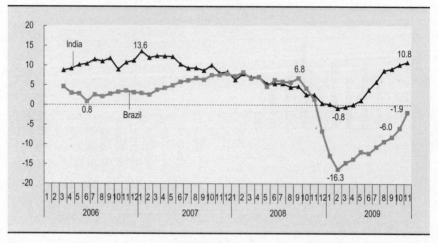

Figure 6

**BRAZIL AND INDIA: PERCENTAGE CHANGES IN INDUSTRIAL
PRODUCTION, 2006–2009**

(Year-on-year moving quarterly averages)

Source: Instituto Brasileiro de Geografia e Estatística; and Central Statistical Organization of India.

experienced the opposite trend (figure 6). The global crisis forced a strong slowdown in industrial activity in both Brazil and India in the last quarter of 2008. However, the negative impact on the Brazilian manufacturing sector was much more severe than in India. Between December 2008 and February 2009, Brazilian industrial production witnessed an average monthly decline of -16.3 per cent compared with the same period in the previous year. In contrast, industrial production in India experienced only a small contraction (-0.8 per cent) in the same period. Although Brazilian industrial production has seen a slow recovery since February 2009, it had not returned to the average monthly growth rates witnessed before the 2008 global crash. In contrast, since May 2009 Indian industrial production has grown at an accelerated pace: between September and November 2009, it registered an average monthly growth of 10.8 per cent compared with a drop of -1.9 per cent in Brazil.

Figure 7

**BRAZIL AND INDIA: PERCENTAGE CHANGES IN REAL GDP
BEFORE AND AFTER THE GLOBAL ECONOMIC CRISIS**

(Quarterly changes)

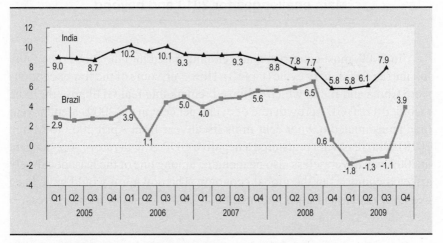

Source: Instituto Brasileiro de Geografia e Estatística; and Reserve Bank of India.
Note: Real GDP at factor cost for both countries.

Before the 2008 financial crisis, the Indian economy was decelerating due to the RBI's anti-inflation policy (figure 7), and it slowed down even more rapidly immediately after being hit by the global economic crisis. However, since the first quarter of 2009, the Indian economy has shown a remarkable capacity for recovery and growth – a very unlikely result if there had not been a quick and vigorous response of both monetary and fiscal policy. In Brazil, in marked contrast, there was a sharp slowdown in real GDP growth in the fourth quarter of 2008, falling into a recession in the first quarter of 2009.

IV. Brazil and India in the post-global crisis: Main challenges for 2010 and beyond

In 2009, most countries that were integrated into the global economy fell into a recessionary cycle (table 3). However, some of the few exceptions were China and India, which achieved remarkable real GDP growth. India recorded a real GDP growth rate of over 6 per cent in the 2009 calendar year (and an estimated 6.9 per cent in its fiscal year from April 2009 to March 2010). Brazil, having registered a negative GDP growth rate of -0.2 per cent in 2009, can nevertheless also be included among one of the least negatively affected countries in the global economy. The downturn would have been deeper if Brazil had not implemented a second round of more aggressive

Table 3

REAL GDP GROWTH RATES IN SELECTED COUNTRIES, 2008–2011

(Per cent)

Countries/regions	2008	2009[a]	2010[b]	2011[b]
Brazil	**5.1**	**-0.2**	**4.7**	**3.7**
India	**7.3**	**6.9**	**7.9**	**7.8**
China	9.6	8.7	10.0	9.7
Russian Federation	5.6	-9.0	3.6	3.4
Mexico	1.3	-6.8	4.0	4.7
United States	0.4	-2.5	2.7	2.4
Euro Area	0.6	-3.9	1.0	1.6
Japan	-1.2	-5.3	1.7	2.2
United Kingdom	0.5	-4.8	1.3	2.7
Canada	0.4	-2.6	2.6	3.6
Newly industrialized Asian economies[c]	6.1	-1.2	4.8	4.7
ASEAN-5[d]	4.7	1.3	4.7	5.3

Source: Central Bank of Brazil; Instituto Brasileiro de Geografia e Estatística; Reserve Bank of India; and International Monetary Fund, *Economic Outlook*, January 2010.

a   Except for Brazil, data referring to the other countries are estimated.
b   Forecast.
c   Hong Kong (China), Republic of Korea, Singapore and Taiwan Province of China.
d   Indonesia, Malaysia, the Philippines, Thailand and Viet Nam.

Table 4

**BRAZIL AND INDIA: SELECTED MACROECONOMIC
INDICATORS, 2008–2010**

(Per cent of GDP, unless otherwise indicated)

	Brazil			India		
Selected macroeconomic indicators	*2008*	*2009*	*2010*	*2008*	*2009*	*2010*
Unemployment rate (per cent)*ᵃ*	7.9	8.1	7.2	7.2	6.8	n.a.
Consumer price change (per cent)	5.9	4.3	4.9	9.1	11.2*ᵇ*	8.8*ᵇ*
Gross investment	18.7	16.7	18.6	40.0	39.4	40.4
Primary fiscal balance*ᶜ*	3.5	2.1	3.3	-2.6	-3.0	n.a.
Nominal fiscal balance*ᵈ*	-1.9	-3.1	n.a.	-5.9	-6.5	n.a.
Gross public debt	57.9	62.9	n.a.	78.2	81.7	81.2
Current account balance	-1.7	-1.5	-3.0	-2.6	-1.9	-2.1
External debt*ᵉ*	12.1	14.1	n.a.	19.5	19.2	19.8
Gross international reserves (US$ billion)*ᶠ*	193.8	238.5	240.5	252.0	300.7	327.9

Source: Central Bank of Brazil; Instituto Brasileiro de Geografia e Estatística; Brazilian Development Bank (BNDES); and International Monetary Fund.
  Note: n.a.: not available.
    a Yearly average, except for 2010 in Brazil, where rate refers to January.
    b Industrial workers 2001 weights.
    c Indicator for Brazil in 2010 refers to yearly target.
    d Interest expenditures included.
    e End-period.
    f Data for Brazil in 2010 refer to January; for India in 2010 data are estimated for end-period.

monetary and fiscal policies from March 2009 onwards. Indeed, since mid-2009, the Brazilian economy has exhibited remarkable resilience. Although the International Monetary Fund forecast in January 2010 a real GDP growth rate for Brazil of 4.7 per cent and 3.7 per cent for 2010 and 2011, respectively (against 7.9 per cent and 7.8 per cent, respectively, for India), the Brazilian Government and private institutions expect that real GDP might increase by an average of over 5 per cent per annum during that period.

If the global recession ends in 2010, there are at least two reasons for expecting vigorous and sustained economic growth in Brazil over the next few years. First, most of the basic macroeconomic indicators are sound (see table 4). Second, the ratio of gross investment/GDP in Brazil is not only much lower than it is in India, but it is still very low for guaranteeing sustained growth in the long run. However, unless there is an unexpected

Table 5

INVESTMENT IN SELECTED SECTORS IN BRAZIL, 2005–2013

(Actual and projected, in R$ billion at 2009 constant prices)

Sectors	Brazilian R$ billion		Real growth rate
	2005–2008	2010–2013	
Oil and gas	201	307	52.7
Mineral extractive industry	53	42	-20.2
Manufacturing industry	90	142	57.7
Infrastructure	199	257	29.0
Total	**543**	**748**	**37.7**

Source: Brazilian Development Bank (BNDES).
  Note: Current values were deflated by the gross fixed capital formation deflators of the Instituto Brasileiro de Geografia e Estatística.

external shock or an erratic economic policy, gross fixed capital formation in Brazil could reach 22 per cent (or more) of GDP in 2013 as a result of actual and projected investments in the near term.

According to Brazilian Development Bank projections, new investment in selected sectors in Brazil for the period 2010–2013 is expected to amount to R$ 748 billion (US$415 billion) (excluding current and expected investment in housing construction and other services) (table 5). This represents an increase of 37 per cent in real terms (or around 7 per cent per annum) in comparison with the period 2005–2008.

In spite of this, both Brazil and India will face some challenges to avoid strong macroeconomic disequilibrium. For instance, policymakers in both countries will have to think about how to manage adverse effects of the current and expected large foreign capital inflows on the nominal and (given the domestic and international price deflators) real exchange rate. Indeed, both Brazil and India will have to manage the effects of a real overvaluation of their currencies as a result of the expected increase in their current-account deficits.[27]

In the case of India particularly, on the one hand, the prompt response in the form of a countercyclical fiscal policy was one of the main reasons for its relatively vigorous growth in 2009; on the other hand, the rapid increase in both its fiscal deficit and gross public debt (see table 4) signals that, since "there is no free lunch", India's policymakers will have to make a strong fiscal adjustment as soon as the fiscal stimuli are withdrawn. Needless to say, this is one of the principal challenges for most countries in the world, especially the developed ones.

Another considerable challenge for Indian policymakers is how to fight the high and increasing inflation rate which is predominantly the result of supply-side channels, especially rising food prices.[28] However, as recognized by the RBI (2010b), once there is a strong risk of transmission of high food prices to other non-food prices through wage-price revisions, the main issue for monetary policy is to manage inflation expectations and, at the same time, to avoid an undesirable deceleration of the Indian economy.

V. Conclusion

In September 2008, when Brazil and India faced the first effects of the global crisis through the financial channels, they might have been expected to experience similar adverse impacts, especially in terms of a downturn of economic activity. However, India turned out to be one of the few countries in the world that escaped the recession in the middle of the global "storm". Although the Indian economy decelerated in the immediate aftermath of the global crisis (in the last quarter of 2008), in early 2009 it showed signs of a rapid recovery. India's real GDP growth rate was over 6 per cent in the 2009 calendar year (and was estimated at 6.9 per cent for the April 2009 to March 2010 fiscal year), which was a remarkable performance and enough to lead to the conclusion that the Indian economy was much less adversely affected than the Brazilian economy which fell into recession in the same year.

Three main reasons explain the resilience of the Indian economy to the recessionary impacts of the global crisis. The first is that Indian foreign exchange regulations, in spite of being relatively open to investments in the stock market, are still highly restrictive to investments in both government treasuries and most fixed-income assets. Therefore, under a regime which somewhat restricts external financial integration – a rare situation in most developing countries in the late 2000s – policymakers were able to restore positive expectations more effectively, even though the global economy was being driven in the opposite direction. The second reason is related to the speed and intensity with which the RBI reduced the basic interest rates. This decision was essential to signal to markets that the priority was to prevent a sharp slowdown or even a possible shrinking of economic activity. The third reason is that the first round of fiscal stimuli was adopted quicker and with much more intensity than it was in Brazil.

One could cynically point out that a more (initially) conservative response of both monetary and fiscal policy could have put Brazil onto a more sustainable recovery and growth path than India.[29] However, the main argument to support the much more vigorous response from Indian economic policy to the negative impacts of the global crisis is that Indian society is not willing to pay for the luxury of deviating from an economic growth path which has lasted almost 30 years and exchanging it for one year of recession and the risk of a slow recovery. It seems that Indian policymakers have learned that giving priority to growth is not incompatible with responsible management of other macroeconomic variables that preserve internal and external macroeconomic equilibria. In Brazil, after more than 25 years of semi-stagnant growth, it seems that policymakers are now also more convinced of this lesson.

Notes

1   For an idea of the important role of economic policy as a countercyclical mechanism, in the 1974-1975 crisis in the United States, the Treasury, after posting a fiscal surplus of around US$ 6 billion (0.43 per cent of GDP) in 1973 (at the peak of the economic boom of the 1970s), ended 1974 with a fiscal deficit of US$ 3.6 billion (0.24 per cent of GDP), which soared to a whopping US$ 63.4 billion (3.87 per cent of GDP) deficit in 1975 (Minsky, 1986: 31).

2   Based on Friedman (1968), it could be pointed out that the role of monetary policy is exclusively to assure the stability of price levels. However, this hypothesis is

questionable in both theoretical and empirical terms (see, for instance, Tobin, 1965 and 1970; and Davidson, 2003).

3   If this rupture is of a global nature, exports also decrease suddenly and sharply.

4   Nouriel Roubini (2008) was one of the few dissonant voices who warned people of the high risk of the global economic crisis. In February 2008 he presented a written testimony to the United States House of Representatives' Financial Services Committee connecting the "current United States recession and the risks of a systemic financial crisis".

5   In October 2008, 47 per cent of Brazil's gross public debt had a two-year maturity compared with a five-year maturity for 70 per cent of India's total debt. See Brazil's Central Bank and Reserve Bank of India websites (respectively, at: http://www.bcb. gov.br and at: http://www.rbi.org.in).

6   While the average annual variation of real GDP in Brazil was 2.4 per cent between 1980 and 2000 (see Instituto Brasileiro de Geografia e Estatística (IBGE) website at: http://www.ibge.gov.br), in India it reached 5.6 per cent (see Reserve Bank of India website at: http://www.rbi.org.in).

7   The repo rate is the rate at which the RBI lends to private and public sector banks, while the reverse repo rate is the opposite.

8   The SELIC overnight rate is Brazil's basic interest rate used as a reference by monetary policy. It is expressed in annual terms as the average rate weighted by the volume of one-day operations guaranteed by federal government securities and carried out at SELIC through committed operations.

9   In an interview, the RBI's economic researchers pointed out that due to the still high Indian public debt, the inflation target should not be a priority of monetary policy.

10 The terms *repo* and *reverse repo* mean, respectively, injection and absorption of liquidity (RBI, 2008: 56).

11 This strategy was confirmed in an interview with the economic research department of the RBI. In the period immediately before the worsening of the global crisis, the main focus of RBI monetary policy was to reduce the long-term inflation rate to around 4.5 per cent per annum, a level that would be considered "tolerable for a democratic society", but "now (that is, after Lehman Brothers' bankruptcy in September 2008), the priority of monetary policy is to sustain economic growth" (interview of the author with RBI officials).

12 Hausmann (2008: 13–14) seeks to explain, econometrically, why the short-term interest rates in Brazil are so high. He shows that they are significantly high owing to the high basic interest rates and the "abnormally" high compulsory rates.

13 The Commission on Growth and Development, sponsored by the World Bank and other foreign public institutions, is composed of economists from many countries, such Robert Solow and Michael Spence (from the United States), Montek Singh Ahluwalia (India) and Edmar Bacha (Brazil) among others.

14 In the words of the president of the RBI, "in the scope of the conventional monetary policy, besides the reduction of the compulsory deposits, we aggressively reduced the basic interest rate" (Subbarao, 2009: 4).

15   In the proceedings of the December 2008 meeting of Brazil's Central Bank Council of Monetary Policy (COPOM), the Brazilian monetary authorities justified the decision to keep the basic interest rate unchanged (at 13.75 per cent per annum) as follows: "the probability of some localized inflation pressure might be reducing. However the COPOM understands that effectively transmitting to the consumer price indices depends on the inflation expectations, which are still over the inflation target path." This evaluation was done even taking into account that: (i) the year-on-year consumer price index in November 2008 was 4.2 per cent and the inflation rate for the subsequent 12 months, as mentioned in the Proceedings, was expected to reach 5.34 per cent; and (ii) the inflation target for 2008 was 4.5 per cent, with a +2 to -2 percentage point of tolerance margin (Central Bank of Brazil, 2008).

16   This does not include the additional investments announced in April 2009 for the housing construction stimulation programme, which will be implemented in the second round of countercyclical measures (Ministry of Finance, 2009).

17   In Brazil, between the third and the last quarter of 2008, the growth rate of gross fixed capital formation (on a year-on-year basis) declined from 19.7 per cent to 3.8 per cent, household consumption fell from 7.3 per cent to 2.2 per cent, and exports from 2 per cent to -7.0 per cent. However, despite this depressionary environment, the year-on-year growth rate of government consumption showed a decline from 6.4 per cent to 5.5 per cent. In contrast, in India, the dramatic year-on-year increase in government consumption, from 6.5 per cent to 26.8 per cent in the same period, was able to partially offset the strong year-on-year deceleration of both gross fixed capital formation (from 29.9 per cent to 22.1 per cent) and of exports (from 13.3 per cent to 4.6 per cent), as well as keeping the quarterly growth rate of household consumption almost unchanged (from 7.1 per cent to 6.1 per cent). These figures were calculated by the author based on IPEA data for Brazil (at: http://www.ipea.gov.br) and on data from the International Monetary Fund for India (at: http://www.imf.org).

18   In its report on the 2008-2009 fiscal year, the RBI indicated that the primary fiscal balance was initially estimated as a surplus of 1.1 per cent of GDP in the fiscal year 2008-2009, but was then restated as a deficit of 2.5 per cent of GDP. It is also important to point out that Indian Government estimates for the current fiscal year, 2009-2010, indicate a significant increase in the primary and nominal fiscal deficits (to 3 per cent and 6.8 per cent of GDP respectively) (RBI, 2009: 12).

19   See the Central Bank of Brazil website at: http://www.bcb.gov.br.

20   According to the decoupling hypothesis, the greater relative importance of Asian countries (particularly China) in world GDP would be able to prevent the recession in the United States from spilling over to the global economy. In an important paper, Akin and Kose (2007: 6) had already clarified the decoupling debate, showing empirical evidence that "while the impact of the North (in terms of economic growth) on the Emerging South groups has declined over time, it has not changed much on the latter one."

21   *O Globo*, 4 October 2008.

22   Agência Brasil, 28 November 2008.
23   *Thaindian News*, 3 November 2008.
24   *The Economic Times*, 28 January 2009.
25   In April 2009, the Brazilian government submitted an amendment to the Law of Budget Guidelines to the Congress, proposing the temporary reduction in the primary fiscal surplus target of 3.8 per cent to 2.5 per cent of GDP with the aim at releasing further funds for increasing public investment and other government expenditures.
26   In Brazil, the impact of the global crisis on industrial production was immediate and happened prior to its negative impacts on exports. Indeed, the manufacturing sector had already begun to slow down in October and then registered a drop in November 2008 (see IBGE database at: http://www.ibge.gov.br). In India, both exports and industrial production were adversely affected in October 2008.
27   Among other measures, policymakers from developing countries should not discard capital controls, if necessary. Unlike the last decade, even the International Monetary Fund has recently adopted a more favourable position towards this kind of measure. In an official position note, Ostry et al. (2010: 20) concluded that "capital controls on certain types of inflows might usefully complement prudential regulations to limit financial fragility and can be part of the toolkit."
28   According to the RBI (2010b: v), "on year-on-year basis, the Wholesale Price Index (WPI) headline inflation in December 2009 was at 7.3 per cent, whereas WPI inflation excluding food articles was 2.1 per cent."
29   This is the position of the former chairman of the Central Bank of Brazil, Armínio Fraga, who recently declared to the Brazilian press that "a conservative management helped to take Brazil out of recession in two quarters". *O Globo,* 23 February 2010.

References

Akin Ç and Kose MA (2007). Changing nature of north-south linkages: Stylized facts and explanations. IMF Working Paper 280 (WP/07/280). Washington, DC, International Monetary Fund, December.
Barbosa N (2010). Latin America: Counter-cyclical policy in Brazil: 2008-2009. *Journal of Globalization and Development*, 1 (1): 1-14.
Central Bank of Brazil (2008). Proceedings of the December 2008 Meeting of the Brazil Central Bank's Council of Monetary Policy. Available at: http://www.bcb.gov.br.
Comission on Growth and Development (2010). *Post-Crisis Growth in Developing Countries*. A Special Report of the Commission on Growth and Development on the Implications of the 2008 Financial Crisis. Washington, DC, World Bank.

Davidson P (2003). *Financial Markets, Money and the Real World.* New York, Edward Elgar.

Friedman M (1968). The role of monetary policy. *American Economic Review* 58 (1): 1–17, March.

Hausmann R (2008). In search of the chains that hold Brazil back. Cambridge, MA, Harvard Kennedy School and Center for International Development, Harvard University, August.

Keynes JM (1936). The General Theory of Employment, Interest and Money. London, Macmillan Press.

Keynes JM (1937). The general theory of employment. *Quarterly Journal of Economics*, 51: 209–226. Reprinted in *The Collected Writings of John Maynard Keynes*, vol. XIV. London, Macmillan, for the Royal Economic Society, 1973 edition.

Keynes JM (1942). A letter to James Meade (June 16, 1942). In: *The Collected Writings of John Maynard Keynes*, vol. XXVII. London, Macmillan, for the Royal Economic Society, 1980 edition.

Krugman P (2009). The Return of Depression Economics and the Crisis of 2008. New York, W.W. Norton & Company.

Ministry of Finance (2009). Atravessando a Crise Mundial. Conference of the Brazilian Minister of Finance Guido Mantega. Available (in Power Point version). Available at: http://www.fazenda.gov.br.

Minsky H (1982). Can "It" Happen Again? Essays on Instability and Finance. New York, M. E. Sharpe.

Minsky H (1986). *Stabilizing an Unstable Economy.* New York, McGraw Hill, 2008 edition.

Nassif A (2007). National innovation system and macroeconomic policies: Brazil and India in comparative perspective. UNCTAD Discussion Paper no. 184. Geneva, United Nations Conference on Trade and Development, May.

Ostry J et al. (2010). Capital inflows: the role of controls. IMF Staff Position Note. Washington, DC, International Monetary Fund, 19 February.

RBI (2008). Macroeconomic and monetary developments. Mid-term review, 2008-2009. Mumbai, October.

RBI (2009). Macroeconomic and monetary developments. Third quarter review, 2008-2009. Mumbai, January.

RBI (2010a). Indian perspective on banking regulation. Speech by Usha Thorat, Deputy Governor, at the International Conference on Financial Sector Regulation and Reforms in Asian Emerging Markets. Mumbai, 8 February. Available at: http://www.rbi.org.in.

RBI (2010b). Macroeconomic and monetary developments. Third quarter review, 2009-2010. Mumbai, January.

Roubini N (2008). The current U.S. recession and the risks of a systemic financial crisis. Written testimony for the House of Representatives' Financial Services Committee Hearing on 26 February 2008.

Subbarao D (2009). Impact of the global financial crisis on India: Collateral damage and response. Paper presented at the symposium on The Global Economic Crisis and

Challenges for the Asian Economies in a Changing World, Tokyo, 18 February 2009. Mumbai, Reserve Bank of India.

Tobin J (1965). The monetary interpretation of history. *American Economic Review,* LV (3): 464-485. June.

Tobin J (1970). Money and income: Post hoc ergo propter hoc? *Quarterly Journal of Economics*, 84 (2): 301–317.

AFRICA AND THE GLOBAL FINANCIAL AND ECONOMIC CRISIS: IMPACTS, RESPONSES AND OPPORTUNITIES

Patrick N. Osakwe

Abstract

Africa has been severely affected by the ongoing global financial and economic crisis. Its impacts are evident in all categories of countries: oil-exporting, middle-income, low-income and agriculturally dependent economies. The crisis has been slowly eroding gains in economic performance achieved by the region since the turn of the millennium. Unlike in the past, African countries responded promptly to the current crisis through the use of countercyclical monetary and fiscal policies. Nevertheless, this paper argues that African policymakers should also prepare themselves to take advantage of global recovery as well as seize any opportunities that might arise from structural changes induced by the crisis.

Introduction

At the dawn of the new millennium, African leaders adopted the New Partnership for Africa's Development (NEPAD) and pledged to change the way they managed their economies, improve governance and lay the foundation for sustainable growth and poverty reduction. The excitement and euphoria surrounding this new attitude to economic management and governance created the impression that Africa had reached a turning point in its development history. It also reinforced the view that the twenty-first

Figure 1

REAL GDP GROWTH RATES IN AFRICA, 1995–2009

(Per cent)

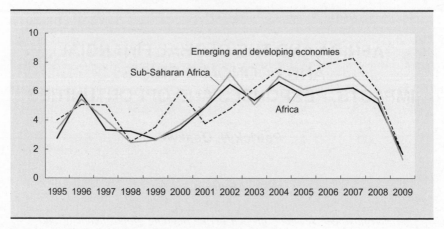

Source: IMF, *World Economic Outlook* database, October 2009.

century could be Africa's century (World Bank, 2000; Hernandez-Cata, Fischer and Khan, 1998). Indeed, in recent years the region has made significant progress in its economic performance, with an average annual growth rate of about 6 per cent over the period 2002–2007 (figure 1). This progress is now being eroded by the global economic and financial crisis that was triggered by events in the United States housing market in the second half of 2007.

When the crisis began, it was assumed that the impact on Africa would be minimal because the region is not well integrated into global financial markets. However, recent developments have shown that this assessment was overly optimistic: the crisis has had a very serious impact on the region. It has led to a decline in the region's real growth rate by between 4 and 4.5 percentage points. It has also reduced prospects for achieving the United Nations Millennium Development Goals (MDGs) in several countries in the region. As a result of the crisis, the number of African countries with growth rates of 5 per cent and above fell from 29 in 2007 to 7 in 2009. Furthermore, the number of countries with negative growth rates increased from 2 to 8 over the same period. It is estimated that the region would need additional

Table 1

PREDOMINANT FORM OF BANK OWNERSHIP IN SUB-SAHARAN AFRICA

Mainly government	Mainly foreign	Mainly local private sector	Foreign plus government	Equally shared
Eritrea	Botswana	Benin	Burkina Faso	Angola
Ethiopia	Cape Verde	Mali	Dem. Rep. of	Burundi
Togo	Central African Republic	Mauritania	the Congo	Cameroon
	Chad	Mauritius	Sierra Leone	Congo
	Côte d'Ivoire	Nigeria		Gabon
	Equatorial Guinea	Rwanda		Ghana
	Gambia	Somalia		Kenya
	Guinea	South Africa		Rwanda
	Guinea-Bissau	Sudan		Senegal
	Lesotho	Zimbabwe		
	Liberia			
	Madagascar			
	Malawi			
	Mozambique			
	Namibia			
	Niger			
	Seychelles			
	Swaziland			
	United Rep. of Tanzania			
	Uganda			
	Zambia			

Source: Honohan and Beck, 2007.

external financing of about US$ 50 billion to achieve pre-crisis-level growth rates (Kaberuka, 2009).

Why did analysts misread the crisis and its impact on Africa? There are two main reasons. First, at the onset of the crisis, there was considerable uncertainty regarding the magnitude of losses sustained by financial institutions in developed countries. Consequently, most analysts underestimated the impact of the crisis on the real sector and the potential for contagious effects on developing countries through trade and capital flows (Pisani-Ferry and Santos, 2009). Second, most analysts did not fully recognize the role of foreign bank ownership in the transmission of the crisis to Africa. Although the region is not well integrated into global financial markets, foreign ownership of banks is quite high in several African countries, and this made them vulnerable to repatriation of funds by the foreign banks to their home countries in response to the crisis (table 1).

Against this background, this paper examines the impact of the financial and economic crisis on Africa, identifies policy responses by African governments and institutions, and discusses potential opportunities created by the crisis that should be seized by African policymakers. The paper is organized as follows. Section I puts the current crisis in historical perspective, pointing out important differences between this crisis and the Great Depression. Section II examines the impact of the crisis on Africa, while section III presents policy responses to the crisis by African governments and institutions. Section IV explores how the region could seize opportunities created by the crisis to lay a solid foundation for sustained growth and development. The last section offers concluding remarks.

I. The crisis in historical perspective

As the world tries to come to grips with the devastation caused by the current financial and economic turmoil, it is important to note that financial crisis is not a new phenomenon. It is to a large extent an unpleasant aspect of the dynamics of market economies. There was a very serious crisis in the 1930s and, more recently, there were financial crises in Mexico in 1994 and in East Asia in 1997–1998. The scale and depth of the economic collapse caused by the current crisis has led analysts and policymakers to compare it to the Great Depression of the 1930s (Collyns, 2008). It is true that the current crisis has a lot in common with the Great Depression. For example, they both originated in the United States and spread quickly to other parts of the globe. Furthermore, both crises led to a significant reduction in business confidence and threatened the payments and settlements systems.

Despite these similarities, it is important to note that the scale and duration of the current crisis has not yet reached those observed during the Great Depression. For example, in the United States, available evidence indicates that during the Great Depression the industrial production index declined by 34 per cent between the first and the ninth quarter of the crisis, while in the current crisis it declined by 11 per cent (figure 2). The Great Depression began in the third quarter of 1929, whereas the current recession

Figure 2

UNITED STATES INDUSTRIAL PRODUCTION DURING
THE GREAT DEPRESSION AND THE CURRENT CRISIS

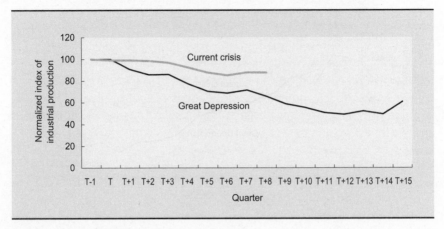

Source: Computed by author, based on data from Econstats.
   Note: T is the beginning of the recession for each of the crises, and the indices have been normalized
   so that they are 100 in the immediate quarter preceding each crisis.

began in the fourth quarter of 2007, although it was not evident until the collapse of the investment bank, Lehman Brothers, in September 2008. Moreover, the decline in United States industrial production since the onset of the current crisis has not reached the scale experienced during the Great Depression (figure 2).

With regard to the stock market, the magnitudes of the decline in the first six quarters of both crises were similar, but the duration was much longer during the Great Depression (figure 3). In particular, in the current crisis the Dow Jones Industrial Average index recovered sharply in the seventh quarter (T+6) whereas it took about 15 quarters before it recovered during the Great Depression. Nevertheless, it should be noted that the current crisis is still unfolding, and the final impact could approach that of the Great Depression. So far, however, it has not reached the scale and duration of the Great Depression.

Figure 3

DOW JONES INDEX DURING THE GREAT DEPRESSION AND THE CURRENT CRISIS

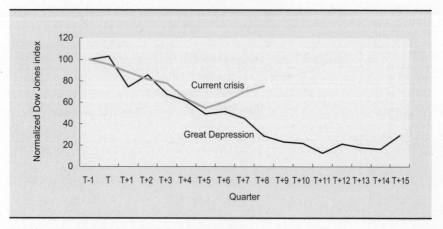

Source: Computed by author, based on data from Econstats.
  Note: T is the beginning of the recession for each of the crises and the indices have been normalized
  so that they are 100 in the immediate quarter preceding each crisis.

Apart from the differences in scale and duration, the current crisis differs from that of the Great Depression in a number of other ways. First, unlike in the 1930s, it is taking place in a more globalized world, as a result of which contagion effects are quite high. Second, developing countries are beginning to play an increasingly important role in the world economy. Third, some developing countries are highly vulnerable because of their dependence on foreign aid and other sources of external finance. Fourth, there are a growing number of multilateral organizations charged with the responsibility of maintaining stability in the global economy. Although they are not as effective as they could be, they are nevertheless playing important roles in reducing the impacts of the crisis. Fifth, since most countries now have more flexible exchange-rate regimes, the real effects of the current crisis should be less severe (Osakwe and Schembri, 2002). During the Great Depression, the exchange rates of most countries were tied to the value of gold (the gold standard), which meant that the exchange rate could not play the role of a shock absorber. Finally, we now have a better understanding of the need, as well as the instruments, for countercyclical policies during downturns.

II. Impacts of the crisis on Africa

The financial and economic crisis has had severe impacts on the financial and real sectors of African economies, with serious consequences for growth and poverty reduction. Countries such as Botswana, Seychelles and Equatorial Guinea have been the worst affected, with growth rates estimated to have declined by 10.3, 8.5 and 5.4 per cent, respectively, in 2009. The crisis affected Africa through four main channels: exchange rates, stock markets, capital flows, and trade and commodity prices.

A. Exchange rates

The financial sector was the first to be affected by the crisis, with several countries experiencing greater volatility in their exchange rates and stock markets. Between the third quarter of 2008 and the first quarter of 2009, the currencies of six African countries depreciated against the United States dollar by 30 per cent or more (table 2). The Seychellois rupee was the most affected, with a depreciation of 108 per cent, followed by the Zambian kwacha which depreciated by 54 per cent over the same period. External factors as well as domestic policies account for the varied impact of the crisis on African countries. For example, the rapid collapse of copper prices was one of the main factors underlying the sharp depreciation of the Zambian kwacha, and it amplified the effects of the depreciation caused by the rise of the United States dollar against most currencies. In the case of Seychelles, unsustainable macroeconomic policies and foreign debt problems forced it to abandon its exchange-rate peg in November 2008, resulting in high exchange-rate volatility.

Rapid and unanticipated movements in exchange rates are costly because they have negative consequences for investment, output and growth (Agbeyegbe and Osakwe, 2005). It is interesting to note that the crisis poses challenges for both floating and managed currencies in the region

Table 2

DEPRECIATION OF AFRICAN CURRENCIES AGAINST THE UNITED STATES DOLLAR, FROM 2008/THIRD QUARTER TO 2009/FIRST QUARTER

30 per cent or more	15–29 per cent	Less than 15 per cent
Congolese (DRC) franc	Botswana pula	Angolan kwanza
Lesotho loti	Gambian dalasi	Burundian franc
Namibian dollar	Ghanaian cedi	Egyptian pound
Seychellois rupee	Kenyan shilling	Ethiopian birr
Swazi lilangeni	Malagasy ariary	Liberian dollar
Zambian kwacha	Mauritian rupee	Malawian kwacha
	Nigerian naira	Moroccan dirham
	Tunisian dinar	Mozambican metical
	Ugandan shilling	Sierra Leonean leone
	West African CFA franc[a]	South African rand
	Central African CFA franc[b]	Sudanese pound

Source: Computed using data from IMF, *International Financial Statistics* database, March 2010.
  a   Used by Benin, Burkina Faso, Côte d'Ivoire, Guinea-Bissau, Mali, Niger, Senegal and Togo.
  b   Used by Cameroon, Central African Republic, Chad, Congo, Equatorial Guinea and Gabon.

(Ltaifa, Kaendera and Dixit, 2009). In countries with floating currencies, it has increased exchange-rate volatility, with serious consequences for long-term investment. In countries with managed currencies and above-trend inflation rates, interventions aimed at halting the depreciation of the local currency resulted in appreciation of the real exchange rate and reduced export competitiveness (Ltaifa, Kaendera and Dixit, 2009).

B.   Stock markets and bank balance sheets

The crisis has also affected African countries through its impact on local stock markets. Since the onset of the crisis there has been an increase in stock market volatility in the region. Between the end of 2007 and 22 January 2010, the Nigerian stock exchange index declined by 62 per cent and the Kenyan and Egyptian exchange indices by more than 30 per cent (table 3). There has also been a significant reduction in market capitalization in most stock markets. For example, between 2007 and 2008, the Namibian stock market lost about 55 per cent of its market value and the Mauritius

Table 3

CHANGES IN AFRICAN STOCK EXCHANGE INDICES, 2007–2010

(Per cent)

Country	Index	End 2007 to end 2008	End 2007 to 22 Jan. 2010
Ghana	GSE All Share index	58.1	-17.0
Malawi	Malawi All Share index	25.6	6.3
United Rep. of Tanzania	DSEI	21.3	16.3
Sudan	Khartoum Index	-7.3	
Botswana	DCI	-16.5	-13.3
Uganda	USE All Share Index	-21.4	
South Africa	FTSE/JSE All Share Index	-26.3	-6.5
Zambia	Lusaka All Share Index	-29.1	-27.0
Kenya	NSE 20 Share Index	-35.3	-33.4
Mauritius	SEMDEX	-36.1	-8.0
Namibia	NSX Overall Index	-40.1	-18.9
Nigeria	NSE All Share Index	-45.8	-62.0
Egypt	EGX 30	-56.4	-34.9

Source: Author's calculations, based on data from the African Securities Exchanges Association (ASEA), 2008; and weekly report of Securities Africa.

stock exchange lost 41 per cent. Ghana, Malawi and the United Republic of Tanzania (Dar es Salaam) are the only countries with exchanges that experienced gains in market capitalization over the same period (figure 4). The significant declines in net worth in stock markets increased the number of non-performing loans and caused deterioration in bank balance sheets in some countries. In 2009, several banks in Nigeria suffered significant losses from non-performing loans, forcing the central bank to inject funds into these institutions. There is also evidence that some banks in the United Republic of Tanzania had problems of non-performing loans and received support from the Government (IMF, 2009).

Figure 4

CHANGES IN STOCK MARKET CAPITALIZATION IN SELECTED AFRICAN COUNTRIES, 2007–2008
(Per cent)

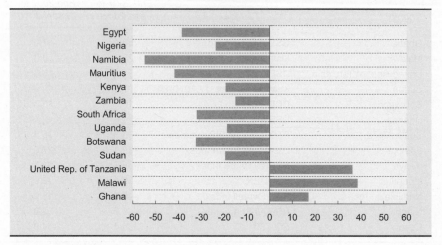

Source: Author's calculations, based on data in ASEA, 2008.

C.   Trade and commodity prices

Trade is one of the key channels through which the crisis has had a devastating effect on African economies. This is not surprising given the fact that African countries generally have high trade-GDP ratios. Over the period 2003–2006, the average trade-GDP ratio for sub-Saharan Africa was 68 per cent, although 20 countries in the region had ratios above 80 per cent. While trade data for some African economies for 2009 are not yet available, available data indicate that the crisis has had a negative impact on trade in several countries. For example, Algeria's merchandise exports fell by about 53 per cent in the third quarter of 2009 compared with the same quarter in 2008. Countries such as Burundi, Mauritius, Nigeria, South Africa and Tunisia also experienced a significant reduction in merchandise exports over the same period (figure 5). On the import side, Mauritius, Morocco, Nigeria, Sierra Leone, South Africa and Tunisia saw a more than 25 per cent decline over that period.

Figure 5

**CHANGES IN MERCHANDISE EXPORTS OF SELECTED AFRICAN
COUNTRIES, 2008/THIRD QUARTER–2009/THIRD QUARTER**

(Per cent)

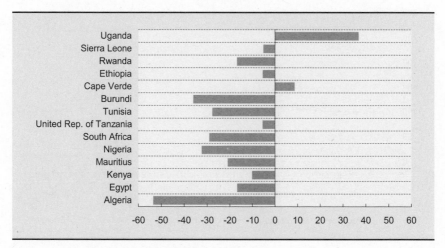

Source: Author's calculations, based on data from WTO website, at: http://www.wto.org/english/res_e/
statis_e/quarterly_world_exp_e.htm.

The slowdown in trade flows was due to declining import demand in key export markets, a shortage of trade finance and falling commodity prices. Since the crisis began, several countries in the region have experienced difficulties in obtaining trade credit. For example, Nigerian banks found it difficult to access trade credit in the United States and Europe. Furthermore, there has been an increase in the risk premium facing African countries in international capital markets, resulting in a serious adverse impact on their access to credit. Falling prices of key African commodity exports over the period 2008 and 2009 also contributed to the decline in Africa's merchandise trade. The price of crude oil fell by more than 50 per cent in February 2009 compared with the same month in 2008, and the prices of copper, coffee and cotton fell by over 20 per cent over the same period. Indeed, the prices of five major commodity groups exported by African countries declined significantly between September and December 2008 (figure 6).

Figure 6

PRICES OF SELECTED COMMODITY GROUPS, 2005–2009

(Index numbers, 2005 = 100)

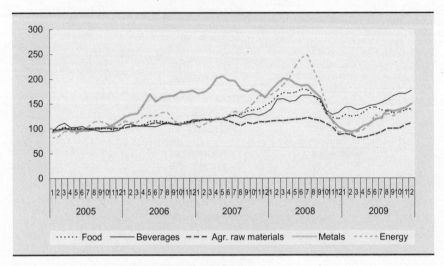

Source: IMF, *International Financial Statistics*, March 2010.

D.   Capital flows

The financial crisis has also affected capital flows to the region. Foreign direct investment (FDI) flows to Africa declined by 36 per cent in 2009 relative to 2008, reflecting partly the fall in global demand for commodities resulting from the crisis (UNCTAD, 2010). The crisis affected the two main components of FDI: greenfield investments and cross-border mergers and acquisition (M&As). For example, M&As declined by 73 per cent between 2008 and 2009. Reduced FDI flows have had a more severe impact in countries such as Chad, Equatorial Guinea, Gambia, Liberia and Seychelles, that have average FDI-GDP ratios above 10 per cent.

Remittances are another form of capital flows that have been affected by the crisis. The annual growth rate of remittance flows to sub-Saharan Africa fell from 47.6 per cent in 2007 to -3 per cent in 2009 (figure 7). The main reason for this decline is that the reduction in economic activities in developed countries has reduced opportunities for African migrants. Cape

Figure 7

GROWTH RATES OF REMITTANCE INFLOWS, 2007–2010[a]

(Per cent)

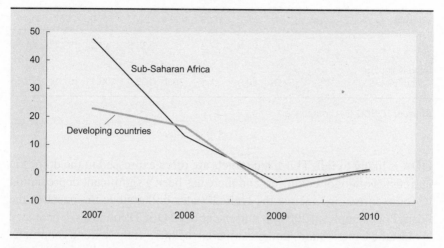

Source: World Bank, *Migration and Development Brief*, 3 November 2009.
  a Estimates and forecasts.

Verde, Gambia and Lesotho are particularly vulnerable because remittances account for over 10 per cent of their GDP. On the other hand, although North African countries receive large inflows of remittances, the reduction of these inflows does not affect their economies as badly because they represent a small percentage of their GDP.

There are concerns that the crisis may result in reduced official development assistance (ODA) to Africa, as developed countries have had to spend large amounts of money to bail out financial institutions and stimulate their economies. Although final aid data for 2009 are not yet available, recent evidence indicates that aid flows to Africa increased from US$ 39 billion in 2007 to US$ 44 billion in 2008 (table 4). Nevertheless, there are several reasons why the crisis may have a negative impact on aid flows to the region. First, aid flows tend to be procyclical in the sense that they increase during booms and fall during downturns. Second, aid commitments and targets are often set as a proportion of gross national income, implying that as income in the donor countries declines due to the crisis, the amount of

Table 4

NET ODA DISBURSEMENT BY ALL DONORS

(Billions of dollars)

Recipients	2000	2001	2002	2003	2004	2005	2006	2007	2008
Africa	15.6	16.8	21.8	27.3	29.7	35.5	43.5	39.1	44.0
All developing countries	49.8	52.3	60.9	71.1	79.4	108.0	106.1	107.1	128.6

Source: OECD-DAC database.

ODA is likely to fall. Third, aid targets are often expressed in the domestic currencies of donor countries, and there has been a significant depreciation of some currencies against the United States dollar since the onset of the crisis. For example, in 2009 the currencies of 12 OECD countries depreciated against the United States dollar compared to 2007.[1] If these trends continue, the monetary value of aid expressed in United States dollars is likely to decline. Fourth, in recent years OECD-DAC (Organisation for Economic Co-operation-Development Assistance Committee) donors have co-financed aid projects in developing countries through triangular cooperation with non-traditional donors such as Brazil, India, Malaysia and South Africa. To the extent that DAC donors reduce funding for these projects in response to the crisis, it may also lead to a reduction in support by non-traditional donors. This would have significantly adverse effects on the implementation of triangular cooperation projects.

E. Impact of the crisis on poverty

The slowdown in economic activities in Africa since the onset of the crisis has had a negative impact on poverty. According to recent estimates by the United Nations Department of Economic and Social Affairs (UNDESA), the number of people in the region living below the poverty line of US$ 1.25 a day grew by 14 million between 2008 and 2009 (United Nations, 2009). One of the channels through which the crisis has affected poverty in Africa is from falling government revenues in several countries since the crisis began. Recent estimates indicate that in sub-Saharan Africa government revenue (excluding grants) fell from 25 per cent of GDP in 2008 to 21 per cent in 2009. Revenue declines of this magnitude reduce the ability of governments to finance health, education and infrastructure projects, thus inhibiting poverty alleviation efforts. The crisis has also affected poverty through an increase in unemployment. It is estimated that the unemployment rate in sub-Saharan Africa increased from 8 per cent in 2007 to 8.2 per cent in 2009,[2] and in North Africa it increased from 10.1 per cent to 10.5 per cent (ILO, 2010). There has also been an increase in the share of workers in vulnerable employment as well as in the share of the working poor in total employment.[3] In sub-Saharan Africa, between 2008 and 2009 the share of workers in vulnerable employment increased from 76 per cent to 77 per cent, and the share of the working poor in total employment increased from 59 per cent to 64 per cent (ILO, 2010).

III. African policy responses

Although the global financial and economic crisis did not originate in Africa, countries in the region reacted to it in a swift manner, both at the national and regional levels. At the national level, several countries set up task forces to monitor the evolving situation in developed countries and the impact on their economies. For example, the Democratic Republic of the Congo, Kenya, Nigeria and Rwanda had national committees advising their governments on the crisis and how to cushion its impacts. Furthermore, many countries adopted policy measures covering the following broad areas: liquidity injection, interest rate changes, recapitalization of banks and regulatory changes, fiscal policy and trade promotion. The specific measures adopted have varied across countries, reflecting differences in availability of resources, macroeconomic fundamentals and vulnerability to the crisis. For example, countries such as Equatorial Guinea and Nigeria that accumulated significant reserves during the last commodity boom had fiscal space to expand domestic demand and offset some of the decline in external demand. On the other hand, countries such as Ghana and Seychelles that had huge fiscal deficits before the crisis had less room to pursue countercyclical policies.

Monetary policy has played an important role in Africa's response to the crisis. Central banks in Botswana, Egypt, Kenya, Mauritius, Namibia, Nigeria, South Africa, Swaziland and Tunisia reduced interest rates following the onset of the crisis. Countries such as Nigeria and Tunisia also took steps to either inject liquidity or increase its flow in domestic money markets. Furthermore, several countries, including Algeria, Kenya, Nigeria and Mali, attempted to recapitalize and strengthen their domestic banks. Some countries implemented measures to boost trade as an important element in stimulating their economies: for example, Liberia reduced trade tariffs, Tunisia increased allocations for export-related business travel, and Madagascar devalued its currency to increase its export competitiveness.

Many countries in the region, such as Cape Verde, Egypt, Gabon, Kenya, Morocco, Namibia, Nigeria, Tunisia, South Africa and the United Republic of Tanzania, implemented fiscal stimulus packages designed to boost growth and offset declines in export demand. The size of the fiscal injections varied: South Africa spent US$ 4.2 billion, Nigeria US$ 1.6 billion, the United Republic of Tanzania US$ 1.3 billion and Kenya US$ 0.3 billion (United Nations, 2009). Interestingly, the fiscal package unveiled by the United Republic of Tanzania represents 6.4 per cent of its GDP, while those of Nigeria and South Africa constituted only 0.7 and 1.5 per cent of their GDP respectively. The fiscal injections made by African governments were mostly for financing infrastructure and other public investments. As a result of these fiscal stimuli and other measures, it is estimated that sub-Saharan Africa's fiscal balance (including grants) shifted from a surplus of 1.2 per cent of GDP in 2007 to a deficit of 4.8 per cent in 2009 (IMF, 2009).

African leaders have also taken measures at the regional level to cushion the impact of the crisis. In November 2008, African ministers of finance and governors of central banks met in Tunis to deliberate on the financial crisis. At the end of the meeting, they set up the Committee of Ten, comprising African ministers of finance and central bank governors to monitor the crisis and make policy recommendations on how to reduce its impact on Africa. The committee is made up of representatives of the following countries and central banks: Algeria, Botswana, Cameroon, Egypt, Kenya, Nigeria, South Africa, the United Republic of Tanzania, the Central Bank of West African States (BCEAO) and the Central Bank of Central African States (BEAC). The committee held its first meeting in Cape Town (South Africa) on

16 January 2009, the second in Dar es salaam, (United Republic of Tanzania) on 11 March 2009, the third in Abuja (Nigeria) on 14 July 2009 and the fourth in Cape Town (South Africa) on 21 February 2010. The committee has been playing a pivotal role in articulating Africa's position on the financial crisis as well as on the reform of the international financial architecture.

Africa has also responded to the crisis through its regional institutions. For example, the African Development Bank (AfDB) took several actions to enable countries of the region to gain greater access to long-term finance. It established a US$ 1.5 billion Emergency Liquidity Facility to support AfDB eligible countries, it provided a US$ 1.5-billion loan to Botswana for infrastructure development (AfDB, 2010), and it established a US$ 1-billion Trade Finance Facility to improve access to trade credit. These measures have enhanced resource flows to the region at a time when major sources of external finance are drying up.

IV. Seizing opportunities created by the crisis

The financial and economic crisis represents a major setback for African countries because it has eroded the significant gains made in economic performance since the turn of the millennium. It has also led to the drying up of major sources of external finance needed to increase investment and boost growth. Nevertheless, the crisis presents opportunities for the region in two key areas. First, it has generated interest in reform of the international financial architecture and greater awareness of the need to increase Africa's voice and participation in the global governance of institutions that make decisions affecting the lives of people in the region. African countries have expressed concerns about the functioning and governance of these institutions for decades, but with little success in influencing significant reforms. The current crisis has exposed the weaknesses inherent in the present institutional set-up. Consequently, there is growing interest among both developed and developing countries in reforming the international financial architecture as an important step towards building a more democratic system of global governance. African countries have to seize this opportunity to increase their voice and participation in global governance. This requires reconciling sometimes diverse national interests, adopting common positions on key global issues, and forming alliances with other developing countries to increase their bargaining power.

The crisis also presents opportunities for Africa to further diversify its export markets. Most emerging-market economies are recovering faster from the crisis than developed countries. This implies that they may be key drivers of growth in the world economy in the near to medium term. There is likely to be an increase in demand for commodities to support growth in these economies, which could create an opportunity for African countries to diversify their export markets and reduce vulnerability to external shocks emanating from developed countries. It is important, however, that African governments use the proceeds from any increase in demand for their commodities to develop productive capacities and induce structural change so as to reduce their dependence on primary commodities in the medium to long term.

There is growing interest in greening the economy as a way to weather the crisis and achieve sustainable growth. This is likely to lead to a significant shift in policy, government spending and investments from high-carbon to low-carbon activities. In particular, it may induce changes in consumption patterns as well as increase investments in clean technologies, renewable energy and climate-friendly products. Given their factor endowments, African countries have a comparative advantage in the production of renewable energy (e.g. solar power) and should seize any opportunities from potential structural changes that may arise from the growing emphasis on low-carbon sectors and technologies. In this regard, African countries need to increase investment in infrastructure, both at the national and regional levels, to reduce transactions costs of trade and increase their international competitiveness. In addition, they need to improve the business environment, strengthen efforts to boost human capital, and maintain political as well as macroeconomic stability. Support to the region from developed and emerging economies in the form of technology transfer would also greatly boost their growth prospects.

V. Concluding remarks

The global financial and economic crisis has led to the drying up of important sources of development finance in Africa and jeopardized recent efforts to boost growth and reduce poverty in the region. Before the onset of the crisis, the region had made significant progress in economic performance, reflecting the combined effects of improvements in macroeconomic policies, higher commodity prices, better governance and more support by development partners. Although the current crisis was externally induced, African countries responded swiftly and, where possible, adopted countercyclical policies that reduced the potentially negative impact on output. Consequently, several countries now have widening fiscal deficits which they will have to monitor closely to ensure that they do not lead to medium- and long-term macroeconomic instability. There is also the need for African policymakers to make greater efforts towards transforming the structure of their economies to reduce vulnerability to external shocks. In this regard, African countries should prepare themselves to take advantage of the potential opportunities that may arise from the present crisis by investing in national and regional infrastructure development, strengthening efforts to increase human capital, and maintaining political and macroeconomic stability. The challenges are enormous but not insurmountable.

Notes

1   Based on annual data, the 12 OECD countries whose currencies depreciated over the period 2007– 2009 are: Australia (7.3 per cent), Canada (6.3 per cent), Hungary (10.1 per cent), Iceland (93 per cent), Mexico (23.6 per cent), New Zealand (17.6 per cent), Norway (7.4 per cent), Poland (12.8 per cent), the Republic of Korea (37.2 per cent), Sweden (13.2 per cent), Turkey (19 per cent) and the United Kingdom (28.3 per cent).

2   This is likely to be an underestimate given the poor quality of labour market data for
      Africa.
3   This is the proportion of employed who are working but fall below the accepted poverty
      line.

References

AfDB (2010). Africa in the wake of the global financial and economic crisis: Challenges
     ahead and the role of the bank. African Development Bank Policy Briefs on the
     Financial Crisis, no. 1, Tunis.
Agbeyegbe T and Osakwe PN (2005). Real exchange rate volatility and the choice of regimes
     in emerging markets. *Journal of Asian Economics*, 15: 1005–1022.
ASEA (2008). *African Securities Exchanges Association Yearbook*. Cairo, The Egyptian
     Exchange.
Collyns C (2008). The crisis through the lens of history. *Finance and Development*,
     45: 18–20.
Hernandez-Cata E, Fischer S, Khan MS (1998). Africa: is this the turning point? IMF Papers
     on Policy Analysis and Assessment no. 98/6, Washington, DC.
Honohan P and Beck T (2007). *Making Finance Work for Africa.* Washington, DC, World
     Bank.
ILO (2010). *Global Employment Trends*. Geneva, International Labour Office.
IMF (2009). Sub-Saharan Africa: Weathering the storm. *Regional Economic Outlook*.
     Washington, DC, October.
Kaberuka D (2009). Start this engine: Africa's policymakers should prepare for global
     recovery by priming their private sectors. *Finance and Development*, 54–55, June.
Ltaifa N, Kaendera S, Dixit S (2009). Impact of the global financial crisis on exchange rates
     and policies in sub-Saharan Africa. IMF Africa Department Working Paper no. 09/3,
     Washington, DC.
Osakwe PN and Schembri LL (2002). Real effects of collapsing exchange rate regimes: an
     application to Mexico. *Journal of International Economics*, 57: 299–325.
Pisani-Ferry J and Santos I (2009). Reshaping the global economy. *Finance and Development*,
     46: 8–12.
UNCTAD (2010). *Global Investment Trends Monitor*. Geneva, 19 January.
United Nations (2009). *World Economic Situation and Prospects 2010* (pre-release). New
     York, United Nations.
World Bank (2000). Can Africa claim the 21st century? Washington, DC, World Bank.

LOOKING FORWARD

POLICY AGENDA

THE REPORT OF THE STIGLITZ COMMISSION: A SUMMARY AND COMMENT

Alejandro Márquez

Abstract

The Stiglitz Commission's Report is summarized with a view to presenting a reader-friendly account of its main ideas for readers who lack the time to read the entire report. The chapter reproduces the structure of the report with a summary of each of its sections, and concludes with a final comment. The report discusses, inter alia, the role of market fundamentalist doctrines and global imbalances as sources of the latest global economic and financial crisis. It views the crisis as just another symptom (as were the energy and food crises that preceded it) of a malfunctioning international financial and economic governance structure in need of reform.

Introduction

The Report of the Commission of Experts of the President of the UN General Assembly on Reforms of the International Monetary and Financial System (2009), written by a commission chaired by Joseph Stiglitz (more commonly referred to as the Report of the Stiglitz Commission) contains powerful insights. It was mandated by the President of the sixty-third session of the United Nations General Assembly with the mission to diagnose the causes of the crisis, evaluate its impacts (focusing on developing countries) and propose an agenda for reforming the international financial and economic architecture.

The report is the result of 11 months of collaborative work by a commission of 17 members, plus one rapporteur and two special representatives from 18 countries. The President of the United Nations General Assembly, d'Escotto Brockmann, who commissioned the report, could not have chosen a better suited person to chair the commission. Joseph Stiglitz, winner of the Nobel Prize in 2001, is one of the most famous and respected economists of our time. He is a particularly well-known critic of the international financial institutions and the World Trade Organization (WTO), having presented his diagnoses of their shortcomings and proposals for reforms in his bestseller books, such as *Globalization and its Discontents* (2002), *Fair Trade for All: How Can Trade Promote Development* (2005, with Andrew Charlton as his co-author) and *Making Globalization Work* (2006). The other members of the commission represented all the continents, with a majority from the South, and comprised academic economists, politicians and senior managers in leading institutions.[1] The report is not an academic paper, but rather an economic and political analysis along with policy statements. As with many such reports involving experts from a variety of backgrounds, this report is a compilation of many ideas, in some instances presented somewhat haphazardly. To provide a better understanding of the report, a pocket book has been published recently (Stiglitz, 2010).

The latest financial crisis could be used as a catalyst for undertaking many needed reforms of the existing international financial order. This is the basic message of the report. However, one of its drawbacks, as with many other similar policy documents, is that it is too long and written in a style that limits its potential readership. The purpose of this chapter is to present a summary of the report's main ideas using less technical language.

The structure of this chapter, which follows that of the report, contains a summary of each of the report's sections. It concludes with this author's comments on the report.

I. Report's introduction

Causes and consequences of the crisis

The way in which the crisis that originated in the United States in 2007 has spread throughout the world shows that the international financial governance structure lacks the appropriate tools and mechanisms to deal with such situations. This is especially problematic for developing countries. For them the crisis can be seen as a negative externality, since they were not responsible for generating it but are now suffering from its adverse effects, reflected in lower output and employment. Within these countries, the impacts on the poorer strata will be long lasting if social spending has to be cut because of the adverse conditions. The seriousness of this situation is better understood with the following example: if, because of temporary cuts in social spending, some infants start to suffer from malnutrition, this temporal shock could affect them for their entire lives. Thus, what started as a financial crisis and spread as an economic crisis to developing countries, could produce a social crisis with long-lasting effects in both developed and developing countries, if proper action is not taken.

To ensure that reforms to the international financial architecture reflect the needs of developing countries, changes in its governance structure should allow them to have more voice, at least to reflect their ever-growing economic importance, which until now has not been taken into account. Any proposals for reform of the governance structure of international finance will also need to address the issue of how best to handle recovery from the actual crisis. This means that reforms not only should aim at achieving long-term objectives, such as a more equitable and sustainable growth path and the creation of decent jobs, but they should also address more short-term problems affecting global poverty, such as food security and insufficient financial aid.

It should be emphasized that this is not only a financial crisis, but an economic one too. Even though it started with disruptions in the financial sector, these were in part due to macroeconomic problems, such as the building up of global imbalances and growing income inequalities between and within countries.

Policy responses to past crises

Past global crises had long-lasting impacts in many countries, especially on their poorer citizens, because one of the first responses by the affected countries was to cut social spending. The reduced levels of social expenditure remained in place even after recovery, and, coupled with other "reforms" such as liberalization of capital accounts, this prepared the ground for the next crisis. The recovery process was guided by the international financial institutions (IFIs), which were created to resolve such issues, not to worsen them, as unfortunately was the case during the Asian crisis of the late 1990s.

As a consequence of the flawed policy recommendations of the IFIs, many of the affected countries decided to embark on their own independent strategies, to prevent future crises, including aggressive foreign reserve accumulation. However, this created negative externalities at the global level because of its impact on global imbalances.

The global dimension of the latest crisis calls for a global response

The danger of countries embarking on unilateral strategies to deal with the crisis without any form of international coordination could lead to a sub-optimal level of stimulus spending in rich countries and perhaps no stimulus package at all in the poorer ones. This would be the case if national governments, fearing that some of the resources of their stimulus packages might leak through imports from other countries, would be compelled to reduce the amount of the stimulus and resort to protectionist measures to ensure that most of the money spent benefits the local economy. Such a move would hamper global economic recovery, and indeed, this was precisely what deepened the Great Depression of the 1930s. This is an issue that should be seriously pondered since the G-20 had pledged in 2008 not to engage in protectionism. However, by 2009 almost all of its members broke their promises, engaging in protectionist practices, even against developing countries.

The amount of subsidies that the financial and non-financial sectors in developed countries have received because of the crisis is also a problematic issue at the global level, since most developing countries cannot even dream of matching such a level of support for their industries. This gives an advantage to developed-country firms and creates more or less the same effects as protectionist policies. For example, the assisted banks are encouraged to increase domestic lending at the expense of lending to developing countries. Therefore it is urgent to increase the level of funding that also contributes to stimulus packages in developing countries for helping their financial sectors and allowing these countries to implement countercyclical policies, especially with respect to social spending.

However, the way resources are provided to developing countries to help them cope with crises has to be reformed, since the conditionalities attached to such assistance by the IFIs in previous crises have often done more harm than good. The reforms should not allow these institutions to require the implementation of procyclical policies in the aftermath of crises, which result in permanent cuts to social spending, or to require reforms that could increase instability, such as capital-account liberalization.

Basic principles for reforms

Collective action, both domestic and global, is needed to reduce the influence of markets in the financial, economic and ecologic spheres, and to increase government intervention, since one of the causes of the latest crisis was excessive deregulation, especially in the financial sector.

Policies implemented in developed countries to deal with the crisis should not exacerbate global imbalances. These imbalances could worsen since many developing countries will not be able to implement comparable countercyclical policies, because of lack of resources or because of the conditionalities imposed on them if they request assistance from the IFIs. If this issue is not addressed, the future growth of many developing countries could be badly affected.

Impact on developing countries

The borrowing constraints of most developing countries during the crisis may force their governments to pursue procyclical fiscal policies, since their tax revenues will fall forcing them to cut some spending. Not only is it becoming more difficult for these countries to access international finance, but also major international financial agents are repatriating their capital out of them. Many governments are unable to prevent this because of past binding bilateral or multilateral agreements which liberalized capital flows.

It is in the interest of global recovery for the IMF to help developing countries adopt countercyclical policies, as the effects of procyclical policies by developing countries will not only adversely affect these countries but also the overall global economy. If the IMF does not pursue this objective, these countries might feel encouraged to further accumulate international reserves, a policy that would continue to feed the global imbalances, thereby impeding the global recovery process. The global economic system would also be affected by policy responses of the developed countries, which could hurt developing economies because of the asymmetries in the availability of financial resources in the two groups of countries.

II. Macroeconomic issues and perspectives

A global response to the crisis needs to take into consideration the constraints of the most vulnerable developing countries. Global coordination is also important since it can enhance the effects of domestic policies. In addition, when designing domestic policies to cope with the crisis, governments should avoid implementing policies that may have a beggar-thy-neighbour effect. Lastly, since many developing countries do not have the resources necessary to adopt policies to cope with the crisis, official development assistance needs to be increased.

Sources of the crisis

The focus on the origins of the crisis should not overstress policy failures and omit market failures. The financial markets "mismanaged risks and misallocated capital" (p. 24). Had the markets done their job correctly, low capital costs should have led to increases in productivity and not to increases in inequality, as happened in the United States.

Part of the explanation of why this crisis occurred in the first place lies in the *laissez-faire* doctrine that has inspired economic, financial and macroeconomic reforms for several decades. The doctrine is based on an almost blind belief in the benefits of markets and a distrust of government intervention.

The greater intensity with which the process of globalization has been pursued has also contributed to an increase in the spread of the negative effects of the turmoil throughout the world.

Some developing countries reinforced their policies of reserve accumulation, which they had initiated after the Asian crisis to serve as a buffer against financial volatility. This volatility was a particular threat because of the unsustainable growth of consumption in the United States, which grew faster than incomes and was encouraged by an explosive combination of low interest rates, poor risk mismanagement and inadequate financial regulations.

Among the negative effects of globalization, not only has it increased the volatility of GDP growth but also income inequality in various ways. As mentioned before, in developed countries, particularly in the United States, inequality has risen, and developing countries have also been experiencing a similar trend. Inequality has increased among different groups of developing countries as well as between developed and developing countries. This trend has affected the evolution of the crisis.

Within developed countries, this trend of increasing inequality has been exacerbated by the implementation of a less progressive tax structure, leading in some cases to a tax reduction of 10 percentage points for the top tax bracket. This partly explains the increase in public debt in some OECD countries, especially in Europe, where countries have had to finance their social welfare systems in a context of stagnating gross domestic product (GDP).

The recent oil price boom, exacerbated by financial speculation, had negative effects on the terms of trade of many countries. It also disproportionally hurt the poorest segments of their populations because of its effect on food prices, which also rose due to a greater emphasis on growing crops for biofuels instead of food crops.

The institutions responsible for global macroeconomic management failed to prevent the build-up of global imbalances. It could even be argued that the global imbalances, concretely reflected in massive international reserve accumulation, were a direct consequence of the mismanagement of institutions like the IMF during the Asian and other emerging-market crises of the 1990s (p. 27). During these crises, the high political and economic costs that countries helped by the IMF had to pay (in terms of accepting harsh conditionalities such as procyclical fiscal policies) induced them to pursue unilateral policies that would protect them from future external shocks, so as to avoid having to resort to IMF assistance in the future.

The inclination of emerging-market economies to accumulate reserves was strengthened by their strong GDP growth fuelled by credit expansion in the United States and rising commodity prices.

A globally coordinated response

Countries cannot export their crises by devaluating their currencies as they did at the end of the 1990s, because the current crisis is a global one.

A globally coordinated response to the crisis needs to address the challenges posed by possible free-riding by small open economies, and a lower level of fiscal stimuli than what is needed – because of debt concerns – as well as an emerging protectionist bias. A global stimulus would make the recovery process less fragile. On the other hand, protectionist measures by developed countries would have a disproportionately harmful effect on developing countries.

Monetary policy

Because interest rates are near zero, and therefore cannot be reduced any further in the United States and in some other developed countries, the burden of the crisis response has to fall on fiscal expansion. Nevertheless, there is room for credit expansion, even if it means direct intervention by governments, since banks are proving to be excessively cautious following the collapse of a number of large banking institutions. Lastly, these conventional and unconventional monetary interventions should not raise concerns that they will increase the risk of inflation, at least until employment and incomes show signs of recovery.

Bailouts

Many developed countries provided bailouts for financial and non-financial enterprises in response to the financial crisis. These bailouts have to be considered in terms of the desired future development of the financial industry. In order to avoid crises like the latest one, there needs to be greater emphasis on the role of financial intermediation, in particular for small and medium-sized enterprises (SMEs). Consideration should also be given to reducing the predominance of the financial sector.

One of the motivations for writing this report was to stress the idea that badly designed bailout plans can produce a negative externality for developing countries, since such bailouts can divert capital flows away from these countries. A new design for the international financial architecture should provide for better risk management, more stable sources of funding and more credit to SMEs in developing countries to improve their long-term growth potential. Unfortunately, past experience has shown that the opposite occurs. That is, the international financial system has produced procyclical flows of capital that have resulted in developing countries bearing the greatest risk, especially through the exchange rate risk.

The role of central banks

One questionable traditional belief conditioning the behaviour of central banks has been that price stability is a necessary and almost sufficient condition for achieving "economic growth and financial stability" (p. 35).

If insurance markets in the private and public sector are insufficiently developed in some developed countries, the situation in developing countries is even worse, especially when coping with exchange rate risks. This is one of the reasons why countries in which central banks that also intervened in the foreign exchange market and controlled capital flows have fared better that those where central banks focused more strictly on targeting inflation.

The effects that a tighter monetary policy or changes in administered prices have had on the consumer price index when the source of inflation is imported have not proved to be sufficient to counter inflation; instead a tight monetary policy in such a case has dampened economic growth in many developing countries.

Economic and financial stability cannot be achieved if central banks do not prevent the formation of bubbles in asset markets, and if monetary policy is not better coordinated with fiscal and social policy.

Risks and policy trade-offs

Diagnosing the presence of bubbles in an economy is not an easy task, but this is not a sufficient reason for not trying to prevent their formation through policy measures.

The structural change in the financial sector in the past few decades, with the increasing importance of securitization and excessive leverage and a diminished role of common bread and butter banking, created problems that generated the crisis. Financial sector reform should give priority to re-establishing a well-functioning system, and should try to insulate the real sector from the negative externalities of a malfunctioning financial system.

Impacts on developing countries

Financial protectionism is another negative effect of financial globalization that appears to be exempt from sanctions by the global governance structure for finance and trade.

Developing countries cannot compete with the credit guarantees being offered in developed countries, which have reinforced capital repatriation (p. 39). This is the consequence of offering banks an insurance against credit defaults stemming only from firms in their own country. The fact that the richer countries can offer their firms more credit guarantees contributes to further disparities in the international arena.

The ability of developing countries to pursue countercyclical fiscal policies is also limited by market forces and the current state of global finance. Constraints on the ability to raise revenues domestically are compounded by limitations on accessing external resources due to the unwillingness of foreign sources to lend in the current juncture, unless at high interest rates.

In addition to financial protectionism, there has been a wave of more traditional protectionism in the form of bailouts for non-financial firms, which developing countries are not able to match. In some cases, developing countries that have signed some type of preferential agreements are required to treat foreign-owned firms on their territory as domestically owned ones. This further reduces the scarce resources that such governments may have at their disposal to help their real sectors.

Another problem that has to be solved at the global level is that, while developed countries are applying countercyclical fiscal policies and bailouts, developing countries that had to seek assistance from the IFIs have once again been forced to apply procyclical measures. This contributes to increasing the risk differential between developed and developing countries instead of decreasing it. To build a fairer world, "counter-cyclical policies, social protection measures, infrastructure development, and credit guarantees" (p. 40) should also be policy options for developing countries.

Funding for developing countries

Funding with low conditionalities should be made available to developing countries to help them cope with the effects of developed countries' protectionist measures. It is important to state that the current level of funding for developing countries to help them deal with shocks is insufficient. However, an increase in funding should not be at the expense of official development assistance (ODA). Any reduction of ODA could lead to unnecessary increases in poverty and the undermining of global solidarity. It could even harm the global recovery process. Additional funding could come from the emission of additional Special Drawing Rights (SDRs) or the transfer of part of them from developed countries to developing countries.

III. Reforming global regulation to enhance global economic stability

The economic crisis and the failure of financial market regulation

The basic functions of a financial market are to "manage risk, allocate capital, and mobilize savings, all at the lowest possible transaction costs" (p. 47). However, financial markets were not working well in many developed countries, especially in the United States, where the crisis originated. This is particularly worrisome since the weight of the financial sector in GDP in many of these economies is quite considerable, and the sector had been growing at unsustainably rapid rates, a trend that is highly correlated with the risk of financial crises.

The debt burden caused by this crisis in developing countries that are able and willing to help their financial sectors will impair their growth potential, because resources that could have been invested in "education, health, infrastructure, and technology" (p. 47) will no longer be available.

This crisis will exacerbate inequality, because even before its onset, compensation schemes in the financial sector increased inequalities, and after the crisis the biggest burden will be borne by the poorest and less educated citizens.

Re-engineering financial market regulation is of the utmost importance. Advances in economic theory have shown that financial markets produce outcomes that are far from efficient because of the presence of informational asymmetries.

Regulatory problems

Financial markets cease to be efficient once the implications of imperfect and asymmetric information are taken into account. This theoretical breakthrough is also backed by historical and econometric studies that show that financial markets do not self-correct, experience market failures and can be a source of systemic risk that can affect an entire economy. As the regulatory regime has neither kept pace with advances in theory nor with financial innovations, it was ill-equipped to prevent the current crisis.

A growing understanding of the need for regulation

New financial instruments require new regulations. But even if new regulations are put in place, regulators should believe in them in order to implement them effectively (p. 49). In the United States, there was a general mood of distrust in the usefulness of such regulations and this impaired the development of an effective regulatory regime.

The emergence of financial institutions that are considered "too big to fail" has made it utopian to think that whenever such an institution is in trouble, the government will not try to enforce a bailout in one way or another. Since financial institutions are well aware of this, the only way to reduce the resultant systemic moral hazard is to couple such bailouts with an effective regulatory regime that would prevent financial institutions from engaging in excessive risk-taking.

Regulatory structures and institutions

Discussions about financial regulation need to take place multilaterally, since, as the past and present crises have shown, in a financially and economically globalized world problems in medium or big economies can easily spread throughout the whole system.

Reforms to the financial system should be comprehensive. They should involve micro issues concerning the behaviour of financial institutions but they should also deal with macro issues such as the stability of the financial sector and how it affects macroeconomic stability.

However, discussions should not be limited only to regulation; rather, they should focus on the broader subject of financial policy, of which regulation is just a part. Financial policy can be understood as State interventions that will help align the private benefits that the financial sector seeks with the social benefits that it should produce. Thus it should deal with issues such as making the financial market accessible to everybody and creating needed markets, such as student loans.

Governments should compare the costs of regulations with their benefits. A given regulatory framework can be costly, but, as the present crisis shows, flawed or incomplete regulations can result in even higher costs to society.

The argument that more regulation will reduce the pace of innovation in the financial sector may be self-defeating, since innovations in this sector have increased systemic risk in recent years.

The following sections present some principles of financial market regulation.

The purposes and general principles of financial regulation

One of the reasons why there are special regulations for the financial sector relating to consumer and investor protection is that the services offered by financial institutions cannot be evaluated easily shortly before, during or shortly after they are provided.

Regulations have to focus on predatory lending, as this crisis has shown. Governments need to protect individuals with a low capacity for assessing the risk associated with some investments against financial institutions that may be tempted to benefit from such individuals.

Because the core activities of banks (i.e. to hold individuals' deposits and give loans to companies) are of systemic importance, regulation of these institutions needs to be more comprehensive than that of non-financial firms. However, during the build-up to the crisis, these core activities became less relevant due to the emergence of a "shadow banking system" (p. 54). This system was pioneered by some banks in the form of off-balance-sheet entities, which, although performing very similar activities to those of banks with important systemic effects, were not subject to the same types of regulations as deposit taking banks. The cause of the crisis was strongly related to the failures of such shadow institutions.

The key role of trust and confidence and the role of regulation

The role of confidence in the financial system is crucial for its functioning. Without it, individuals will not agree to lend capital to financial institutions or will start taking their money out of them. Confidence needs to be restored by a regulation that allows a stronger presence of the government in the sector, since experience shows that self-regulation and private risk-rating agencies have not prevented financial institutions from trying to hide their risk positions from regulators and investors alike.

Transparency and incentives

The remuneration scheme for executives based on stock options and regulatory arbitrage are mechanisms that create incentives for reducing transparency. Moreover, much of the damage from the crisis was caused by off-balance-sheet investment vehicles put in place to make profits from regulatory arbitrage.

Following the idea that regulation should not only assure transparency but should also promote it, increases in capital adequacy requirements should be implemented for banks paying their executives with stock options. This would increase transparency by reducing the incentives for such practices.

Boundaries of financial regulation

The tradition of having different regulations and regulators just because the names of the instruments and institutions are different has to change. For instance, when engaging in similar activities, deposit-taking banks and non-deposit-taking banks should be regulated under similar rules and regulators. Financial regulation must go beyond this traditional shortcoming and be designed and applied in a comprehensive way, taking into consideration the economic functions of the instruments and institutions dealt with (pp. 60 ff).

Special attention must be given to the coherence of different regulatory frameworks, both at the national and international levels, to reduce the risk of regulatory arbitrage. This coherence of the regulatory framework needs to be focused more carefully on "systemically important activities, instruments, and institutions" (p. 61).

Moreover, special attention should be given to institutions where governments are bearing explicit or implicit risks, for instance through the provision of deposit insurance or when the size of an institution can create systemic risks that are prevented by bailouts or debt nationalizations. The systemic importance of such an institution should be clearly defined according to "leverage, size, exposure to retail investors, and/or degree of correlation with other activities" (p. 61).

Micro-prudential versus macro-prudential regulation

Micro-prudential regulation, when aimed at consumer protection, refers to protecting consumers from financial institutions, especially those consumers who find it difficult to identify the risk of the instruments offered to them. On the other hand, macro-prudential regulation should focus on overseeing the entire banking system, to check systemic risk indicators such as "leverage, the failure of large, inter-connected institutions, and systemically important behaviour and instruments and their interactions with the economic cycle" (p. 61). Both regulations should seek to enhance macroeconomic stability.

Regulations should cover all financial institutions and instruments, even if, as noted above, more emphasis should be placed on regulating the systemically important ones. A comprehensive regulation would diminish the risk of future financial crises, since identifying sources of systemic risk is difficult *a priori*. Another benefit of this approach to regulation is that it would tackle regulatory arbitrage.

IV. International institutions

The need for new global economic governance

The fact that the response of the IFIs to the global financial and economic crisis has been inadequate is reason enough for a serious debate on reforming them. Furthermore, these institutions did little to prevent, or even promoted, the conditions that ultimately led to the crisis.

In order to function properly, the IFIs have to restore their credibility *vis-à-vis* developing countries. To achieve this, they need to give developing countries a fair share of voice and representation in their governance. The fair share of voice should not be measured solely according to their economic weight, but even if this were to be the only guiding principle, it should be noted that their economic weight now is far more important than it was in the 1940s, when the governance structure of most IFIs was created based on this principle.

The current financial and economic crisis is not the only challenge the world has faced in recent years. This crisis follows previous food and energy crises, which severely affected many developing countries, and is taking place in the context of an increase in inequality within and among countries as well as in the context of climate change. All these interconnected challenges pose a threat to the traditional pattern of globalization.

Globalization can be characterized as being market-led, and thus requires a corresponding development of the international governance structure, which, until now, has been lagging behind the economic integration process. This process has increased the role of international externalities that need to be addressed, as well as the role of public goods that need to be provided at the global level. In this sense, a very important public good is the stability of the international economic system.

The existing system

The current international economic governance structure is based on three institutions created after the Second World War: the IMF, the World Bank and the WTO (successor to the General Agreement on Tariffs and Trade, GATT). These three specialized agencies, two of them under the United Nations umbrella (the IMF and the World Bank), were created in the hope that their coordinated efforts would bring sustained growth. Their activities were complemented by specialized United Nations agencies such as the International Labour Organization (ILO) and the Food and Agriculture Organization of the United Nations (FAO).

Apart from these institutions, exclusive groups of nations – within the G-7, G-8 or G-20 – have also attempted to deal with the governance challenges posed by globalization. Even though the G-7 has been involved in many negotiations with developing countries, the main weakness of these types of exclusive groups is that they leave out too many countries that should also have a say in global matters. The future governance structure should encompass all countries – developed, developing and least developed – and encourage exchanges with existing forums.

Global Economic Coordination Council

The segmented landscape of international institutions today is in need of overall coordination, under what the report calls a Global Economic Coordination Council (p. 87). Such an institution would be able to grasp the big picture, keeping an eye on major trends affecting the global economy and the adequacy of the world's economic governance structure to face the challenges posed by such trends.

International panel of experts

Since the creation of the Global Economic Coordination Council could be conceived as a long-term goal, the first step to achieve it should be the creation of an international panel of experts that would be charged with identifying and following trends that influence global systemic risks. This panel could also start to analyse the global economic governance structure with a view to identifying its deficiencies.

The panel of experts should be of a multidisciplinary nature in order to be able to identify social and environmental challenges as well. The members should also be representative of the different geographic regions of the world and of countries at different levels of development. Lastly, the panel should not perform research on its own but rather tap into the existing knowledge pool of subjects it will be focusing on.

The mandate and governance of the proposed Global Economic Coordination Council

In the long-term, the Global Economic Coordination Council should be part of the United Nations system, with equal status to that of the General Assembly and the Security Council. It would be responsible for analysing global risks and providing leadership whenever collective action is needed to solve issues. It could also coordinate the actions of existing global institutions and promote their accountability.

The International Monetary Fund

The IMF, a very important part of the global financial architecture, is mandated to ensure global financial and economic stability. One major problem with this institution is that its policy recommendations have been embedded in the market fundamentalist ideology, which is one of the causes of the current crisis. The other major obstacle that impairs its effective functioning is its governance structure, in which developing countries have less than their fair share of voice, as already pointed out by the G-20. Therefore, these two problems need to be addressed in reforms of this institution.

Governance of IFIs

As already noted, there is a growing consensus that developing countries should have a greater voice in IFIs, in proportion to their economic weight but also to their role as recipients of the services provided to them, especially in the case of the least developed countries.

The voting mechanism in the IMF also needs to be revised. The double majority condition (i.e. that a motion needs the approval of 85 per cent of the voting power and 60 per cent of the voting members to pass) required for revising the Articles of Agreement, should also be required for the selection of key posts (such as those of the Managing Director and of the chair of the

IMF Committee), as well as for approving important policy measures and for access to lending. Such a reform would strengthen the sense of ownership of the member countries.

In addition, the IMF should ensure the highest level of transparency in its operations.

V. International financial innovations

The global reserve system[2]

The prevailing dominance of the dollar as a global reserve currency and as an international means of payment dates back to the time of the Bretton Woods agreement, when the only currency that remained convertible to gold was the dollar. It maintained its dominance even after the collapse of this exchange rate system in 1971, when the United States Government decided to relinquish the dollar's gold convertibility and a system of floating exchange rates developed, which allowed the emergence of some other competing reserve currencies. This post-Bretton Woods system has "proven to be unstable, incompatible with global full employment, and inequitable" (p. 109).

The global exchange rate system has a "deflationary bias" (p. 109) because there is more pressure on countries with a deficit in their current account to correct it than for countries with a surplus. Of course, the exception to this trend is the United States, which is under no pressure to correct its current-account deficit because it is the issuer of the main global reserve currency. This, combined with the greater mobility of capital flows since the introduction of the global flexible exchange rate regime, has increased exchange rate volatility and the instability of the global financial system.

To prevent recurrent balance-of-payments crises, that became more common after the collapse of the Bretton Woods system, many developing countries chose a strategy of accumulating large amounts of international reserves denominated in hard currencies. This self-insurance mechanism led to a resource transfer towards the United States and other developed countries.

To address all these issues many observers have proposed a revival of Keynes's idea of creating a global reserve currency issued by a global central bank. This is a feasible idea, which the international community should consider implementing to ensure a stable growth path secured by a stable global reserve system.

Instability

Whenever agents start to lose confidence in the dollar and in its role as a global reserve currency because of an excessively soft monetary policy, the United States Federal Reserve reacts by sharply increasing interest rates, as happened in the late 1970s and early 1980s. This affects the global exchange rate system in a contractionary way, with heavy repercussions on developing countries.

If many countries were to decide to have a current-account surplus, this would result in declining world income unless the United States agreed to being the "deficit country of last resort" (p. 111) and increased its deficit even more.

Self-insurance and deflationary bias

The procyclicality of capital flows promoted debt accumulation in hard currencies in developing countries during boom periods, financing sustained increases in current-account deficits. This situation often culminated in balance-of-payments crises and domestic financial crises in the deficit countries.

To avoid this, especially after the Asian crisis in the late 1990s, developing countries have accumulated large amounts of international reserves as a self-insurance policy in the absence of an appropriate international financial and economic architecture to prevent or address such crises.

If proper measures are not taken to help developing countries cope with the current crisis, the risk of reinforcing the trend towards reserve accumulation will increase and with it a surge in protectionist trade policies and beggar-thy-neighbour exchange rate policies, which will hamper the recovery process.

With the existence of a global reserve currency, not tied to the external position of a particular country, the excessive liquidity problems associated with the dollar as the main reserve currency would be less likely to occur. On the other hand, such a global reserve system also has to be designed in a way that would reduce incentives for currency reserve accumulation and thus reduce global imbalances.

Sovereign debt defaults and the existing system

Many developing countries have experienced sovereign debt defaults since the 1980s. This can be considered a major external challenge to their development because such defaults have translated into long periods of increasing poverty and unemployment. As is the case for developed countries in the current crisis, many of the previous debt crises involved private debt that was "nationalized" because the indebted financial institutions or other companies were judged "too big to fail" (p. 121).

The bargaining processes during these debt defaults often produced insufficient write-offs – at least not enough to insure a sustainable debt path – and thus often led to follow-up crises.

An International Debt Restructuring Court

Debt work-out processes should be based on the "principles of human-centred development, of sustainability, and of equity in the treatment of debtors and their creditors" (p. 123). This is why an "International Debt Restructuring Court" (p. 124) is needed at the global level similar to such courts that already exist at the national level.

Its functions could go beyond dealing with sovereign debt defaults by also considering private-debt-related issues that involve several jurisdictions in order to prevent a home country bias in work-out processes. This has been an important issue in the current crisis.

Innovative risk management structures

The volatility and procyclicality of international capital flows has necessitated measures to enable developing countries to better manage the openness of their financial sectors and thus avoid feeding boom-bust cycles, currency and maturity mismatches as well as debt default episodes. Some examples of innovative ways of providing finance to developing countries include bonds linked to GDP growth and commodity prices, or the development of local currency bond markets.

IFIs such as multilateral development banks should play the role of market makers to help develop these innovative instruments. Since they would generate more social than private benefits in the initial stages, they would not be developed by the private sector. The successful experience of the World Bank as a market maker when it introduced carbon credits in accordance with a proposal in the Kyoto Protocol could serve as an example of how such a proposal could be implemented (p. 127). The World Bank or other regional development banks could extend loans to developing countries, and the servicing of those loans could be linked to their GDP performance. Thereafter, the banks could sell the loans in the international financial markets either directly or in a securitized way.

Innovative sources of financing

The difficulty in meeting funding commitments for development assistance and in allocating resources for global and regional public goods has produced a set of innovative ideas relating to the provision of such needed resources.

One potential source of revenues is domestic taxes raised for achieving global objectives. The objectives and design of these taxes should be internationally coordinated. Other sources of revenue could come from taxes on carbon dioxide emissions or from auctioning emission permits. Such a policy would have a dual effect: on the one hand it would reduce emissions contributing to climate change in developed countries, and on the other hand it would enable an increase of funding for development assistance in developing countries that could also be used to help mitigate climate change in those countries.

VI. The report's concluding comments

Causes of the crisis: failed policies and misguided philosophies

Finding a sustainable solution to this crisis (i.e. a strong recovery coupled with lower risk of a follow-up crisis) requires a sound diagnosis of its causes. The diagnosis made in this report stresses that the main cause of this crisis lay in failed policies, based on misguided philosophies that allowed its rapid spread from the United States to the rest of the world.

Apart from domestic institutional deficiencies, shortcomings in the global financial and economic governance structure played a major role in the crisis. These institutions, guided by market fundamentalism, failed to foresee the build-up of the crisis. Indeed, they forced countries to follow policies – such as promoting the "export of toxic products, flawed regulatory philosophies, and deficient institutional practices" (p. 132) – that contributed to the eruption of the crisis and its spreading around the world. This market fundamentalism which guided the policies of the IFIs, predominantly the IMF, has posed a challenge for most developing countries.

What has been done

A worsening of the latest crisis was prevented by many governments correctly reacting in a coordinated way by implementing stimulus packages. It is worth emphasizing that many of these packages included a "green" component, thereby addressing both short- and long-term challenges.

What needs to be done

A sustainable way out of the crisis requires policies that address both short- and long-term challenges, many of them related to achieving more social equity, promoting welfare in developing countries and taking into consideration environmental protection. This report has viewed this crisis as a symptom – similar to the previous energy and food crises – of a more complex set of failures that need to be addressed at the global level.

Some common themes of analysis throughout the report

This is a crisis that has to be seen as a global one, and thus its challenges have to be addressed at the global level. The incentives for some developing countries to accumulate foreign reserves in an unsustainable way resulted from a flawed global financial and economic governance structure.

The report also stresses that there have been double standards in policy advice for developing countries compared with how developed countries have reacted to the crisis: while developing countries going through financial crises in the past were forced by IFIs to follow procyclical policies, developed countries during this crisis applied fully-fledged countercyclical policies. Even if, in their response to the latest crisis, some developing countries are also applying some fiscal stimuli and rescue packages, the differences in resources between North and South make the global effects highly asymmetrical. Moreover, they have led to capital flowing away from developing countries that have implemented sound macroeconomic policies, and towards developed countries that were at the origin of the crisis.

Another recurrent theme throughout the analysis is that financial and economic globalization has outpaced existing global institutional capacity to cope with or prevent its adverse effects. If the global institutions cannot be reformed to cope with this challenge, new ones should be created. One important international institution that is missing is an independent and politically neutral one that could continuously monitor the fitness of the international financial and economic governance structure.

Some key recommendations

Helping developing countries is both a matter of global solidarity and self-interest. Another debt crisis in these countries is not desirable, and providing assistance with procyclical conditionalities attached would only unfairly increase risks for these countries, while countercyclical policies are being pursued in industrialized nations. In case some developing countries face difficulties, both debtors and creditors should be able to count on a re-engineered sovereign debt default work-out system, as proposed in this report.

Some of the proposals of this report overlap with those made by the G-20, but there are also some differences, which mainly concern scarcely discussed but crucial issues, such as the deficiencies of the global reserve system, the global imbalances in trade and capital flows, the problems posed by financial institutions considered "too big to fail" and the importance of giving developing countries more voice in the IFIs.

The goal of this report has been to convince the international society that there is room for improving how the global economy works, especially in promoting well-being in developing countries. Part of this goal could be achieved by institutionalizing the coordination of economic policy at the global level through a proposed Global Economic Coordination Council. A precondition for a peaceful world is the strengthening of global solidarity at times of environmental or economic crises.

The United Nations is the only global body, comprising all countries, that has the legitimacy to deal with the broad economic, social and environmental challenges discussed in this report. It should not be forgotten that this institution was created in response to severe crises in the past, such as the Great Depression and the Second World War. Therefore this crisis represents an opportunity to increase its role in the international financial and economic governance structure.

VII. Comment

The report of the Stiglitz Commission, in line with its mandate, attempts to analyse the latest economic and financial crisis and formulates policy alternatives from the viewpoint of developing countries. The latter comprise around 150 countries from three continents which are economically, politically, socially and culturally heterogeneous. To find common agreement among so many disparate voices is virtually impossible. Nonetheless, it is important to articulate developmental aspects in the debates about the causes of the crisis and the necessary policy changes needed. The majority of developing countries, in particular the least developed, are not represented in the G-20, and normally play only a marginal role in most supranational institutions. It is to the credit of this report that it reflects their common interests. Some key proposals of the report, especially the call for new global institutions to better manage a development-friendly globalization process, to overhaul the global currency system and to contain global imbalances, are not found in the policy statements of the G-20 or in those of other influential entities. Also, the normative values to which the authors adhere go beyond what is found in other policy documents and economic analyses. They display a commitment to development, greater equity, global solidarity and peaceful cooperation of countries, irrespective of political, ethnic or cultural backgrounds.

The report provides an incisive diagnosis of why the crisis occurred. The link between market fundamentalist doctrines at the domestic level and within IFIs, which led to the intensification of globalization since the end of the 1970s and to improperly handled and frequent economic, social and environmental crises throughout the world, is clearly stated. The role of global imbalances in this crisis, resulting from the decision of some developing countries to accumulate excessive international reserves as a means of self-insurance against global instability is also clearly presented. What is not clearly stated is the weight of certain large surplus countries such as China, Japan and other Asian economies, as well as Germany,[3] and how their actions have crowded out exports from other developing countries.

Since the report clearly states that the United States was at the epicentre of the crisis, it should also have mentioned which countries – developed and emerging – embarked on a policy of unsustainable surplus accumulation.

The report advocates a greater voice for developing countries in the international arena, which will clearly find support, especially from many observers from these countries. However, it should not be forgotten that some of these countries disregard human rights domestically, and discriminate against political and ethnic minorities. None of this is mentioned in the report even though it deals not only with economic issues, but also with social and environmental ones.

The report tends to avoid naming specific countries or institutions directly so that readers need to read between the lines. Some parts of the report are vague or couched in overly diplomatic language, and the report is not well structured and contains some redundancies. Nonetheless, the fact that the report will help propagate key ideas more than compensates for these rather minor shortcomings. Many of the ideas need further elaboration and research, apart from academic and political discourses, but they do set an agenda for global governance for the years to come.

Notes

1   The Commission members were: Andrei Bougrov (Russian Federation), Yousef Boutros-Ghali (Egypt), Jean-Paul Fitoussi (France), Charles A. Goodhart (United Kingdom), Robert Johnson (United States), Jomo Kwame Sundaram (United Nations), Benno Ndulo (United Republic of Tanzania), José Antonio Ocampo (Colombia), Pedro Páez (Ecuador), Yaga Venugopal Reddy (India), Avinash Persaud (Barbados), Rubens Ricupero (Brazil), Eisuke Sakakibara (Japan), Heidemarie Wieczorek-Zeul (Germany), Yu Yongding (China) and Zet Akhtar Aziz (Malaysia). Rapporteur: Jan Kregel (United States). Special Representatives of the President of the General Assembly: Francois Houtart (Belgium) and Ali Boukrami (Algeria).
2   The report uses the terms "reserve system" and "currency system" as equivalents.
3   Germany is not accumulating reserves but its huge current-account surplus certainly adds to the problem of global imbalances.

References

United Nations (2009). Report of the Commission of Experts of the President of the United Nations General Assembly on Reforms of the International Monetary and Financial System, 21 September. Available at: http://www.un.org/ga/econcrisissummit/docs/FinalReport_CoE.pdf (accessed on 1 June 2010).

Stiglitz J (2010). *The Stiglitz Report: Reforming the International Monetary and Financial Systems in the Wake of the Global Crisis*. New York and London, The New Press.

REFORMING MACROECONOMIC POLICIES IN EMERGING ECONOMIES: FROM PROCYCLICAL TO COUNTERCYCLICAL APPROACHES*

Ricardo Ffrench-Davis

Abstract

Macroeconomic fundamentals are among the most relevant variables for economic development. The commonly accepted approach in mainstream thinking and among international financial institutions in recent years emphasizes macroeconomic balances of two pillars: low inflation and fiscal balances, with open capital accounts. We call these "financieristic" macroeconomic balances, and believe this approach underlies the present global financial and economic crisis. It implies a clear disregard for the overall macroeconomic environment for producers. As a consequence, in many emerging economies (EEs) "sound macroeconomics" (low inflation and fiscal discipline) is observed in parallel with slow growth, a high level of unemployment and low use of productive capital, which are the result of unstable aggregate demand, outlier macro prices and volatile capital flows.

In order to provide a macroeconomic environment conducive to sustained growth, a third pillar must be added, which is linked to the productive

* Based on Ffrench-Davis (2006a). These issues are discussed in further detail in Ffrench-Davis, 2006b. The author appreciates the valuable contributions of Heriberto Tapia and Rodrigo Heresi, and comments received in a seminar of the Commission and at the 2009 Latin American Studies Association (LASA) Congress in Rio de Janeiro.

side of the economy. The behaviour of aggregate demand at levels consistent with potential GDP growth is a crucial part of a third pillar for real macroeconomic balances, which neoliberal approaches have frequently failed to consider. Similarly, other crucial ingredients are well-aligned macro prices, such as interest and exchange rates. This paper analyses alternative macroeconomic environments faced by firms and workers in the productive side of the economy (the producers of GDP), and the interrelationships between financial and real variables.

Introduction

The successful control of inflation and budget deficits has been a general trend among Latin American economies over the past two decades. However, the economic and social performance of many of those economies has been disappointing during that period. In spite of theories that predict economic development convergence with developed countries, a significant number of developing economies have displayed a divergence instead, and are experiencing a worsening of their already unsatisfactory social indicators such as poverty and income distribution. As a matter of fact, while the East Asian economies have been converging with developed countries, with annual rates of per capita GDP growth of 3.8 per cent in 1990–2007 compared with 1.7 per cent in the United States, Latin America has only matched the United States growth rate.

One main reason for the poor performance of several EEs is the absence of a comprehensive approach to macroeconomics beyond the necessary emphasis on the control of inflation and budget deficits. Moreover, in some countries (particularly in Latin America), explicit consideration for the real side of the economy has been disregarded. This narrow view has contributed to the deficient effects from the implementation of reforms associated with the Washington Consensus (Ffrench-Davis, 2008), and it still underlies the design of macroeconomic policies and the policy recommendations of international financial institutions (IFIs).[1]

Real macroeconomic balances are crucial for achieving a more dynamic and equitable form of development. Therefore it is relevant to learn how these balances are obtained, how sustainable and comprehensive they are, how consistent they are with macrosocial balances, and how they affect the variables underlying potential GDP (GDP*).

From the productive point of view, efficient macroeconomic policies must contribute to: (i) using the available productive capacity by raising the rate of utilization of labour and capital in a sustainable manner; (ii) fostering capital formation; and (iii) increasing productivity through improvements in factor quality and their more efficient allocation. These are the three cardinal elements that can generate endogenous growth and increase the GDP growth rate during the transition to a new stationary level.[2] A high average rate of use of capacity implies reconciling the levels of actual aggregate demand and potential supply, and achieving a suitable mix of tradables and non-tradables as well as appropriate macroeconomic relative prices, such as interest rates and exchange rates. Capital formation and actual total factor productivity (TFP) of that capital are vitally dependent on the quality of those balances.

For macroeconomic policies to make the most effective contribution to development, it is necessary to adopt a comprehensive overall view, which: (i) systematically takes into account the effects of those policies on productive development, (ii) reconciles the macroeconomic and macrosocial balances in a similarly integrated manner, and (iii) leads to trends that are sustainable over time.

The performance of the Latin American economies has been driven by a macroeconomic environment where the main agents – governments, entrepreneurs, workers and investors – have been facing sizeable fluctuations in aggregate demand, economic activity and macro prices. Significant successes in reducing inflation and improving fiscal responsibility have not been enough to achieve stability in the environment in which producers – both labour and capital – operate. Consequently, although overall GDP also responds to complex processes related to micro and meso structures, wrong macroeconomic policies have been one main factor responsible for the volatile and disappointing behaviour of output. This paper focuses on the definition of macroeconomic balances, and their overall impacts on growth.

As capital flows have played a dominant role in emerging economies since the 1970s, their effects are central to the discussion in this paper.

The paper is organized as follows. Section I defines macroeconomic balances for sustainable growth. The analysis involves two contrasting approaches to macroeconomic balances that emphasize the relative weight of real versus short-term financial factors in economic decisions: a two-pillar financieristic balance, and a three-pillar real macroeconomic balance for development. It explores why financial instability has significant real permanent effects as a result of the gap between potential GDP and its actual utilization (referred to here as *output gap* or *recessive gap*); the positive dynamic implications of holding low output gaps for capital formation and actual TFP are stressed. Section II examines the connection between external shocks and the macroeconomic environment, highlighting the challenges confronting policymakers in dealing with the real business cycle and with destabilizing intertemporal macroeconomic adjustments. Section III analyses the role played by short-term segments of financial markets and the predominance of financial speculation and rent-seeking at the expense of investments in productive activities. Section IV concludes.

I. Real macroeconomic balances

There is broad consensus that macroeconomic "fundamentals" are among the most relevant variables for promoting economic development. However, there is widespread misunderstanding as to what constitutes "sound fundamentals" and how they can be achieved and sustained.

The operational definition of macroeconomic balances has become so narrow that in many Latin American countries "a sound macroeconomic policy", viewed as maintaining low inflation and small public deficits or surpluses, has been observed to coexist with slow growth, high unemployment and low capital utilization resulting from unstable aggregate demand and outlier interest and exchange rates. This section broadens the view of macroeconomic balances by also taking into account the relationship between financial and real variables.

A. A two-pillar macroeconomic approach

The approach that has been in fashion in mainstream thinking and among IFIs, even up to the present, emphasizes macroeconomic balances of two pillars: low inflation and fiscal balances. It clearly omits consideration of the overall macroeconomic environment for producers, which includes other very influential variables such as aggregate demand, and interest and exchange rates. We call the two pillars "financieristic" macroeconomic balances.

This financieristic approach evidently includes other ingredients as well, but the hard, relevant objective is the achievement of the two pillars noted above. It assumes that fulfilling that objective leads to productive development if the economy is liberalized (that is with the addition of microeconomic reforms, several of which have in fact been undertaken). This has been the established approach for about two decades, and continues to be the basis of the "remaining agenda" pushed by IFIs, particularly the IMF (see, for example, Fischer, 1993; Singh, et al., 2005; and Singh, 2006). Additionally, a frequent assertion in the more recent conventional literature is that an open capital account imposes macroeconomic discipline on EEs.[3] Indeed, this approach assumes, sometimes explicitly or frequently implicitly, that a full opening of the capital account would help impose external and fiscal balances, and consequently automatically generate an aggregate demand that is consistent with productive capacity. However, it is well documented that this is not the usual experience in the frequent cases of external, positive and negative, financial and terms-of-trade shocks experienced by EEs (Ffrench-Davis, 2006a, ch. VI; Williamson, 2003). Understandably, concern for those two financial balances is justified, especially since several Latin American countries have suffered from hyperinflation. When present, this phenomenon rightly tends to become such a dominant concern that an anti-inflationary policy often becomes the leading and imperative objective of economic policies. Hyperinflation processes (see figure 1.C) have been the consequence of public deficits that are out of control and the printing of money to finance them.

In the 1990s, Latin American countries were successful in reducing inflation to single-digit levels and in balancing their fiscal budgets. Fiscal deficits averaged 1–2 per cent of GDP (though of course varying among

Figure 1

MACROECONOMIC INDICATORS IN SELECTED
LATIN AMERICAN COUNTRIES, 1976–2007

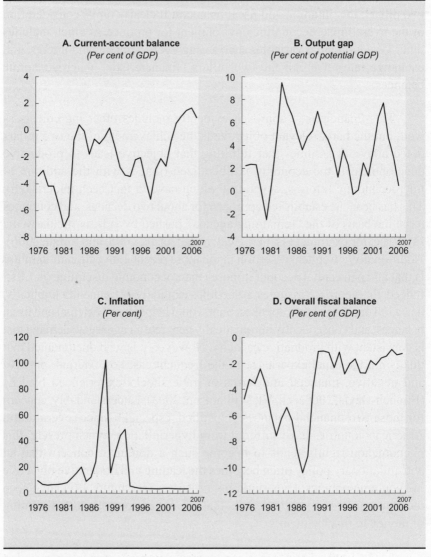

Source: Author's calculations, based on ECLAC data; and Hofman and Tapia, 2004.
Note: The selected countries are: Argentina, the Bolivarian Republic of Venezuela, Bolivia, Brazil, Chile, Colombia, Costa Rica, Mexico and Peru. Averages were weighted using GDP at 1980 constant prices.

countries) in 1994 and 1997 – the two years preceding the two recessive shifts of the 1990s.[4] Increases in money supply to finance public expenditure had become weaker or disappeared. Thus, many of these countries fulfilled the main requirements of neoliberal macroeconomic balances (see figures 1.C and 1.D).[5]

Clearly, the two-pillar macroeconomic approach was not enough. At the same time, there was an increasing external deficit (see figure 1.A) that implied a greater degree of vulnerability. In boom periods, the excess of expenditure over domestic production or income was concentrated in the private sector (Marfán, 2005). In fact, during the boom stages of the economic cycle, while the external deficit (financed with capital inflows) worsened, the public sectors of many countries in the region registered marked improvements between the 1980s and 1990s until they were hit by the contagion effects of the Asian crisis. Growth of current-account deficits was frequently caused by the increased net expenditures of the private sector in the 1991–1998 period. This outcome was the combined result of the large supply of foreign financing and permissive domestic macroeconomic policies which allowed their destabilizing effects to transmit into the domestic economy; it is noteworthy that those procyclical policies were usually praised by financial markets. Consequently, after the turbulences of 1994 (Tequila crisis), 1997–1998 (Asian crisis) and 2008 (global crisis), a significant recessive output gap reopened, with severe adverse effects on growth and equity (Ffrench-Davis, 2006a).

B.   Toward real macroeconomic balances: Three pillars

Financial macroeconomic balances alone cannot produce an environment that is conducive to high and sustained growth; a third pillar must be added, linked to the productive side of the economy. The behaviour of aggregate demand at levels consistent with potential GDP (also called productive capacity, installed capacity, or production frontier) is a crucial component of a third pillar of real macroeconomic balances. Also important are well-aligned macro prices, such as interest and exchange rates. Frequently, these prices and aggregate demand have been outliers (out-of-equilibrium) in neoliberal experiences, as reflected in economies working either quite below potential GDP (the most frequent result), or at full capacity but with a booming aggregate demand and a large external deficit.

One of the most fundamental macroeconomic balances refers to the rate of utilization of productive capacity. In economies with inflexible price systems and *incomplete* factor markets, both positive and negative shocks provoke successive adjustments. The results are greater disparity between supply and aggregate demand, with a consequent gap between potential productive capacity and the use made of it, particularly in the "stop" stages that follow the "go" stages. Unstable demand in a stop-and-go setting inevitably means a lower average net use of productive capacity and a lower average actual productivity than in a situation of stable proximity to the productive frontier. Naturally, the larger the instability, the larger will be the recessive output gap.

C.   *Instability, growth and equity*

Behind the emergence of output gaps is the extreme instability of GDP growth rates. As shown below in figure 4, Latin America has experienced volatile business cycles, with intense contractions and expansions. Evidently, the production frontier poses a limit to the recovery of actual GDP; only temporarily can actual GDP exceed potential GDP, while in recessive situations actual GDP can be notably below potential GDP. The implication of this annoying asymmetry is that average actual GDP under conditions of real macroeconomic instability is significantly lower than the average production frontier. This asymmetry, intrinsic to economic reality, has significant implications for defining the doses or degree of emphasis placed on the diverse objectives and policies, and for empirical research and econometrics (see Ffrench-Davis, 2006a, ch. III, section 2).

The magnitude of the gap between effective demand and the production frontier has important static and dynamic effects. First, it affects the ex post productivity and profitability of the projects implemented. Second, higher rates of capital utilization mean that the average level of employment is higher and that the given labour force combines with a larger stock of physical capital in actual use. Higher actual productivity means that the

Figure 2

OUTPUT GAP AND INVESTMENT RATIO IN SELECTED LATIN AMERICAN COUNTRIES, 1970–2009

(Per cent)

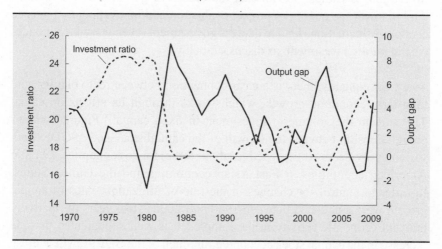

Source: Ffrench-Davis, 2006a; and updates, based on ECLAC, 2010; and Hofman and Tapia, 2004.
Note: Averages for Argentina, the Bolivarian Republic of Venezuela, Bolivia, Brazil, Chile, Colombia, Costa Rica, Mexico and Peru. The investment ratio is the share of fixed capital formation in actual GDP. The output gap is the difference between potential and actual GDP as a share of potential GDP.

potential welfare of labour and rentiers (wage earners and profit makers) can improve in line with the higher average rate of use of capacity. If wages and profits grow, then fiscal revenue will grow as well. Consequently, workers, entrepreneurs and the government will be able to sustain higher consumption and investment, with a net positive effect on overall economic welfare. Third, in the dynamic dimension, there are several effects of the degree of stability. Higher rates of utilization, and the consequent increase in actual average productivity (in standard econometrics it would appear as a rise in TFP), will tend to stimulate investment in new capacity.[6] For the supply of investment to expand effectively, investors must perceive a real improvement in the short term, and expect that the reduction in the recessive output gap will be sustained in the medium to long term.

Figure 2, which shows the close association between the output gap and capital formation in Latin America, reflects one of the main negative effects of the underutilization of productive factors. This relationship responds to several factors:[7] (i) if there is plenty of idle capacity, there is less incentive to invest in new productive assets; (ii) a volatile environment deters irreversible investment (Pyndick, 1991); (iii) the recessive gap and its fluctuations tend to lower the quality of project evaluation and innovation; (iv) intense economic fluctuations tend to depress government revenues, which induces cuts in public investment, as discussed below.

Consequently, there is a clear connection between real volatility and long-term economic growth, which works through its effects on actual TFP and on the volume of investment in fixed capital.[8] Figure 3 shows the relationship between the growth of the capital stock and of GDP (both variables divided by the respective labour force) for 26 economies: 19 Latin American economies, 6 East Asian economies and the United States. In order to control for changes in the rate of utilization, rates of annual growth were calculated between 1980 and 2006 – two years of relatively buoyant economic activity in the sample.[9] It is well documented that the increase in the capital stock accounted for much of the GDP growth in those economies.[10]

Moreover, most of the differences in growth between the Latin American countries and the more dynamic countries of East Asia are attributable to the rapid growth of capital stock. Figure 3 also illustrates the "disappointing" non-convergence of Latin Americas with the more developed countries. In fact, the United States and the East Asian countries have been growing faster than almost all the Latin American region (where Chile is an outlier, but it only began to converge rapidly in the 1990s).

Another dynamic consequence of lower macroeconomic volatility is a tendency towards greater equity.[11] This links comprehensive real macroeconomic balances with *macrosocial* balances (including poverty and income distribution). Indeed, low-income sectors, with less human capital and with small and medium-sized enterprises, have less capacity to react to continuous abrupt changes. During periods of expansion, the rate of inflation normally accelerates, and it is the poor who have problems protecting their assets and income against the "inflation tax". The period of downward adjustment tends to be accompanied by falling wages and employment, along with a shift from formal to informal markets (Tokman, 2004). This

Figure 3

EMERGING ECONOMIES AND THE UNITED STATES: GROWTH OF CAPITAL STOCK AND GDP, 1981–2006

(Average annual percentage growth rate per member of the labour force)

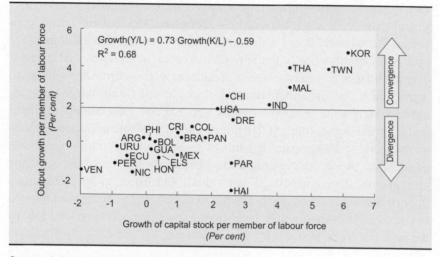

Source: Author's calculations; and Ffrench-Davis, 2006a.
Note: Capital stock and GDP in 1995 prices. Capital stock was calculated using the perpetual inventory method, assuming an average working life for capital of 30 years.

has a negative impact on consumption and on the wealth of low-income groups. A pro-cyclical behaviour of the share of lower income groups in overall consumption, but with a downward bias, should be expected under conditions of instability.[12] Thus, instability is a significant source of inequity, and it rewards speculation and windfall gains at the expense of productive activities and TFP.

Real volatility also has an impact on public finances, because during recessions there is a drop in tax proceeds that translates into cuts in expenditure (as happened during the debt, tequila and Asian crises). Maintaining excessive expenditure cuts in essential items for several years undermines efforts to improve factor quality and hinders the full utilization of installed capacity, thus lowering any efficiency of changes in production that might be under way.

The Latin American experience shows that an efficient combination of financial and real macroeconomic balances has been lacking. In the 1990s, successful inflation reduction was partly due, in a number of cases, to exchange-rate appreciations through the so-called *exchange rate anchor*. In fact, the vast majority of Latin American countries revalued their currencies in real terms between 1990 and 1994, between 1995 and 1997, and again between 2004 and 2008. Furthermore, many countries that exhibited high rates of underutilization of their productive capacity, with renewed access to external finance or improved terms of trade, as well as currency revaluations were able to increase their rates of resource utilization while reducing inflation (see white arrows in figures 1.A, 1.B and 1.C). Supply available in the form of non-exports (GDP not exported) was able to respond rapidly to the increased aggregate demand, with generally falling average rates of inflation. Appreciation-cum-trade liberalization, caused the recovery in aggregate demand, both by individuals and firms, to be increasingly import-intensive (see Ffrench-Davis, 2006a, ch. IV). This caused imports to rise to an excessively high level from a level that had been kept low by the previous recession.

In the countries whose currencies had appreciated the most, with bigger and faster growing external deficits led by financial flows, price stabilization tended to be more rapid. However, they also became more vulnerable, as the gap between domestic spending and actual GDP (the external deficit) grew wider and external liabilities rose apace. As was to be expected, external creditors became increasingly sensitive to political and economic "bad news," which led to broad crises around 1995, 1999 and 2009.

The sharp recovery of GDP growth to 5.3 per cent in 2004–2008 is undoubtedly a positive development, but it took place after six years of large disequilibria (1998–2003), when there was a significant output gap.[13] This long period signifies a costly failure of domestic macroeconomic policies to keeping the economy close to the production frontier. That failure was compounded by the pro-cyclical behaviour of international trade and finance.

II. External shocks and real macroeconomic balances

In order to cope with real volatility it is crucial to understand its causes. External shocks are a major source of macroeconomic fluctuations in EEs. It is possible to identify at least three sources of positive external shocks to which economic activity can respond positively insofar as installed capacity is available. The first source is an increase in export prices. However, swings in external prices are largely transitory; if the economy accommodates to a transitorily high price and abundance of foreign currency, the probable subsequent downward adjustment in economic activity usually will be traumatic. A second source of external shocks is changes in international interest rates. These influence the volume of capital inflows, as well as affecting national income – since a drop (rise) in external interest rates increases (reduces) the national income of a net debtor – and the foreign currency market. A third source of external shocks, which has been the main determinant of macroeconomic instability in Latin American countries since the 1970s, is the sharp fluctuations in the volume of capital flows. In this respect, private capital flows other than FDI are particularly noteworthy because of their volatility.

Figure 4 shows the systematic association between swings in aggregate demand and external shocks. In other words, in recent decades, generally real volatility has had an external origin, which has been notably stronger than domestically originated shocks. In the late 1970s and the 1990s there were sizeable capital surges, while recent years have been marked mostly by significant terms-of-trade changes. Figure 5 shows that changes of actual GDP have been sharply associated with fluctuations in aggregate demand. The pro-cyclical external shocks have usually been multiplied by subsequent domestic pro-cyclical policies. In the last four decades, aggregate demand swings have led GDP changes both in the periods of boom and recession that have affected the region. Usually, it is only subsequently that domestic policies have played a role in moderating or exacerbating the effects of external shocks.

Figure 4

**GROWTH OF AGGREGATE DEMAND AND EXTERNAL SHOCKS
IN SELECTED LATIN AMERICAN COUNTRIES,1989–2007**

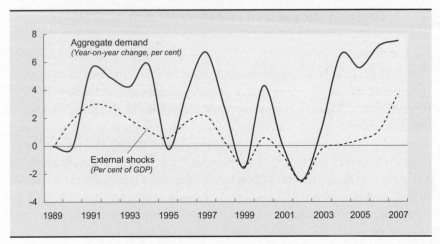

Source: Author's calculations, based on data from ECLAC.
Note: The countries covered are: Argentina, the Bolivarian Republic of Venezuela, Bolivia, Brazil,
Chile, Colombia, Costa Rica, the Dominican Republic, Ecuador, El Salvador, Guatemala, Haiti,
Honduras, Mexico, Nicaragua, Panama, Paraguay, Peru and Uruguay. External shocks result
from net transfers, capital inflows and factor payments and the improvement in the terms of trade,
measured as a share of GDP.

In fact, the causality has been twofold. On the one hand, shocks have
been essentially exogenous: the overall supply of capital flows, world interest
rates, and the evolution of the terms of trade are generally independent of
economic policies in EEs. On the other hand, exposure to shocks and the
intensity of their effects are affected by some domestic factors. Indeed, the
degree to which external shocks are reflected in GDP growth is strongly
determined by: (i) the initial gap between actual GDP and the production
frontier; (ii) the nature of the domestic economic policies implemented,
especially the macroeconomic ones; (iii) the expectations of economic
agents; and (iv) political events.

In an "ideal" adjustment process in a perfectly flexible and well-
informed economy with *complete* and homogeneous factor markets, excess
aggregate demand is eliminated without any drop in the rate of use of

Figure 5

GROWTH OF GDP AND AGGREGATE DEMAND IN SELECTED LATIN AMERICAN COUNTRIES, 1989–2007

(Annual percentage change)

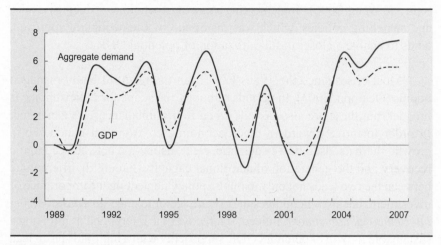

Source: Ffrench-Davis, 2006a, and updating, based on data from ECLAC.
Note: For countries covered, see note to figure 4.

capacity. On the other hand, in the typical setting of an economy with price inflexibility and imperfect factor mobility, the implementation of neutral, demand-reducing policies, for instance in the context of a shock in the capital account, usually leads to a significant drop in domestic production. This is because such policies reduce demand for both tradable and non-tradable goods and services, thus giving rise to unemployment especially in the latter sector. This confirms the significant implications of price inflexibility, factor immobility, incomplete markets and flaws in information during adjustment processes in the real economy. They explain why adjustment usually occurs significantly below the production frontier.

In fact, in adjustment processes in the real world, a sharp reduction of demand tends to cause a decline in production, which gives rise to a lower rate of utilization of installed capacity and discourages capital formation (figure 2). The addition of switching policies that influences the composition of output and expenditure may cushion the decline in economic activity.

Such policies may be global – such as the exchange rate – or they may be more sector-specific. The East Asian countries provide examples of the successful use of extremely selective policies, and also of notably effective adjustment processes (Amsden, 2001; Kaplan and Rodrik, 2001; Mahani, Shin and Wang, 2006). Implementing a mix of expenditure-reducing policies and switching policies, which was dismissed by the neoliberal approach, tends to enable a closer to full utilization of potential GDP.

Most crises since the 1980s have been the result of badly managed booms (Ocampo, 2003). In periods of boom, the scope for policy choice is broader, but these are also periods when future imbalances are generated. In order to move towards a macroeconomic environment conducive to growth, there needs to be a systematic, clear distinction between economic recovery and the generation of additional capacity. Failure to differentiate between the two leads not only to public policy neglecting the importance of investment, but also encourages the private sector to undergo a *destabilizing intertemporal adjustment*. Indeed, if a recovery is interpreted as allowing a sustainable growth of potential GDP, supposedly with a high TFP, it can lead to feeling richer and increasing consumption (thus crowding out national savings), while not really being richer. Thus macroeconomic policy should be guided by making a sharp distinction between creating new capacity and using existing capacity.

In fact, if capital inflows or improved terms of trade stimulate processes of recovery in economies that have high unemployment of productive factors, actual productivity rises because of an increase in the rate of utilization of potential GDP. Subsequently, agents and authorities (and also many researchers, e.g. Ffrench-Davis, 2006a, ch. III) may confuse the jump in actual productivity that is based on the utilization of previously idle labour and capital with a structural increase in the sustainable speed of productivity improvements. From the point of view of "rational" consumers, they tend to assume that there is an increase in their permanent income. Consequently, the market response would tend to be an intertemporal upward adjustment of consumption, with the external gap covered by capital inflows, as long as the supply of foreign savings is available. That implies a crowding out of domestic savings, which results from agents' decisions based on biased information.[14] As a result, the intertemporal adjustment ends up being destabilizing.

The increased availability of funds tends to generate a process of exchange-rate appreciation. And the expectations of continued, persistent appreciation encourage additional inflows from dealers operating with maturity horizons in line with the expected appreciation of the domestic currency. For allocative efficiency and for export-oriented development strategies, a macro price – as significant as the exchange rate – led by capital inflows conducted by short-termist agents reveals a severe policy inconsistency. The increase in aggregate demand, pushed up by inflows and appreciation, and a rising share of the domestic demand for tradables, artificially augments the absorptive capacity and the demand for foreign savings. Thus, exogenous changes (like fluctuations in the supply of funds) are converted into an endogenous process, leading to domestic vulnerability due to the potential reversibility of inflows. In the case of a transitory improvement in the terms of trade, a similar destabilizing process can occur, with an excessive increase in consumption and a weakening in the generation of productive capacity in tradable sectors that are intensive in domestic inputs (i.e. the Dutch disease).

Figure 6 shows that the evolution of real exchange rates has responded to a large extent to financial flows, rather than to the real forces behind the current account. The volatile components of flows have been short-term portfolio investments, while flows of greenfield FDI are fairly stable. In some periods, the mid-term volatility of financial flows has been reinforced by significant fluctuations in the terms of trade. Actually, between 2003 (still a recessive year for Latin America) and 2007 (during a period of significant recovery), the terms of trade explained most of the elimination of the binding external financial restrictions that had kept Latin American countries operating below the production frontier during the period 1998–2003 (see Ocampo, 2007).

Therefore when actual output is reaching close to the production frontier, more active counter-cyclical policies are needed to regulate the expansion of aggregate demand. Moreover, with a closing recessive output gap, the role of policies to enhance productive development (and increase potential output) becomes crucial. In fact, it is essential to keep the rate of expansion of demand in line with the growth of productive capacity (and also with sustainable external financing). Otherwise, if passive macroeconomic policies are adopted in situations of positive external shocks (such as lower

Figure 6

**LATIN AMERICA: NET CAPITAL INFLOWS AND
REAL EXCHANGE RATE, 1980–2009**

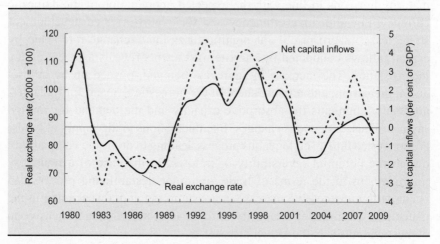

Source: Ffrench-Davis, 2006a, and updating, based on ECLAC figures.
Note: The real exchange rate is defined in terms of US dollars per unit of local currency.

international interest rates, improved terms of trade, or increased supply of capital inflows) or those of a domestic nature (a boom in the construction sector or in the demand for durable goods or stocks and bonds), then the economy will be subject to inflationary pressures and/or a growing gap between expenditure and output. In all events, a future adjustment in the opposite direction will usually build up.

In brief, it is necessary to further improve the capacity to implement real macroeconomic policies by including a counter-cyclical mix, in order to reconcile the proximity of the economy to the production frontier with sustainability and price stability. However, as documented by Kaminsky et al. (2004) for a sample of 104 countries, the opposite has tended to occur.

III. Financial development, financierism and productivism

Financial development is a key ingredient for economic development.[15] Channelling financial resources to sectors of higher productivity improves overall efficiency in the economy and enhances economic growth. However, financial markets are imperfect and quite incomplete in EEs. In a world of uncertainty, incomplete insurance markets, informational costs and contagious changes of mood, as well as ex ante and ex post valuations of financial assets may be radically different, to the point that market corrections may be abrupt, overshooting and destabilizing (Stiglitz, 2000; 2005).

A.   *Financierism empowered by neoliberal reforms*

A distinctive feature of macroeconomic management in the transition of the most successful EEs towards the level of development of more advanced countries has been the predominance of *"productivistic"* over *"financieristic"* dimensions. Development has been led by the "real" side, with financial aspects at its service. This policy correlation is contrary to the neoliberal approach and to the standard thesis of financial liberalization as one of the most essential inputs for development.

This financieristic neoliberal approach has been adopted by many EEs, with the dominance (or strong influence and powerful lobbying) over macroeconomic decisions of financial agents with a short-term perspective. The growing link with the international financial system facilitated the disassociation with the needs of domestic productive systems and encouraged capital flight during periods of domestic crises. In short, total openness to international financial markets (as witnessed in the 1990s in most EEs) can dismantle comprehensive efforts at domestic stabilization, and tends to lead to integration into more speculative segments of world markets. In contrast, insertion into the world economy should be aimed at promoting long-term capital inflows, accompanied by access to technology and export markets.

From the mid-1990s, campaigning and elected Latin American leaders became regular visitors to Wall Street. In addition, when newly elected political authorities had to nominate their economic authorities, the international mass media exerted strong pressures for their preferred candidates – the "market's candidate", with "market" denoting the financial markets that have short-term horizons. The strengthening of this dimension has provoked a growing duality, worrisome for democracy, in the constituencies or "voices" taken into account by authorities in EEs. The present features of globalization are increasing the distance between policymakers and financial agents vis-à-vis the domestic agents (workers and firms and fiscal tax proceeds) that are bearing the consequences. Thus, an outcome of the specific road taken by globalization has been that experts in financial intermediation – a microeconomic training – have all too often been a major influence on the evolution of domestic macroeconomic balances and their volatility.[16]

Pressures from international financial markets have pushed some governments to offer guarantees to financial investors as a means of gaining credibility beyond what is consistent with growth and equity, and even beyond what is necessary to achieve short-term credibility with international financial markets. As shown by the Argentinean case in the 1990s, if public commitments go beyond the capacity that a democratic country can bear, the result may be praises in the short term but a net loss of credibility in the medium and long term.

The case of Chile in its return to democracy in 1990 is an outstanding example of differences between the productivistic and the financieristic dimensions: while domestic and foreign financial media praised the liberalization policies under the military rule of Pinochet, Chile recorded its lowest investment ratio in the last half of the century. By contrast, the reforms of the 1990s – including regulation of financial inflows, some tax increases, labour reforms to strengthen workers' bargaining power and significant increases in minimum wages – were initially received with concern and criticism by large private entrepreneurs and the financial sector, while the investment ratio reached historical peaks. This successful combination was made possible by adopting a three-pillar macroeconomic approach in the early 1990s (see Ffrench-Davis, 2010, chapter VIII).

B. Rational pro-cyclicality of short-term financial markets, and irrational policymakers following their advice

It becomes highly unlikely to be able to escape from financieristic traps without a traumatic adjustment. Such adjustments usually involve an overshooting to outlier exchange or interest rates and the emergence of considerable liquidity constraints, which together generate a very unfriendly macroeconomic environment for firms and labour.

An outstanding feature of the most recent currency and financial crises in East Asia and Latin America is that they involved mainly those EEs which were considered by IFIs and financial agents as being highly "successful".[17] Indeed, risk rating agencies had been awarding them with increasingly better grades,[18] as a result of which they attracted large private capital flows and falling spreads, which grew in parallel with accumulating rising stocks of external liabilities.

Given that voluntary flows cannot take place without the willing consent of both debtors and creditors, why did neither agent act in a timely manner to curb flows well before the crises? Both regions had become vulnerable through a combination of large external liabilities with a high short-term or liquid share, credit booms, currency and maturity mismatches, significant external deficits, appreciated exchange rates, high price/earnings ratios in the stock market and high luxury real estate prices, plus low domestic investment ratios in the case of the Latin American countries. In parallel, agents specialized in microeconomic aspects of finance placed in the short-term or liquid segments of capital markets acquired a dominant voice in the generation of macroeconomic expectations. Why are these voices intrinsically pro-cyclical?

There is an extremely relevant body of literature about the causes of financial instability – such as the asymmetries of information between creditors and debtors, and the lack of adequate internalization of the negative externalities that each agent generates (through growing vulnerability) – which underlie the cycles of abundance and shortage of external financing (Krugman, 2000; Rodrik, 1998; Stiglitz, 2000; Harberger, 1985). Beyond those issues, as stressed by Ocampo (2003), finance deals with the future, and evidently concrete "information" about the future is unavailable.

Consequently, the tendency to equate opinions and expectations with "information" contribute to herd behaviour and multiple equilibria. Notorious contagion, first of over-optimism and then of over-pessimism, has been observed in many of the financial crises experienced by EEs over the last three decades.

During all recent generalized expansive processes, there has been an evident contagion of over-optimism among creditors. Rather than displaying an "appetite for risk", in those episodes agents supplying funding underestimated or ignored risk. With respect to debtors, in periods of over-optimism, the evidence is that most debtors do not borrow with the idea of a default and expectations of being rescued or benefiting from a moratorium. On the contrary, expectations of high yields tend to prevail: in fact, borrowers are also victims of the syndrome of financial euphoria during boom periods.

However, over and above these facts, there are two additional features of the creditor side that are crucially important. One feature is the particular *nature of the leading agents* acting on the supply side. There are natural asymmetries in the behaviour and objectives of different economic agents. The agents predominant in the financial markets are specialized in short-term liquid investments, operate within short-term horizons, and therefore are highly sensitive to changes in variables that affect returns in the short run.[19] The second feature is the gradual spread of information among prospective agents on investment opportunities in EEs. Agents from different segments of the financial markets gradually become drawn to these economies once they become aware of the new and profitable opportunities available there.

From the supply-side, this explains why the surges of flows to EEs over several periods – 1977–1981, 1991–1994, mid-1995–1998, and 2004–2007 – were *processes* that went on for several years rather than one-shot changes in supply. This points to the relevance for policy design to make a distinction between two different types of volatility of capital flows: short-term ups and downs, and medium-term instability. Medium-term instability causes several variables – such as the stock market, real estate prices and the exchange rate – to move persistently in a given direction, providing "wrong certainties" to the market of one-sided movements of prices and returns. It encourages additional capital flows and the seeking of economic rents, rather than gains due to differentials in real productivity, until it becomes evident that increased prices and returns are not sustainable. Private capital flows, led by mid-term volatility (or reversibility) of expectations, usually have a strong and costly pro-cyclical bias.

On the domestic side, high rates of return were potentially to be gained by creditors from capital surges directed to EEs. At the time of their financial opening up in the 1980s and early 1990s, Latin American economies were experiencing recession, depressed stock and real estate markets, as well as high real interest rates and, initially, undervalued domestic currencies. Indeed, by 1990, the prices of real estate and equity stocks were extremely depressed and the domestic price of the dollar was comparatively high (ECLAC, 1998; Ffrench-Davis and Ocampo, 2001).

In such a context, there is potentially space for very profitable capital inflows. Flows should continue until rates of return converge, as would happen naturally over the long term. The direction of expected adjustments in any emerging-market economy that moves from a closed to an open capital account under those conditions would tend to be similar to those recorded in Latin American countries. The outcome in these countries as well as in East Asia, for instance, was a spectacular rise in stock prices, multiplying an average price index by four in 1990–1994, and in the Latin American countries, after a sharp 40 per cent drop with the Tequila crisis) by two both in 1995–1997 in Latin America, and in 1992–1994 in East Asia (Ffrench-Davis 2006a, table VII.4). All these swings were directly associated with portfolio flows.

Finally, in an incomplete list, the increased supply of external financing in the 1990s generated a process of exchange rate appreciation in most Latin American countries (see figure 6) and more moderately in East Asia. Consequently, expectations of continued appreciation encouraged additional inflows.[20] However, the combination of an open capital account, large liquid liabilities and expectations of depreciation lead, most naturally, to a large outflow, with a large depreciation if the rate is flexible.

For allocative efficiency and for export-oriented development strategies, a macro price – as significant as the exchange rate – led by capital flows conducted by short-termist agents reveals a strong policy inconsistency. The increase in aggregate demand, driven up by inflows and appreciation, and a rising share of the domestic demand for tradables "artificially" augment a country's absorptive capacity and the demand for foreign savings. Thus, as mentioned above, the exogenous change – brought about by transformations in international capital markets – gets converted into an endogenous process, leading to domestic vulnerability due to the potential reversibility of flows.

In brief, the interaction between the two sets of factors – *the nature of agents* and *the process of adjustment* – explains the dynamics of capital flows over time, and why suppliers keep pouring in funds even when real macroeconomic fundamentals worsen. When creditors *discover* an emerging market, their initial exposure is low or non-existent. Thereafter, they generate a series of consecutive flows, which result in rapidly increasing stocks of financial assets in that market. However, the increase becomes too rapid and/or large for an efficient absorption, and, frequently, the absorption is artificially increased by an exchange-rate appreciation and rising real aggregate demand, resulting in a growing external deficit.

At some point, the creditor's sensitivity to negative news is likely to suddenly increase significantly when the country has reached several *vulnerability zones. Both* the accumulation of stocks of assets abroad by financial suppliers until the boom stage of the cycle is well advanced and a subsequent sudden reversal of flows can be considered as *rational* responses on the part of individual agents with short-term horizons. This is because it is of little concern to this sort of investor whether (long-term) the fundamentals are improving or worsening as long as they continue to bring inflows that continue to generate high earnings for them. What is relevant to them is that the crucial indicators from their point of view (i.e. prices of real estate, bonds and stocks, and exchange rates) can continue to provide them with profits in the near term and, obviously, that liquid markets allow them, if need be, to reverse their decisions in a timely manner. Thus they will continue to supply net inflows until expectations of an imminent reversal build up. This explains why they may suddenly radically change their opinions about the economic situation of a country whose fundamentals, other than liquidity in foreign currency, remain fairly unchanged during a shift from *over-optimism* to *over-pessimism.*

Naturally, the opposite process, of a resumption of inflows, tends to take place when the debtor markets have "sufficiently" adjusted downwards. When this happens, the process of continued inflows can be sustained for some years, as occurred in the periods 1991–1994, 1995–1997 and 2004–2008.

In conclusion, economic agents specialized in the allocation of financial flows, who may be highly efficient in their field but operate with short-term horizons, "by training and by reward", have come to play a leading role in determining macroeconomic conditions and policy design in EEs. This implies that a financieristic approach gains predominance over a productivistic approach. In contrast, growth with equity requires improving the rewards for productivity enhancement rather than financial rent-seeking in search of capital gains. This calls for a need to rebalance priorities and voices.

IV. Concluding remarks

Emerging-market economies have experienced a sharp paradox: while agreeing on the importance of macroeconomic balances, they have encountered a common situation in which the outcome has been costly disequilibria for large segments of the real economy: labour and physical capital. Indeed, that reveals a severe real macroeconomic disequilibrium.

In order to deal with these inefficiencies, EEs need to adopt a macroeconomic approach that focuses not only on stabilization of the price level and on the control of fiscal deficits (as advocated by the mainstream approach), but also on external balances (key in open economies) and real variables, which affect the link between present and future. Achieving real balance in the use of productive capacity (i.e. the utilization of the productive factors – capital and labour – at their potential level) is crucial to the evolution of actual income, social equity, structural or "full employment", tax revenues, capital formation and future growth.

Real macroeconomic balances – including aggregate demand that is consistent with productive capacity, sustainable (non-outlier) exchange rates and interest rates, fiscal responsibility and moderate inflation – are essential for growth and equity. Given the pro-cyclicality of financial flows (and terms of trade), one prerequisite for achieving those macroeconomic balances is the comprehensive regulation of capital flows. The positive outcome of such regulation would be a macroeconomic environment conducive to development actually development-friendly. Naturally, for regulating volatile financial flows, developing countries must have several alternatives at their disposal, and be able to choose a flexible set of policies that are strongly counter-cyclical and well adapted to their specific economic structures, the degree of development (completeness) of their markets, and the democratic objectives of their respective societies. In addition, any eventual reform of the international financial architecture must provide sufficient policy space for the needed improvement of macroeconomic policies in emerging-market economies.

Notes

1   See, for example, Singh, 2006.
2   Related discussions can be found in Agénor and Montiel, 1996; Aghion and Durlauf, 2009; ECLAC, 2004 and 2010; Easterly, Islam and Stiglitz, 2001; and Rodrik, 2006.
3   A recent IMF working paper (Tytell and Wei, 2004) examines the disciplinary effect of financial globalization on macroeconomic balances, focusing on the two pillars in fashion – low inflation and fiscal balances – and disregarding the other components of a comprehensive set of real macroeconomic balances. A different robust view is developed in another IMF occasional paper by Prasad et al. (2003).
4   It is inconsistent to assert that fiscal deficits were the cause of currency or financial crises on the basis of fiscal figures that refer to the period after the turmoil (for instance to 1998–1999); clearly, this would be indicative not of a cause but of a consequence of the crises.
5   Also, economic reforms succeeded in improving export dynamism. However, trade reforms during episodes of appreciating real exchange rates frequently ended up causing an excessive destruction of tradable activities whose output (referred to as importables

or import substitutes) was directed to domestic markets. Likewise, export development has remained too concentrated in commodities with low value added, which limits the transmission of export dynamism to the rest of the economy (see Agosin, 2007; Ffrench-Davis, 2006a, chs. IV and V).

6   One significant explanatory variable of the low investment ratio recorded in Chile during the period 1974–1989 (the Pinochet Dictatorship) is the large average output gap predominating in that period (Ffrench-Davis, 2010, ch. I). The large size of the gap was associated with sharp and abrupt drops, with gradual macroeconomic recoveries.

7   The negative effect of volatility on investment has been found to be statistically significant by a number of econometric studies (see, for example, Aizenman and Marion, 1999). Aghion et al. (2005) and Ramey and Ramey (1995) tested econometrically the connection between volatility and growth, and found a significant negative relationship.

8   Other two key relationships are an increase in potential productivity, brought about by technological change, and the formation of human capital. It must be borne in mind that technology frequently needs to be embodied in factors of production (physical and human capital) in order to be part of the production function. Even intangible technology associated with the organization and generation of institutions usually requires investment in equipment and infrastructure, and depends on a more highly skilled labour force.

9   We are assuming that all countries had fairly similarly high rates of utilization of factors in 1980 and 2006, in which case the rise in actual and potential GDP is similar.

10   The exceptions are Haiti, a country in turmoil as a result of internal conflicts that have conspired against the use of its productive capacity, and Paraguay, where the capital stock series are biased by the construction of huge dams, which has a lagged effect on production. Barring these two cases, the explanatory power of the regression (measured by R^2) increases to 92 per cent.

11   Inequality, in turn, has a negative effect on the formation of human capital, the quality of democracy, and consequently on economic growth (Bourguignon and Walton, 2007; Alesina and Rodrik, 1994).

12   See, for example, Dutt and Ros, 2005; Lustig, 2000; Morley, 1995; Rodrik, 2001; World Bank, 2003.

13   In 2004–2008, pulled up by strengthened world economic activity and sharply improved terms of trade, the output gap fell significantly. While potential GDP was expanding in the order of 3 per cent, actual GDP rose 5.3 per cent in that five-year period. Thus the recessive gap, part of the previous macroeconomic disequilibria, was progressively corrected.

14   As highlighted by Aghion and Durlauf (2009), the low savings ratios underlie the lack of conditional convergence of developing countries, and particularly Latin American countries. We stress that low savings are partly a consequence of recessive gaps led by two-pillar macroeconomics and a subsequent discouragement to productive investment.

15   See a recent contribution by Aghion and Durlauf, 2009.

16   See interesting comments in Bhagwati (2004) on the lobbying of "Wall Street" financial agents and their negative implications for trade.

17   For further details, see Ffrench-Davis, 2006a, chapter VI, and Williamson, 2003.

18   Reisen (2003) points out that risk rating agencies usually follow the market. Nonetheless, they play a significant destabilizing role because they tend to reinforce over-optimism and over-pessimism.

19   Persaud (2003) argues that modern risk management by investing institutions (such as funds and banks), based on value-at-risk measured daily, works pro-cyclically in boom and bust periods. Pro-cyclicality is reinforced by a trend towards a homogenization of the mood of financial agents (as they converge through herd behaviour). A complementary argument by Calvo and Mendoza (2000) examines how globalization may promote contagion by discouraging the gathering of information and by strengthening incentives for imitating market investment portfolios.

20   For short-termist agents, actual and expected profitability increase with the appreciation process. That same process, if perceived as persistent, would tend to discourage investment in the production of tradables intensive in domestic inputs. Therefore the exchange rate trend during the expansive or boom stage is most relevant because of its policy implications. It is at this stage that external imbalances and currency and maturity mismatches are, inadvertently, generated.

References

Agénor P-R and Montiel PJ (1996). *Development Macroeconomics*. Ewing, NJ, Princeton University Press.

Aizenman J and Marion N (1999). Volatility and investment: Interpreting evidence from developing countries. *Economica*, 66(262), May: 157–179.

Alesina A and Rodrik D (1994). Distributive politics and economic growth. *The Quarterly Journal of Economics*, 109: 465–490.

Aghion P and Durlauf S (2009). From growth theory to policy design. Working Paper 57, Commission on Growth and Development, World Bank, Washington, DC. Aghion P, Angeletos G, Banerjee A and Manova K (2005). Volatility and growth: Credit constraints and productivity-enhancing investment. NBER Working Paper No. 11349. Cambridge, MA, April.

Agosin MR (2007). Trade and growth: Why Asia grows faster than Latin America. In: Ffrench-Davis R and Machinea JL, eds., *Economic Growth with Equity: Challenges for Latin America*. New York, Palgrave Macmillan.

Agosin M and Ffrench-Davis R (2001). Managing capital inflows in Chile. In: Griffith-Jones S, Montes M and Nasution A, eds., *Short-Term Capital Flows and Economic Crises*. New York, Oxford University Press and United Nations University/World Institute for Development Economics Research.

Amsden AH (2001). *The Rise of "The Rest": Challenges to the West from Late-Industrializing Economies*. New York, Oxford University Press.

Bhagwati J (2004). *In Defense of Globalization*. New York, Oxford University Press.

Bourguignon F and Walton M (2007). Is greater equity necessary for higher long-term growth in Latin America? In: Ffrench-Davis R and Machinea JL, eds., *Economic Growth with Equity*. New York, Palgrave.

Calvo G and Mendoza E (2000). Rational contagion and the globalization of securities markets. *Journal of International Economics*, 51: 79–113.

Dutt A and Ros J (2005). Contractionary effects of stabilization and long-run growth. IPD Working Paper, Macroeconomic Task Force, University of Columbia, New York.

Easterly W, Islam R and Stiglitz J (2001). Volatility and macroeconomic paradigms for rich and poor countries. In: Dreze J, ed., *Advances in Macroeconomic Theory*. London, Palgrave.

ECLAC (1998). *Políticas para mejorar la inserción en la economía mundial* (second edition). Santiago, Chile, CEPAL/Fondo de Cultura Económica.

ECLAC (2002). Growth with Stability: Financing for Development in the New International Context. ECLAC Books, No. 67, Santiago, Chile.

ECLAC (2004). *Productive Development in Open Economies*. Santiago, Chile.

ECLAC (2010). La hora de la igualdad: brechas por cerrar, caminos por abrir, Período Ordinario de Sesiones, Brasilia.

Ffrench-Davis R (2006a). *Reforming Latin America's Economies after Market Fundamentalism*. New York, Palgrave Macmillan.

Ffrench-Davis R (2006b). From Financieristic to Real Macroeconomics: Seeking Development Convergence in Emerging Economies, Commission on Growth and Development Working Paper No. 44, Washington, DC.

Ffrench-Davis R (2008). Growth challenges for Latin America: Reforms – What has happened, why and how to reform the reforms. For the Commission on Growth and Development, December.

Ffrench-Davis R (2010). *Economic Reforms in Chile: From Dictatorship to Democracy* (second edition). London, Palgrave Macmillan.

Ffrench-Davis R and Ocampo JA (2001). The globalization of financial volatility. In: Ffrench-Davis R, ed., *Financial Crises in "Successful" Emerging Economies*. Washington, DC, Brookings Institution Press/ECLAC.

Fischer S (1993). The role of macroeconomic factors in growth. *Journal of Monetary Economics*, 32(3): 485–512.

Harberger A (1985). Observations on the Chilean economy, 1973-83. *Economic Development and Cultural Change,* 33, April: 451–472.

Hofman A and Tapia H (2004). Potential output in Latin America: a standard approach for the 1950-2002 period. *Estudios Estadísticos y Prospectivos* 25, ECLAC, December.

Kaminsky G, Reinhart C and Végh C (2004). When it rains, it pours: pro-cyclical capital flows and macroeconomic policies. NBER Working Paper 10780, Cambridge, MA, September.

Kaplan E and Rodrik D (2001). Did the Malaysian capital controls work? NBER Working Paper No. 8142, Cambridge, MA.

Krugman P (2000). Crises: The price of globalization? Presentation at the Symposium on Global Economic Integration: Opportunities and Challenges organized by the Federal Reserve Bank of Kansas City at Jackson Hole, Wyoming, 24–26 August. .

Lustig N (2000). Crises and the poor: Socially responsible macroeconomics. *Economía*, 1(1). Washington, DC, Brookings Institution, December.

Mahani Z, Shin K and Wang Y (2006). Macroeconomic adjustment and the real economy in Korea and Malaysia since 1997. In: Ffrench-Davis R, ed., *Seeking Growth under Financial Volatility*. London, Palgrave Macmillan.

Marfán M (2005). Fiscal policy efficacy and private deficits: A macroeconomic approach. In: Ocampo JA, ed., *Rethinking Development Challenges*. Palo Alto, CA, Stanford University Press.

Morley S (1995). *Poverty and Inequality in Latin America: The Impact of Adjustment and Recovery in the 1980s*. Baltimore and London, Johns Hopkins University Press.

Ocampo JA (2003). Capital account and counter-cyclical prudential regulations in developing countries. In: Ffrench-Davis R and Griffith-Jones S, eds., *From Capital Surges to Drought*. London, Palgrave Macmillan/WIDER.

Ocampo JA (2007). La macroeconomía de la bonanza económica latinoamericana. *CEPAL Review* No. 93, December.

Persaud A (2003). Liquidity black holes. In: Ffrench-Davis R and Griffith-Jones S, eds., *From Capital Surges to Drought*. London, Palgrave Macmillan.

Pyndick R (1991). Irreversibility, uncertainty, and investment. *Journal of Economic Literature*, 29(3), September.

Prasad E, Rogoff K, Wei S and Kose M (2003). Effects of financial globalization on developing countries: Some empirical evidence. *IMF Occasional Paper* No. 220, September.

Ramey G and Ramey V (1995). Cross-country evidence on the link between volatility and growth. *American Economic Review*, 85(5), December.

Reisen H (2003). Ratings since the Asian crisis. In: Ffrench-Davis R and Griffith-Jones S, eds., *From Capital Surges to Drought*. London, Palgrave Macmillan.

Rodrik D (1998). Who needs capital account convertibility? In: Kenen P, ed., *Should the IMF Pursue Capital Account Convertibility?* Princeton Essays in International Finance, No. 207, Princeton University, Princeton, NJ.

Rodrik D (2001). Why is there so much economic insecurity in Latin America? *CEPAL Review* No. 73, Santiago, Chile, April.

Rodrik D (2006). Goodbye Washington Consensus, hello Washington confusion? A review of the World Bank's *Economic Growth in the 1990s: Learning from a Decade of Reform. Journal of Economic Literature*, XLIV, December.

Singh A (2006). Macroeconomic volatility: The policy lessons from Latin America. IMF Working Paper 166, International Monetary Fund, Washington, DC, July.

Singh A, Belaisch A, Collyns C, De Masi P, Krieger R, Meredith G, and Rennhack R (2005). Stabilization and reform in Latin America: A macroeconomic perspective of the experience since the early 1990s. Occasional Paper 238, IMF, Washington, DC, February.

Stiglitz J (2000). Capital market liberalization, economic growth and instability. *World Development*, 28(6), June: 1075–1086.

Stiglitz J (2005). Responding to economic crises: Policy alternatives for equitable recovery and development. IPD Working Paper, Macroeconomics Task Force, Columbia University, New York.

Tokman V (2004). *Una voz en el camino. Empleo y equidad en América Latina: 40 años de búsqueda*. Santiago, Chile, Fondo de Cultura Económica.

Tytell I and Wei S-J (2004). Does financial globalization induce better macroeconomic policies? Working Paper 04/84, International Monetary Fund, Washington, DC, May.

Williamson J (2003). Overview: an agenda for restarting growth and reform. In: Kuczynski PP and Williamson J, eds., *After the Washington Consensus: Restarting Growth and Reform in Latin America*. Washington, DC, Institute for International Economics.

World Bank (2003). *Inequality in Latin America and the Caribbean: Breaking with history?* Washington, DC.

A POSSIBLE NEW ROLE FOR SPECIAL DRAWING RIGHTS IN AND BEYOND THE GLOBAL MONETARY SYSTEM

Jürgen Zattler*

Abstract

The paper examines the role that Special Drawing Rights (SDRs) could play in the present global monetary system. Shortly before the old Bretton Woods currency system broke down in 1973, SDRs were generated as artificial reserve money in addition to the dollar. Since then they have played only a marginal role, as the so-called Triffin-dilemma built into the Bretton Woods-System and inducing scarcity of international reserves, no longer applied. Given the obvious weaknesses in the present post-Bretton Woods monetary system, which basically is a dollar standard, this paper argues for a new role for SDRs in contributing to redressing the global imbalances and alleviating the shortcomings of the present system. SDRs could be allocated primarily to countries that lack currency reserves, and reserves presently held mainly in dollars could be diversified if denominated in SDRs. In addition, SDRs could be used for private international transactions, emerging countries' bonds could be issued in SDRs and countercyclical policies could be financed with SDRs. Beyond the monetary system, SDRs could be used to finance global public goods, in particular for implementing policies relating to climate change in developing countries.

* The author wishes to thank Gerhard Ressel for his very useful comments on earlier drafts of this paper and the associated discussions.

Introduction

The world has experienced the worst economic crisis since the 1930s. Even though there are signs that the worst is behind us, there are a number of downside risks to the recovery. Moreover, ensuring that the recovery will be sustainable remains an enormous challenge. In order to meet this challenge, two major issues need to be addressed. First, it is necessary to examine the factors that were at the root of the crisis. Apart from the widely discussed deficiencies in financial regulation, the large and rising global imbalances were another important factor. In this context, it has been pointed out that the current reserve system based on the United States dollar has been partly responsible for those immense global imbalances. The second issue relates to global warming and its potentially disastrous impacts on our well-being. Mitigating climate change is a challenge that requires enormous investments and financing, in particular in developing countries. At the same time, such investments could constitute an important driver for growth and income generation in the years to come.

This paper discusses what role the Special Drawing Rights (SDRs), the "artificial money" issued by the International Monetary Fund (IMF), could play as an element in a strategy for strong and sustainable growth. Section I provides some basic information about SDRs and outlines recent SDR-related developments. Section II discusses the alleged deficiencies in the current dollar-based global reserve system and considers to what extent an enhanced role of SDRs could contribute to improving the stability of the international financial system. Section III explores the potential of SDRs to foster development and the provision of global public goods, such as those that contribute towards reducing global warming.

I. A renewed interest in SDRs

An SDR is an international reserve asset. The allocation of SDRs directly increases recipient countries' international reserves.[1] Member countries have the possibility to exchange their SDRs for freely usable currencies provided by other IMF members. Usually countries with a balance-of-payments deficit exchange SDRs with countries that have a balance-of-payments surplus.

At present, SDRs can be used only in official transactions with the IMF; they cannot be spent in the marketplace. The Fund ensures the liquidity of the SDR through a mechanism whereby members with strong external positions are designated to purchase SDRs from members with weak external positions. Voluntary exchanges between members and prescribed holders in a market managed by the Fund are also possible. The creation of SDRs does not generate money supply per se. For countries that hold on to their allocation, no impact on the money supply would be expected. For allocations that are spent, the ultimate monetary and price impact would essentially depend on the extent to which central banks decide to sterilize the transactions. Therefore, the long-term impact on prices is a reflection of domestic monetary policies rather than the supply of an outside reserve asset. Accordingly, in the post-Bretton Woods system, where money creation is not limited by the amount of reserves, liquidity creation is independent of SDR allocations. In other words, in this system SDR allocations are not needed in order to increase global liquidity.

At present, the value of an SDR is determined by a basket of four currencies: the United States dollar (weight: 44 per cent), the euro (34 per cent), the yen (11 per cent) and the pound sterling (also 11 per cent). This currency basket is reviewed every five years. The SDR interest rate is a weighted average of three-monthly risk-free rates of the four basket currencies. While the SDR interest rate had averaged more than 5 per cent over the past few decades, it declined to about 0.4 per cent in early 2010. Member States of the IMF receive interest payments on their SDR holdings and pay charges on their cumulative allocation of SDRs at the same rate. Therefore, members with holdings equal to their cumulative allocations pay no interest on a net basis.

SDRs were created by the IMF in 1969 to supplement the existing official reserves of member countries. The reform was motivated by the inherent constraints on supply reserve assets (gold and dollars) under the Bretton Woods system of fixed exchange rates. The allocation of SDRs made it possible to create liquidity and reserve assets deliberately, independently of the dollar. But until recently only two general allocations of SDRs had been made (in 1970–1972 and in 1979–1981) amounting to a cumulative total of SDR 21.4 billion.

Since the outbreak of the financial and economic crises, the issue of SDRs has once again become the subject of debate. Participants at the G-20 Summit in London in April 2009 pledged to support growth in emerging-market countries and developing countries by boosting the IMF's lending resources to $750 billion. This commitment was a response to a worsening of the reserve position of many developing countries along with a drying up of external financing, although prospects for some other developing countries improved. Overall, the World Bank (2010) is projecting an external financing gap of $305 billion for developing countries in 2010.[2]

As part of this package, the G-20 leaders committed to supporting a general allocation of SDRs equivalent to $250 billion and urged implementation of the 1997 decision to allocate SDRs to "new" members.[3] That decision was approved by the IMF Board in September 2009. According to the IMF's Articles of Agreement, SDR allocation is based on the IMF quota system, whereby IMF member countries receive a share of the issuance corresponding to their IMF quota. Such a quota is based broadly on the relative economic size of the member country, which determines its financial contributions as well as voting power within the IMF. It has been pointed out that this system results in most of the SDRs being allocated to countries that are unlikely to use them. Somewhat less than $100 billion of the proposed emissions would benefit developing countries.

The G-20 commitment was echoed by the recommendations of the Commission of Experts of the President of the United Nations General

Assembly on Reforms of the International Monetary and Financial System (also known as the Stiglitz Commission), chaired by Joseph Stiglitz. However, this Commission went further by advocating a more prominent role for SDRs in the global reserve system. Some of the Commission's proposals were taken up by the Resolution of the United Nations Conference on the World Financial and Economic Crisis and its Impact on Development, adopted in June 2009.

Another recent development is that the IMF has agreed with emerging-market countries to issue bonds denominated in SDRs. China will invest $50 billion in such funds, to be paid in renminbi. Brazil and the Russian Federation also announced their interest in this scheme, thus fulfilling their pledge at the London G-20 summit to participate in boosting the IMF's resources. With regard to China, these steps are part of a new strategy to diversify its currency reserves, to encourage a move towards a global reserve system that is less dependent on the dollar, and to give the renminbi a role in international payment settlements. In this context, China has established foreign currency swaps with a number of developing economies, both within Asia (Indonesia, Hong Kong (Special Administrative Region of China), Malaysia and the Republic of Korea) and outside that region (Argentina and Belarus). In its own interest, China will not rush out of the dollar; but these are signs that China has started, prudently, to diversify its currency reserves, and to invest more of its dollar reserves in short-term maturities.

II. The "Triffin-dilemma" and the shortcomings of the current reserve system

In 1960, Robert Triffin, the Yale economist best known for his critique of the Bretton Woods system of fixed currency exchange rates, argued that the post-Second World War currency system would not be sustainable because it contained an internal contradiction. Williamson (2009:1) explains this dilemma in the following way: "Apart from gold, whose supply was small and erratic, the increase in demand for international liquidity could be satisfied only if the reserve centre, the United States, ran a payments deficit to supply more dollars to the world. But such deficits were bound to undermine confidence in an unchanged link of the United States dollar to gold." It should be pointed out that under the post-war Bretton Woods system, the payments deficit, or more precisely the deficit in the balance of foreign exchange payments, was bound to result from current-account deficits (as capital flows were largely restricted).

To cope with the above problem, one of the proposals was to create additional SDRs in order to supplement the supply of dollars. Due to the expected shortage of reserves and stringent United States monetary policy, this proposal was adopted, and an initial allocation of SDRs was agreed in 1970. However, due to the subsequent shift by the United States towards a very expansionary fiscal and monetary policy and the associated flooding of the world economy with United States dollars, there was no longer a shortage of liquidity. This development led to the breakdown of the post-war Bretton Woods system and the abolition in 1973 of the dollar parity system. There followed a system of floating exchange rates and few rules, in which SDRs did not play a systemic role.[4] Until today, this currency system has not changed fundamentally. However, over time the system has been complemented by a radical liberalization of capital flows.

The question is whether the Triffin dilemma still applies in the circumstances prevailing today, where dollar convertibility has been abandoned, capital accounts have been largely liberalized and flexible exchange rates accepted. Under this system, the United States is no longer obliged to change dollars into gold and to maintain dollar parity with other currencies. However, any increase in the supply of reserves still depends on the United States' balance-of-payments position. But whereas under the post-war system, with its restricted capital flows, the supply of reserves was directly linked to current account positions, this has changed under the current system: with today's largely liberalized capital accounts, the international supply of dollars can equally be provided by capital exports from the United States. The United States can provide a range of liquid assets to the world while at the same time exporting capital, thus running a balanced current account or even a current-account surplus. Therefore, the argument that the United States has to run a current-account deficit in order to provide international liquidity, and that the current dollar-based system will *necessarily* erode confidence in the dollar, does not hold in today's circumstances. However, there are still two shortcomings of the dollar-based reserve system, which relate to issues already highlighted by Triffin, as discussed below.

(a) There is still tension between the objective to increase, or rather to satisfy, the global demand for dollar reserves, and the national objectives of the United States. The *dependence of the supply of global reserves on United States macroeconomic policies* and balance-of-payments positions can generate either an excessive or a limited world supply of reserves. The United States, which issues the dominant international reserve currency in pursuit of national monetary objectives, might have an expansionary or a restrictive impact on the world economy. And indeed, in the past few decades the world has witnessed large swings in the United States' current-account imbalances and associated volatility of the dollar exchange rate. Previous crisis episodes, such as debt crises, commodity price crises, currency crises and interest rate shocks, were partly a consequence of the current, dollar-based currency system (Schulmeister, 2009: 8). This problem became even more acute following a relaxation of controls on capital flows and the associated increase in their volatility. Therefore it is quite clear that the current system is a potential cause of instability in exchange rates and global activity.

(b) While the present system is not necessarily associated with a current-account deficit in the United States, there is at least a *built-in tendency in that country of high, long-lasting and increasing current-account deficits,* and therefore the risk of erosion in the confidence of the value of the dollar. The underlying problem is that there are adverse incentives for national policymakers, with few compensatory coordinating mechanisms. In the United States, there is an incentive to over-consume. International demand for dollars puts pressure on the real interest rate in the United States, and, by stimulating consumption, encourages dissaving, both by the private and the public sector. At the same time, there is little pressure on the United States to curb the associated macroeconomic deficits, as that country has the advantage of being able to borrow at low cost in its own currency, and because there are very few means for exerting political pressure on the country to adjust. But the problem of adverse incentives and lack of coordination applies not only to the United States, as the present situation shows. The growing deficit of the United States is mirrored by an increase in dollar holdings by surplus countries, particularly China.

There are two important reasons why countries strive to accumulate reserves. First, they might wish to "self-insure". Indeed, the present system puts less pressure on surplus countries than on deficit countries (except for the United States as the reserve-issuing country) to adjust. Consequently, there is an incentive for countries to "self-insure" by building up reserves. In particular, developing countries are forced to build up relatively large currency reserves as a means of protecting themselves against adverse external impacts, such as excessive exchange rate volatility (partly associated with the dollar-based system), but also against "shocks" due to short-term capital outflows, adverse movements in the terms of trade and financial crises. Indeed, the past few decades have witnessed a high degree of dollar exchange rate volatility as well as high and increasing volatility in the terms of trade. Also, the financial crisis of the last two decades revealed that developing countries are subject to strong procyclical capital flows. Another factor encouraging developing countries to self-insure might have been IMF policy, which attached stringent conditionality in its support programmes. Indeed, IMF conditionality often pushed countries receiving IMF assistance to adopt over-restrictive policies, which often exacerbated their problems. The experience of developing-country governments during the Asian financial crisis certainly played a significant role in highlighting the importance of self-insuring. The second important reason why countries strive to accumulate reserves is in order to increase their competitive position by intervening in foreign exchange markets. Many export-oriented countries, most notably China, are pursuing this strategy. Their interventions aim at avoiding exchange-rate appreciations and the related loss of competitiveness of their domestic export industries. The relative importance of the two factors in contributing to the rapid increase in reserve holdings by developing countries is debatable, but it is clear that both are playing an important role.

Apart from these two major shortcomings of the current dollar-based reserve system, other deficiencies have also been suggested. In particular, the current system is considered as having a restrictive bias, leading to a tendency towards inefficiency of global aggregate demand in goods and services. This argument was put forward very forcefully by the report of the Stiglitz Commission, which states: "When reserve accumulation is the result of current account surpluses, and not simply the result of tempering the impact of autonomous private foreign capital inflows on the exchange rate, there is a reduction in global aggregate demand" (United Nations, 2009: 112).

The question arises as to why reserve accumulation linked with export surpluses is negatively affecting global aggregate demand. It is certainly true that the accumulated reserves will not translate into effective domestic demand. However, if the central bank holds the reserves, for example in the form of United States Treasury bills, this helps to increase public spending in the United States, while global aggregate demand is not necessarily affected (though the downside is that this feeds macroeconomic imbalances, but this is another issue). Therefore, the argument is not convincing by itself (which does not mean that there are not other features in the current system that adversely affect global aggregate demand).

III. Potential role of SDRs for improving the efficiency of the global reserve system

How could SDR allocations contribute to a more efficient functioning of the global financial and economic system? And, how could the role of SDRs in the global reserve system be fostered in concrete terms?

The allocation of new SDRs already decided by the Fund will provide liquidity-constrained countries with significant unconditional financial resources. It will thereby smoothe their adjustment and allow scope for expansionary policies. Beyond that, the allocation will help those countries meet their reserve asset needs in the years to come. Such an allocation could also contribute to preventing a further aggravation of global imbalances by reducing the need for countries to pursue destabilizing reserve accumulation policies. Without such allocations, many countries may seek to rebuild their currency reserves depleted during the crisis so as to ensure adequate reserve buffers. This would at least make it more difficult to rebalance the global economy. Indeed, a continued build-up of precautionary national reserve holdings would exacerbate international imbalances resulting in serious long-term costs.

Beyond the existing SDR allocations, SDRs could also be used to play a more systematic role in the global financial system. They could help overcome the disadvantages of the current system, notably the dependence of the global reserve supply on the economic policies and politics of the United States which have tended to result in the substantial global imbalances the world has witnessed in recent years. The active use of SDR issuances could contribute to the better adjustment of reserve supply to the demand for reserves. It would help to diversify reserve holdings and risk, as the SDR is a more stable store of value and unit of account compared to its component currencies. According a more important role to SDRs would help reduce the motivation of countries to build up reserves as a kind of self-insurance, because they would be less exposed to the ups and downs of dollar liquidity. If appropriately designed, a new role for SDRs could also contribute to preventing the build-up of imbalances by exerting pressure on the United States to adjust.[5]

There are several, mutually reinforcing ways to foster the role of SDRs in the global reserve system. First, and most importantly, the IMF could provide for further issuances.[6] In particular, SDR could be allocated at times of crisis, where countries would be required to rebuild there SDR holdings once the crisis has passed. Besides, the market for SDRs would have to be increased, for example by fostering the SDR as a privately held asset.[7] The scope of use of SDRs could be extended to become a more broadly accepted means of payment in international trade, in commodity pricing or in corporate book-keeping. Additionally, financial assets could be denominated in SDRs, for example by the IMF through the creation of SDR-denominated securities.

Another option would be to establish a "substitution account" at the IMF, as already discussed in the 1970s. Dollar holders would present their excess dollar holdings to the IMF in exchange for an equivalent amount of SDRs at the current market exchange rate. The SDRs being held in the substitution account could also be used to settle international payments. This could help foster an orderly diversification out of the dollar and influence reserve supply more efficiently.[8] However, the establishment of a substitution account would require agreement on socializing the exchange-rate risk currently concentrated in large balance sheet positions (Mateos y Lago, Duttagupta and Goyal, 2009: 19), for example by the large dollar-holding central banks and investment funds. Shifting the risk from these institutions to the broader IMF membership would certainly be problematic. Why should other IMF members take over a part of the risk, particularly as the high reserves are partly a result of deliberate expenditure promoting policies? Agreement on risk-sharing seems possible, if at all, only as part of a broader deal.

Despite the potential of SDRs to improve the efficiency of the global reserve system, as outlined above, there are also clear limitations on what the SDRs could do. First, it should be stressed that there are limits to the size of accumulated issuances. SDRs constitute a claim on hard currencies: they serve as a reserve currency only because they can be exchanged for hard currencies. SDR issuances allow the use of global reserves in hard currency jointly; in other words, SDRs provide a pooling mechanism with the associated, more efficient use of existing reserves. However, this form of pooling only works as long as there is a sufficient and credible size of the pool in relation to the drawing rights. Besides, a similar pooling effect could be achieved by revamping the relevant IMF facilities (Mateos y Lago Duttagupta and Goyal, 2009, 2009: 11). Secondly, a system in which SDRs play a more prominent role would not be adequate; there would still be the need for a mechanism for coordinating national policies to prevent global imbalances (Kregel, 2009; UNCTAD 2009: 121). Strengthening the surveillance role of the IMF, as well as peer pressure within the G-20, would also be of the utmost importance.

IV. Potential of SDRs to foster development and the provision of global public goods

Apart from its potential to improve the efficiency and stability of the global monetary system, according a more important role to SDRs within the global reserve system could offer other advantages as well, notably greater equity and sustainability. Regarding equity, it has been argued that the current, dollar-based reserve system is associated with two advantages for the United States. First, since that country has the advantage of being able to pay its debts in its own currency, it is not required to settle those debts through a transfer of assets. Secondly, the United States benefits from so-called "seigniorage", which is the gain from issuing the zero-interest asset of money (or the low-interest asset of reserves). On the other hand, the high volatility of the current system is subjecting developing countries to recurrent external shocks and problems of illiquidity, in particular as a result of procyclical capital flows. As outlined above, this might induce them to accumulate large amounts of foreign exchange reserves to protect themselves against shocks, a policy which does not come without costs (the opportunity costs of holding reserves). To the extent that dollar reserves would be substituted by SDR reserves, the above-mentioned advantages for the United States would be curbed.

As mentioned, according to IMF rules, new SDRs are distributed on the basis of member countries' quotas. It has been proposed to make a higher share of SDR issuances available to developing countries by changing the allocation formula in a way that results in larger allocations to developing countries or to countries most in need of reserves. For example, SDRs might be distributed in relation to the size of the demand for reserves in recent years (see, for example, UNCTAD 2009: 22). However, such reforms would not be in conformity with the broad mandate of the Fund. It would require changing the IMF's Articles of Agreement and it would not be in the interest of the wider membership of the Fund. The issue of substance notwithstanding, this proposal does not, therefore, seem to be politically feasible, to say the least.

Another option would be for industrialized countries to commit to voluntarily transferring "their" SDR allocations to developing countries or to international organizations. There are several possible approaches:

(a) SDR donation. Industrialized and surplus countries could donate their SDRs to developing countries or to international organizations. In that case the central bank of the donating country would have to write down the SDR asset in its balance sheet. As this implies a loss for the central bank, such a donation would involve a real (budgetary) cost. Moreover, the donating country would have to service the interest on the SDR liability vis-à-vis the IMF.

(b) Transfer of SDR allocation. Industrialized and surplus countries could transfer their SDR allocations to developing countries. In this case, the recipient countries would take over the SDRs from the transferring industrialized country, and those SDRs would count as an asset as well as a liability in their balance sheets. If the recipient country were to spend the SDRs (i.e. exchange them for hard currency), it would have to pay net interest to the IMF.

(c) Lending of SDRs. Newly issued SDRs could be made available by industrialized and surplus countries to the multilateral development banks (MDBs) through loans or equity finance. For example, an industrialized country could invest the SDRs in bonds issued by a multilateral development bank, such as the World Bank. This would allow the MDBs to enhance their lending capacity for developing countries. The lender country would be entitled to receive interest payments on those bonds.

However, these proposals entail certain risks and downsides. First, in the cases of (b) and (c) above, there is an obvious risk for the recipient countries relating to debt sustainability. Since an SDR is an interest-bearing asset, any transfer or lending arrangements would expose these countries to interest rate variability, along with the associated high risks. The current SDR interest rate is only about 0.4 per cent, but this is a very low level by historical standards; over the past 30 years, it has averaged about 5.5 per cent. Thus reliance on such funding carries an undeniable risk in terms of debt sustainability, particularly for vulnerable and small low-income countries. Besides, development finance is already provided to this group of countries on highly concessional terms. If interest rates were to increase from their present low levels, SDR service charges might overstretch low-income countries' financing capacity. This is particularly the case for those low-income countries where SDRs constitute a relatively high share of their overall exports. Nevertheless, such donations, even when linked with the obligation to service the interest charges, could be very attractive to many developing countries, as the interest rate would probably be much lower than the rate that countries with access to private markets pay on average. Secondly, if the SDRs were used by recipient governments to draw on hard currency and these funds were sold domestically, there would be a risk of real appreciation and loss of international competitiveness (the so-called "Dutch disease"). These drawbacks need to be taken seriously, although they should not lead to abandoning altogether the idea of SDR transfers to developing countries. One important issue here is that if some countries decide to implement such transfers, the funds should be used to foster investment and productivity in recipient countries (in order to avoid the Dutch disease and debt problems) and/or used for crisis-related, time-bound expenditures.

There is another argument against using SDRs to finance development-related investments. SDRs were created to provide international liquidity in order to overcome short-term balance-of-payments difficulties. If they were to be spent for other purposes, such as for meeting development objectives, the question would inevitably arise as to why such financing could not be made available more effectively through regular budgetary allocations by donor governments or by increasing support to multilateral institutions such as the World Bank or IMF facilities. Why transfer SDRs instead of providing the funds through the traditional budgetary appropriations for development cooperation? While this is a fair point, using transfers could be justified for the provision of development-related global public goods such as in the area of climate change mitigation.[9] Indeed, this would be broadly in line with the original concept of SDRs, notably to provide short-term liquidity in case of a balance-of-payments crisis, which is also a utilization that is linked to a global public good, namely "global financial stability".

In this context, the issues raised in the negotiations for a post-Kyoto protocol are complex and challenging. Since the main point of divergence between industrialized and developing countries concerns the issue of financing, the possible use of SDRs could constitute an important element of a deal on future climate-change-related financing. Industrialized countries, and possibly emerging-market countries, could commit to making available, temporarily, "their" SDR allocation for climate protection measures, either directly or through the World Bank and the regional development banks.[10] If necessary, the donor countries could commit to taking (partly) over the interest charges linked to the use of SDRs (which, in most countries, would require going through their respective budgetary procedures). One specific proposal is that industrialized countries invest the SDRs in bonds issued by development institutions (such as the World Bank); in this case the donor country would bear the SDR interest service charges, but would receive the interest from the bonds, thus minimizing its budgetary costs. If the IMF issued SDRs regularly and the major greenhouse gas emitting countries decided to use a part of their allocation for such transfers, this could contribute to a "global green deal" in financing a share of the needed funds for mitigation action. Such a deal could also help trigger a new recovery in the still sluggish world economy, while at the same time ensuring that the recovery focuses on green investments.

V. Concluding remarks

It is clear that the present problems in the global monetary system require comprehensive reforms, including, in particular, better macroeconomic coordination and improved macro-financial surveillance. Thus the potential of SDRs to improve the functioning of the current currency system is limited, as the SDR is essentially a pooling mechanism. However, the role of SDRs in the global reserve system is already increasing, and it is worth discussing in greater depth what longer term role SDRs could play within a more comprehensive reform approach. For example, countercyclical issuances, combined with other reforms (aimed at a broader use of SDRs for official and private transactions), might increase the stability of the international financial system by making it less dependent on the economic policies and politics of the United States. This could also contribute to enhancing the efficiency of the system, as the supply of reserves might be better able to respond to the demands of the world economy. Apart from improving the stability and efficiency of the global financial system, the SDRs could be used to contribute to the provision of global public goods. In particular, major greenhouse gas emitting countries could make available a part of their SDR allocations for climate-related investments in developing countries, thus contributing to a successful conclusion of the ongoing climate negotiations.

Now might be a unique moment to discuss these proposals: both the United States and countries holding sizeable foreign exchange reserves may actually find it more acceptable today than ever before to introduce reforms of the current global monetary system. For the United States, it would provide an opportunity to take policy decisions with less concern about their global impact. For countries holding substantial dollar reserves, it would enable them to diversify their reserves and minimize the risk associated with a depreciation in the international value of the dollar. China, the Russian Federation and other emerging-market economies have already explicitly advocated a new currency system, in which SDRs and the IMF would play a more important role. Moreover, it is in the interest of all countries to ensure that the stalled climate negotiations are revived. Since a major stumbling block in the negotiations in Copenhagen in December 2009 concerned financing, the possible use of SDRs, whereby industrialized countries – and perhaps also emerging-market countries – could commit to making temporarily available their SDR allocations for climate protection measures, could constitute an important element in any revived climate negotiations.

Notes

1   The reserve asset character of SDRs derives from the commitment of members to hold and accept SDRs, and to honour the obligations underlying the operations of the SDR system. Therefore it does not constitute a liability of the IMF.

2   This figure is based on a projection of their total current-account deficits, along with scheduled repayments due on private foreign debt (resulting in total external financing needs of about $948 billion in 2010). It also takes into account the amount of private-sector financing likely to be forthcoming (World Bank, 2010).

3   The 1997 decision concerned a one-time allocation to new IMF members, mostly former communist countries. However, this allocation was agreed only recently, mainly because it had not been accepted earlier by the United States.

4   However, under the new system, the value of SDRs was not fixed solely against the dollar, but rather against a basket of currencies.

5   Such a system could exert a stronger adjustment pressure on the United States, for example, by shifting the exchange-rate risk to the United States Treasury and because concerns about the value of the United States dollar could lead to a shift in favour of SDRs. Besides, once an alternative reserve currency, such as the SDR (but equally the euro or other potential reserve currencies), gains substantial weight, there would be an additional incentive for the United States to adjust, because of the risk of investors moving increasingly away from the United States dollar.

6   As pointed out in the report of the Stiglitz Commission, issuances could actively be used in a countercyclical way, with bigger issuances when growth is below potential and vice versa.

7   At present, SDRs can only be used for official transactions.

8   As Williamson (2009) stresses, it is not possible for the IMF to effectively influence the rate of reserve growth by varying the rate of SDR issuance as long as countries retain the right to accumulate dollars. In order to ensure that SDR issuances influence the total stock of reserves, some form of asset settlement would need to be introduced. Therefore Williamson suggests that countries be required to exchange their own currencies for SDRs and vice versa, for example by establishing a substitution account at the IMF denominated in SDRs.

9   George Soros has repeatedly advocated using SDR allocations for global public goods.

10   The funds would have to be paid back, thus rebuilding the original SDR holdings.

304 *Jürgen Zattler*

References

Kregel J (2009). Some simple observations on the reform of the international monetary system. Policy note. Annandale-on-Hudson, NY, The Levy Economics Institute of Bard College, August.
Mateos y Lago, Duttagupta R and Goyal R (2009). The debate on the international montary system. IMF staff position note, Washington, DC, November.
Schulmeister S (2009). Globalisierung ohne supranationale Währung: Ein fataler Widerspruch. *Ifo Schnelldienst*, 16/2009.
UNCTAD (2009). *Trade and Development Report 2009: Responding to the Global Crisis – Climate Change Mitigation and Development.* New York and Geneva, United Nations.
United Nations (2009). Report of the Commission of Experts of the President of the United Nations General Assembly on Reforms of the International Monetary and Financial System. New York, 21 September.
Williamson J (2009). Understanding Special Drawing Rights (SDRs). Policy brief. Washington, DC, Peterson Institute for International Economics, June.
World Bank (2010). *Global Economic Prospects 2010: Crisis, Finance and Growth in Developing Countries.* Washington, DC.

THE FINANCIAL AND ECONOMIC CRISIS AND GLOBAL ECONOMIC GOVERNANCE*

Detlef J. Kotte

Abstract

The global financial and economic crisis has demonstrated the need for major reforms in the system of global economic governance. Such reforms are necessary in order to reduce the predominant influence of financial markets in determining the conditions under which governments design their macroeconomic and development policies. Dependence on the dollar as the main reserve currency could be reduced by allowing an international institution to create international liquidity to support countries facing an externally caused balance-of-payments or currency crisis. But the key to greater stability is more likely to lie in a multilaterally agreed set of principles and rules for exchange-rate management, accompanied by a framework for macroeconomic policy coordination among the systemically important countries. In developing countries and emerging-market economies the use of capital controls would help stabilize the macroeconomic context for investment in real productive capacity and successful integration into the global economy.

---

* This paper draws on UNCTAD's *Trade and Development Report, 2009*, chapter IV: Reform of the International Monetary and Financial System.

Introduction

The financial and economic crisis that broke out in 2007 has, once again, shown the close connection between financial fragility and current-account imbalances, and between banking and currency crises. It has also shown that macroeconomic and financial imbalances in the developed countries continue to have strong repercussions on growth and stability in developing and emerging-market economies.

As an immediate reaction to the spillover of the financial crisis to the rest of the world, the President of the French Republic, the Prime Minister of the United Kingdom and others boldly called for a "new Bretton Woods" agreement (Financial Times, 2008; Boughton 2009). And at their summit in September 2009, the leaders of the G-20 (2009) committed to "reform the global architecture to meet the needs of the 21st century". However, policy action remained focused on crisis management and short-term stabilization to circumscribe the damage in the real economy, and on strengthening regulation and supervision of financial markets.[1] Such action is necessary and may reduce the risk of crises resulting from "irrational exuberance" in financial markets, but it is insufficient to solve the more deep-seated problems with the current global economic governance system. While financial regulation aims at influencing the behaviour of private actors in financial markets, the global governance dimension relates to an international framework for public action in the management of cross-border financial transactions and exchange rates, and for macroeconomic policies.

This paper first discusses the most glaring shortcomings of the global economic governance system against the background of the recent crisis. It then goes on to propose several elements of reform of the international monetary and financial system that could, in addition to strengthening financial regulation and supervision, help prevent similar crises in the future.

I. The world economy before the crisis

A. Financial fragility

Rapid credit expansion is not necessarily a sign of increased financial fragility. But in the run-up to the financial crisis in the United States, the growing credit was not used for financing projects to expand and upgrade real productive capacity, the returns from which could have serviced the debt. Instead, it was used for financing consumption and speculation. In this regard, the current financial crisis in the United States and other developed countries was not particularly different from previous financial crises in emerging markets. As investors lost a realistic perception of the risks connected with high-yielding assets, speculative bubbles were created in several segments of the financial and real estate markets. In combination with the increasing importance of non-bank financial institutions as providers of finance, the creation of credit itself became increasingly dependent on the behaviour of asset prices: higher prices of existing assets, rather than the creation of new real capital, stimulated further credit expansion through their influence on bank capitalization and increased the value of potential collateral that borrowers could offer (Özgür and Ertürk 2008).

Net capital inflows to countries with current-account deficits fuelled speculation in the markets for high-risk financial assets and real estate. Speculation also increasingly determined prices in the international markets for primary commodities and in foreign exchange markets. Commodity contracts came to be considered by financial investors as an alternative asset class in their portfolios (UNCTAD, 2009a: 25–35).[2] In foreign exchange markets speculation took the form of "carry trade" flows attracted by possible arbitrage profits resulting from interest rate differentials and expectations of additional gains from currency appreciation.

B.   Macroeconomic management and the "confidence game"

Fragility in financial markets as a result of excessive risk taking and herd behaviour would be less of a problem if its costs were borne only by those actors that create it through debt-financed speculative investments. But it has severe impacts on the real sector, as is evident each time a financial crisis leads to a credit crunch, when it becomes difficult, if not impossible, for producers or traders of goods to obtain financing for their activities, thus contributing to recession and rising unemployment. Moreover, with their growing size, financial markets have acquired enormous power to influence macroeconomic outcomes through their impact on key financial prices, and to influence the formulation of economic policy in the direction of reduced government interference in their business.

Over the past 25 years or so economic policy thinking has been shaped more and more by the assumption, derived form neoclassical economic theory, that free markets always lead to optimal outcomes, or at least to outcomes that are preferable to those that can be achieved with State intervention. With progressively greater financial liberalization, macroeconomic and structural policies therefore have been increasingly designed in way that is judged to be "sound" by financial market participants who are assumed to have the appropriate knowledge to make such judgements. For example, surging private capital flows to developing and transition economies have been typically viewed by many observers and policymakers as a sign of strength of the receiving economies, and in the case of developing and transition economies, as beneficial for development. And the growing external deficit of the United States before the current crisis was not considered a serious threat to the stability of the world economy, as financial markets continued to finance it.

More than other financial crises before, the present one, which erupted in the most sophisticated financial market in the world, has demonstrated that the idea that markets produce optimal results when left to self-regulation is wrong. Excessive financial deregulation has not led to a better allocation of productive capital; rather, it has opened new avenues for speculation that is mostly unrelated to the financial system's role of performing service functions in the real economy.

The international dimension to this is that exchange rates are driven up or down by speculator "sentiments", which are typically an extrapolation of past trends into the future that last until speculative bubbles burst, and they have little or no relation to the viability of a given current-account position. Actors in financial and currency markets are not concerned with the proper interpretation of macroeconomic fundamentals; otherwise a number of economies with excessive private debts – including those that were destinations of carry-trade operations, but also the United States – would not have continued to attract large capital inflows. Nor are actors in financial markets concerned with proper assessments of corporate performance or the long-term valuation of real estate; otherwise large bubbles would not have occurred in the stock and real estate markets. Moreover, these actors are not concerned with a correct interpretation of real demand-supply relations in primary commodity markets; otherwise there would not have been excessive commodity price fluctuations. Rather, they are concerned with guessing how certain "news" will influence the expectations and investment decisions of other financial market participants, so as to derive maximum benefits from asset price movements driven by "herd behaviour", regardless of whether this is justified by fundamental economic performance indicators. A pattern of exchange rates that is strongly influenced by financial flows following changes in "market sentiment" is therefore inherently unstable and prone to misalignments.

C. Macroeconomic imbalances

The macroeconomic side of the – finally unsustainable – expansion of debt-financed consumption and speculation prior to the financial crisis is that for many years the United States had been the world's largest net capital importer – the inevitable counterpart to its role as an engine of growth for the world economy – through its increasing trade deficit, which transmitted strong growth impulses to the rest of the world (see table 1).

This process was greatly facilitated by the role of the dollar as the main international reserve currency, thanks to which the United States, distinct from other economies, is under no pressure to adjust to an external deficit. Any excess of its imports over exports can be paid for with its own

Table 1

SELECTED MACROECONOMIC INDICATORS FOR MAJOR DEFICIT AND SURPLUS COUNTRIES, 2001–2007

(Per cent, unless otherwise indicated)

	Real GDP	Domestic demand	Consumption	Exports	Current-account balance (Per cent of GDP) 2001	2007
	Average annual change				2001	2007
China	10.6	7.5	7.9	25.5	1.3	11.0
Japan	1.9	1.2	1.3	9.5	2.1	4.8
Germany	1.2	0.4	0.3	7.8	0.0	7.5
Switzerland	2.1	1.3	1.3	6.1	7.8	9.9
United States	2.8	2.9	2.8	6.0	-3.9	-5.2
United Kingdom	2.6	2.7	2.5	4.8	-2.1	-2.7
Australia	3.3	4.9	3.8	2.6	-2.0	-6.3
Spain	3.4	4.5	4.1	4.2	-3.9	-10.0

Source: OECD StatExtracts; The World Bank, *World Economic Indicators*; IMF, *World Economic Outlook*, October 2009 online databases; and *UNCTAD Handbook of Statistics* database.

currency. Growing dollar reserves of surplus countries seeking to prevent an appreciation of their nominal exchange rates through intervention in the foreign exchange market were mainly invested in United States Treasury bonds. The role of the dollar as the main reserve currency also ensures that the United States financial market is considered by actors in financial markets as a "safe haven" for their investments. Moreover, an increasing share of private capital flowing to deficit economies was invested in high-risk assets because interest rates on less risky assets were very low and foreign banks took advantage of "regulatory arbitrage" (i.e. the possibility of investing in financial instruments that offered higher short-term profits than would have been possible in more tightly regulated financial markets at home).

But the deficit of one economy has to be matched by a surplus in at least one other economy. Therefore, macroeconomic and financial policies in surplus countries matter as much for the emergence of imbalances in international trade and instability in the world economy as do policies in deficit economies (see table 1). The lopsided distribution of domestic demand growth among the leading economies was not only the outcome of fast, mostly debt-driven expansion of demand in the deficit economies (primarily the United States but also other countries like Australia, Spain and the United Kingdom), but also of insufficient domestic demand growth in the main surplus economies, notably Germany and Japan. An exception to this general pattern was China: this economy's large surplus was accompanied by very strong growth of its gross domestic product (GDP) and domestic demand.

The exchange-rate system did not operate in a way that would have generated adjustments towards a more balanced distribution of global demand growth. This was because demand and supply of currencies in the foreign exchange markets were not driven by trade-related transactions but by cross-currency financial flows, which to an increasing extent were unrelated to price and cost developments in the real sector. In this situation, international coordination of national macroeconomic policies would have been especially important to ensure stability in the international trading and financial system.

II. Institutional shortcomings and the case for reform

In the build-up to the financial crisis, the International Monetary Fund (IMF) and the Financial Stability Board failed in what should be their most important function: maintaining international monetary and financial stability. One reason why the IMF has been unable to play a decisive role in the prevention of financial crises has been the limited reach of its surveillance; another has been its definition of "sound" macroeconomic policies.

In the run-up to the crisis it was certainly difficult to fully grasp the problems with the often opaque debt instruments resulting from financial innovation. However, when warnings were issued by institutional observers that the risk of an adjustment crisis was mounting they were ignored by policymakers. For example, three years before the eruption of the financial crisis the Bank for International Settlements had already pointed to the financial and macroeconomic risks associated with the housing bubble in the United States (BIS, 2004: 144–146), and for several years UNCTAD had warned that the increasing current-account imbalances were unsustainable, and that without an internationally coordinated macroeconomic policy effort a "hard-landing" was likely to occur (UNCTAD, 2005, 12–18; UNCTAD, 2007: 19).[3]

Macroeconomic policy surveillance by the IMF has been effective only for countries borrowing from the Fund, but it has been ineffective for countries that are not dependent on IMF financing, including systemically important countries. Also, the IMF has had no influence on the exchange-rate management of the major reserve currencies; neither has it been able to contribute to improving policy coordination among the major deficit and surplus economies with a view to achieving greater compatibility of their macroeconomic policy stances. Similarly, the G-7/8 did not use its influence to resolve the problem of the global imbalances in a concrete manner and discuss common policy action in earnest before the crisis broke out. As policymakers finally discovered that markets have only limited wisdom in judging what is macroeconomically right or wrong, the potential role of public policy in general, not only in terms of regulation of markets but also in terms proactive macroeconomic crisis management, came to be perceived in a different light. The result was a revival of countercyclical policies, including discretionary fiscal action, at the national level, and a modest effort by governments of the leading countries to coordinate such policies at the international level.

A logical step further would be to subject the pattern of exchange rates to greater public scrutiny and discipline, and to institutionalize international coordination of macroeconomic demand management with a view to preventing the build-up of large imbalances, and hence subsequent adjustment crises. This would contribute significantly to greater coherence in the global economic governance system. At present, the World Trade Organization (WTO) provides a multilateral institutional framework for trade policy and international trade relations, but there is an institutional vacuum with regard to monetary and financial policies and international financial activities, even though capital flows, exchange rates and macroeconomic policies can have much more dramatic impacts on other countries than trade policies.

As with tariffs and other trade barriers, any change in the exchange rate of an open economy has international repercussions. Clearly, there are important differences between the impacts of exchange-rate changes and those of tariffs on trade, the most important being that tariffs are product-specific, while exchange-rate changes affect the relative prices of all traded goods and services. But another important difference is that exchange-rate movements generated by the behaviour of financial investors in international currency markets are unpredictable and erratic. As a result, possible gains from international trade and competition are not fully realized and actual gains are unequally distributed, which in turn affect fixed capital formation in tradeable industries.

III. Monetary system reform for crisis prevention

A. A new reserve currency?

In view of the shortcomings of the international monetary and financial system, the role of the dollar as the main international reserve currency has been challenged and the possibility of an alternative reserve asset raised, among others in the report of the so-called Stiglitz Commission (UNPGA, 2009). One proposal, discussed by the Commission and reiterated by some observers (e.g. Bergsten, 2007; Dullien, Herr and Kellermann, 2009:140–144), was first mooted in the late 1970s. This proposal envisaged allowing central banks to deposit dollar reserves in a special "substitution account" at the IMF, to be denominated in Special Drawing Rights (SDRs). Since the SDR is valued as the weighted average of the major currencies, its value is more stable than that of each of its constituent currencies. The exchange-rate risk associated with reserve holdings would thus be shifted to the IMF and would have to be covered either through the generation of higher revenues by that Fund or by guarantees from its member States.

A much bolder step would be to empower an international body to issue an "artificial" reserve currency.[4] This issue is closely connected to that concerning the provision of international liquidity and the question of how the role of the SDR could be strengthened to make it the main form of international liquidity and a reserve asset. With its current mandate, the IMF resembles a "credit union", in the sense that it cannot create its own money but, in principle, can only lend out what has been deposited by member States. As a provider of an alternative reserve asset (and international lender of last resort) the IMF would resemble more a central bank that can issue SDRs against itself, as suggested by Akyüz (2009).[5] In case of need, for example when a temporary current- account deficit arises as a result of external factors, or when an exchange-rate has to be defended against depreciation that is unwarranted by the underlying fundamentals, member States should be allowed to draw on this liquidity with much wider access limits than are presently applied in IMF lending.

Arrangements for access to SDRs should take into account the fact that the need for accessing such liquidity varies not only across countries but also over time. In the medium to long term, it grows broadly in line with global output and the volume of international trade and financial transactions. From the point of view of short-term stabilization of the global economy, it would be appropriate to issue more SDRs when global growth is below potential or during crisis periods, and to issue smaller amounts of SDRs or retire them in periods of fast global output growth.

Such a stronger role of the SDR would probably offer a number of advantages. It would enable easier and more reliable access to international liquidity in times of crisis that would reduce the need for accumulating dollar reserves to counter pressures for currency depreciation when financial markets lose confidence in an economy or a currency. But in a world where capital can move freely this would not prevent large exchange-rate fluctuations or protracted misalignments as long as there continue to be incentives for interest arbitrage and currency speculation. The question of how to ensure that exchange rates are determined in a way that minimizes such incentives thus remains unresolved.

B. Multilateral rules for exchange-rate management

The global economic governance system contributes to sustained growth and employment creation inasmuch as it provides a stable international environment for business decisions related to choices in international trade and to investment in real productive capacity. Erratic movements of exchange rates send wrong or unreliable signals to market participants and harm investment and innovation, while persistent exchange-rate misalignments distort the competitiveness of producers on international markets.

The experiences of the various financial and currency crises since the breakdown of the Bretton Woods system suggest that freely floating exchange rates tend to encourage currency speculation as long as there is national autonomy in monetary policy-making, but also that absolute stability of the *nominal* exchange rate may be counterproductive, because it cannot prevent current-account imbalances resulting from shifts in the *real* exchange rate. Nominal exchange-rate changes are necessary as they reflect diverging cost and price developments across countries. On the other hand, excessive volatility encourages financial speculation and discourages long-term investment. Exchange-rate changes, and in particular *real* exchange-rate changes that have a strong influence on the international competitiveness of all producers, cannot be left to a market that is under the influence of strong speculative forces. But at the same time, exchange-rate manipulation as a means of influencing national trade performance, and thus a process of competitive devaluation, also has to be prevented – a concern that was already central to the architecture of the Bretton Woods system and the creation of the IMF. All these considerations call for a system in which each country would be able to manage its exchange rate flexibly, but within a framework that protects the interest of other countries.

One approach to reforming the international currency system in this direction has been proposed by UNCTAD (2009a and b). Central to this proposal is a multilateral agreement on principles and rules for governing exchange-rate management that focuses on maintaining sustainable current-account positions by keeping the real exchange rate more or less stable. Compliance with these rules and principles would be subject to surveillance by an international body, perhaps a reformed IMF. The initial exchange-rate pattern could be determined by a multilaterally agreed formula that approximately reflects the purchasing power of a currency expressed in all other currencies, similar to the rule that was implicit in the former Bretton Woods system and the European Monetary System before the introduction of the euro. Subsequently, the real effective exchange rates would be kept stable (or within a narrow range) through mandatory adjustments in the nominal exchange rate (Flassbeck and Spiecker, 2007: 279–280). Nominal exchange-rate adjustments would have to be undertaken in accordance with changes in variables such as the GDP deflator, unit labour costs or central bank interest rates, so as to reflect inflationary tendencies and avoid uncovered interest parity.

For certain countries and at certain times, some flexibility in the application of the basic rule may be necessary. For example, the sustainable level of the real effective exchange rate can change with the country's stage of development. Thus, similar to the provision of special and differential treatment in the multilateral trading system, a degree of flexibility could be retained in favour developing countries that still have a long way to go in catching up with developed countries. They could be allowed to keep their exchange rates slightly undervalued with a view to facilitating their domestic manufacturers' entry into global markets, on the one hand, and to providing a degree of shelter for their nascent domestic industries from overwhelming global competition on the other. In certain cases, a fall in export earnings resulting from factors beyond the control of an individual country may also warrant an exception to the basic rule.

The main difficulties in creating such an exchange-rate system are probably the determination of the initial pattern of parities and the implied reduction of national autonomy in exchange-rate management. Thus governments would need to be convinced of the rewards that can be had in return for giving up that autonomy, namely greater stability of the international environment for trade and financial relations and the reduced risk of externally induced financial and currency crises. In addition, trade patterns would be less distorted and the parameters for decision-making by firms with regard to real investment and innovation in order to compete in the globalized economy would be much more stable and predictable, with attendant effects on growth and employment creation in all countries.[6]

C. Complementary reforms

An exchange-rate adjustment mechanism based on multilaterally agreed principles and rules would go a long way in preventing current-account imbalances and excessive boom episodes based on external debt accumulation which are typically followed by financial and currency crises. However, it may need to be supported by additional measures, such as improved international macroeconomic policy coordination in combination with more effective policy surveillance, and active capital-account management. Each of these would also be useful independently of a currency system reform, and may take less time than such a system to gain international approval.

1. Strengthened macroeconomic policy coordination and surveillance

While a multilateral exchange-rate mechanism would minimize the risk of large current-account imbalances emerging from exchange-rate-induced shifts in international competitive positions, it may not be sufficient to correct large imbalances that are the result of big differences in domestic demand growth, as shown in table 1. Therefore, the global economic governance system would gain greater coherence if multilateral trade rules and a multilateral exchange-rate mechanism were complemented by an international body for effective coordination and surveillance of macroeconomic policy. The need for macroeconomic policy coordination has previously been recognized, for example by the Monterrey Consensus. While such coordination has sometimes been used during crises, it would be of particular importance as a means of crisis prevention. In order for IMF policy surveillance to become more effective, all member States need to commit to adhering to recommendations resulting from surveillance exercises. As in the case of the system for exchange-rate determination, such adherence can only be expected if governments recognize the advantages of sacrificing a degree of policy autonomy for the benefit of greater global stability that would result if all governments were to adjust their macroeconomic policies in line with international requirements. It will be especially important to achieve a greater balance in the obligations of surplus and deficit countries, respectively, in efforts to correct emerging current-account imbalances.

Greater effectiveness of macroeconomic policy surveillance also requires that its focus be shifted away from generating market confidence to addressing the needs for countercyclical demand management. Macroeconomic policy coordination and surveillance would not imply imposing a particular policy design on each individual country; rather, it should aim at influencing the overall policy stance, especially of systemically important economies, as it results from the mix of the different components of demand management: monetary, fiscal and incomes policies. Distinct from past practice, monetary policy would need to be judged by the extent to which it is geared to keeping interest rates low to provide favourable conditions for the financing of investment, rather than focusing on narrowly defined inflation targets or on the ability of a currency to attract capital inflows. Fiscal policy would best be assessed against its contribution to stabilizing aggregate demand and employment, rather than against the "ideal" of a balanced budget per se. And incomes policy, the scope of which depends on country-specific institutional frameworks for labour markets, would need to be assessed from a macroeconomic perspective which considers wages as a major determinant of demand, rather than from a microeconomic perspective that considers wages only as the largest component of production costs.

If such an international coordination mechanism had been in place, the large global imbalances that built up before 2008 could certainly have been mitigated, and perhaps even avoided. In such a framework, central banks would have undertaken coordinated intervention to achieve exchange adjustments that the market failed to generate. In addition, restrictive macroeconomic action would have been taken by the authorities in the United States and in other deficit economies experiencing relatively fast growth to slow down the expansion of domestic demand, while in the surplus economies with slow demand growth, including in particular Germany and Japan, as well as some oil exporting countries, more expansionary monetary and fiscal policies would have been appropriate. This could also have included encouraging households to reduce their savings and employers to raise wages in line with, or temporarily in excess of, productivity gains.

2.   Capital controls

Even if the experience of the financial crisis leads to filling some of the gaps in national financial regulation and supervision, the management of cross-border capital flows requires separate attention. Appropriate management of such flows is not only a financial policy issue, in the sense that it may help prevent speculative bubbles and non-transparent and excessive risk-taking by financial institutions; it is also a macroeconomic issue of particular importance for the international competitiveness of producers in emerging markets and developing economies.

The notion that reducing the volatility of international financial flows is a precondition for stable growth and an expansion of international trade guided the Bretton Woods negotiations, which laid the foundation for the post-war governance system for a long period of relative monetary and financial stability in the world economy. In order to achieve this, governments were allowed to introduce comprehensive capital controls to preserve their domestic macroeconomic policy space. While "equilibrating" private international financial flows and those related to "productive" investment were explicitly welcomed, the IMF's Articles of Agreement gave each government freedom to protect their economies against undesirable financial transactions (Helleiner, 2009).

With the end of the Bretton Woods system in the early 1970s and the subsequent wave of liberalization of international capital flows, the idea of capital controls became a taboo in mainstream discussions of appropriate financial policies, as market forces were considered the only reliable guide for the allocation of capital.[7] Some rethinking began in the aftermath of the Asian crisis, and in the context of the present crisis several authors (e.g. Rodrik and Subramanian, 2008; Reinhart and Rogoff, 2008; Bibow 2010) have again provided convincing arguments for the use of restrictions on international capital mobility as a means of reducing the risk of recurrent international financial crises. The experiences of numerous economies, such as Chile, China, Colombia, India, Malaysia, Singapore and Taiwan Province of China, suggest that capital controls can be effective and useful (Epstein, Grabel and Jomo, 2004).

When introduced in a period of crisis, capital-account management mainly takes the form of restrictions on capital outflows. On the other hand, when it is conceived as an instrument for preventing the build-up of speculative bubbles and currency misalignments and for preserving domestic macroeconomic policy space, it primarily implies certain restrictions on capital inflows. Depending on the specific requirements of countries, comprehensive capital-account management can include outright bans of certain types of capital inflows, minimum-stay requirements, as well as reserve requirements or taxes on foreign loans.

Capital-account management could be applied in a countercylical manner by restricting excessive foreign borrowing in good times and controlling capital flight during crises (Rodrik, 2009). In any case, it would certainly be a step forward if surging capital inflows were no longer perceived as a sign of a strong receiving economy, but rather as a potential for disequilibrium, with negative effects on monetary management and trade. The IMF should therefore change its stance by more actively encouraging countries to consider introducing capital controls as provided for in its Articles of Agreement, and advising them on their national implementation (Rodrik, 2009; South Centre, 2008).

IV. Summary and conclusion

Reform of global economic governance needs to aim at greater coherence between the multilateral trading system and international arrangements for the management of monetary and financial relations. So that those relations do not continue to be the source of major macroeconomic and trade imbalances, such reform should seek to reduce the predominance of financial markets in determining the conditions under which governments design their macroeconomic and development policies. Allowing financial markets to continue to exercise strong influence on key economic variables and economic policy decisions would sow the seeds of future crises. Strengthening national regulation and supervision of financial markets is a minimum condition for greater stability; however, it will not be sufficient to prevent the build-up of new imbalances in a system which lacks an effective mechanism of policy coordination among systemically important countries for correcting divergences in macroeconomic policy and growth performance, and where the pattern of exchange rates fails to accurately reflect current-account positions.

In the absence of a deep reform of the international exchange-rate system towards appropriate rules and mechanisms for multilateral intervention in currency markets, there is the danger that an increasing number of countries will continue to aim at an undervalued exchange rate, larger current-account surpluses and higher foreign exchange reserves. The need for such reserve holdings could be reduced by allowing an international institution to create international liquidity to support countries that are facing an externally caused balance-of-payments or currency crises. However, the key to the prevention of protracted imbalances and instability in international financial and trade relations appears to lie in reform of the exchange-rate system and the creation of a framework for more effective macroeconomic policy coordination and surveillance. Exchange rates must be flexible enough to compensate for interest and inflation differentials and stable enough to provide reliable signals for business decisions in the tradeables sector. A multilateral system based on the principle of stability of the real effective exchange rate, as proposed by UNCTAD, would reduce the need for accumulating foreign exchange reserves.

Experience with the current financial crisis has demonstrated even more clearly than other, previous crises that markets do not know better. It also challenges the conventional wisdom that dismantling all obstacles to cross-border private capital flows is the best recipe for countries to advance their economic development. Surging capital inflows are not necessarily a sign of strength, but always a potential source of disequilibrium, and they can have grave repercussions for macroeconomic stability and trade performance. Developing countries may be well-advised to put greater emphasis than in the past on strengthening their domestic financial systems, and to rely on capital inflows only to the extent necessary for the financing of imports of capital goods and technology that help to build domestic production and export capacity.

Notes

1   See the various communiqués and declarations of the G-8 and the G-20, at: www.7.utoronto.ca/ and www.g20.org, respectively.

2   The "financialization" of primary commodity markets, discussed at greater length by Mayer in this volume, is the most plausible explanation for the parallel movement of commodity price indices, stock price indices and the movement of currencies that are especially exposed to carry-trade speculation (UNCTAD, 2009a).

3   UNCTAD's *Trade and Development Report 2007* stated: " ... adjustment is imminent and can be either "soft", involving smooth correction through government intervention, or "hard", involving a painful contraction an crisis in deficit countries with major adverse repercussions for surplus countries" (UNCTAD, 2007, Overview: III).

4   The idea of an international reserve currency to be issued by a supranational financial institution was first advanced by Keynes in his *Treatise on Money*, published in 1930, and later refined by him in his Bretton Woods proposals for an International Clearing Union.

5   The Stiglitz Commission notes that with its current governance structure, the IMF may not be considered neutral enough by all countries to serve as the issuer of such a currency. It therefore proposes that a new "Global Reserve Bank" be created for the purpose.

6   Recognition of these advantages was one of the preconditions for the Bretton Woods system, in which governments sacrificed some monetary autonomy in return for greater stability in the financial markets and more balanced international trade (UNCTAD, 2007c: 47–48).

7   This was despite the fact that the IMF Articles of Agreement continued to provide for the possibility that "members may exercise such controls as are necessary to regulate international capital movements ..." (IMF Articles of Agreement, Article VI, Section 3: Controls of capital transfers).

References

Akyüz Y (2009). *Policy Response to the Global Financial Crisis: Key Issues for Developing Countries*. Geneva, South Centre, Geneva, May.

Bergsten C (2007). Toward a free trade area of the Asia Pacific. *Policy Briefs in International Economics* 07–2. Washington, DC, Peterson Institute for International Economics, February.

Bibow J (2010). Global Imbalances, the U.S. Dollar, and how the crisis at the core of global finance spread to "self-insuring" emerging market economies. *Levy Economics Institute Working Paper,* No. 591. Annandale-on-Hudson, NY.

BIS (Bank for International Settlements) (2004). Annual Report, Basel.

Boughton JM (2009). A New Bretton Woods? *Finance and Development* 46 (1): 44–46, March.

Dullien S, Herr H and Kellermann C (2009). Der gute Kapitalismus. Bielefeld, Transcript Verlag.

Epstein G, Grabel I and Jomo KS (2004). Capital management techniques in developing countries: an assessment of experiences from the 1990s and lessons for the future. UNCTAD/G-24 Discussion Paper Series, no.27. New York and Geneva, United Nations Conference on Trade and Development, March.

Financial Time (2008). European call for Bretton Woods II. 16 October. Available at: http://www.ft.com/.

Flassbeck H and Spiecker F (2007). *Das Ende der Massenarbeitslosigkeit.* Frankfurt, Westend Verlag.

G-20 (2009). Leaders' Statement at the Pittsburgh Summit. 24–25 September. Available at: http://www.g20.org/Documents/pittsburgh_summit_leaders_statement_250909.pdf.

Helleiner E (2009). The contemporary reform of global financial governance: Implications of and lessons from the past. UNCTAD/G-24 Discussion Paper Series, no.55. New York and Geneva, United Nations Conference on Trade and Development, April.

Özgür G and Ertürk K (2008). Endogenous money in the age of financial liberalization. IDEAs Working Paper Series no.05/2008. Reading, International Development Economics Associates.

Reinhart C and Rogoff K (2008). Is the 2007 US financial crisis so different? An international historical comparison. *American Economic Review,* 98 (2): 339–344.

Rodrik D (2009). Let developing nations rule. In: *VOX EU.* 28 January. Available at: http://www.voxeu.org/index.php?q=node/2885.

Rodrik D and Subramanian A (2008). Why we need to curb global flows of capital. *Financial Times,* 26 February.

South Centre (2008). Calls for revamping the global financial architecture. Statement by Board Members of the South Centre. Geneva, 29 October. Available at: http://www.southcentre.org/index.php?option=com_content&task=view&id=871&Itemid=1.

UNCTAD (2005). *Trade and Development Report 2005: New Features of Global Interdependence.* New York and Geneva, United Nations.

UNCTAD (2007). *Trade and Development Report 2007: Regional Cooperation for Development.* New York and Geneva, United Nations.

UNCTAD (2009a). The global economic crisis: Systemic failures and multilateral remedies. Report by the UNCTAD Secretariat Task Force on Systemic Issues and Economic Cooperation. New York and Geneva, United Nations.

UNCTAD (2009b). *Trade and Development Report 2009: Responding to the Global Crisis.* New York and Geneva, United Nations.

UNPGA (2009). Report of the Commission of Experts of the President of the United Nations General Assembly on Reforms of the International Monetary and Financial System. Available at: http://www.un.org/ga/president/63/commission/financial_commission. shtml.